The Making of Tomorrow

By Raoul de Roussy de Sales

MY NEW ORDER

THE
MAKING
OF
Tomorrow

RAOUL de ROUSSY de SALES

REYNAL & HITCHCOCK · NEW YORK

"If we could first know where we are
and whither we are tending, we could
better judge what to do and how to do it."

ABRAHAM LINCOLN

Contents

Introduction

IT is generally recognized that this war is not a war in the ordinary sense of the word but a combination of national and revolutionary struggles.

There are two series of conflicts going on at the same time: the *vertical* conflicts in which nations fight one another, and the *horizontal* conflicts which are ideological, political, social, and economic. The latter transcend boundaries. They are carried on within each country. They overlap purely national allegiances, and disrupt the national fronts. They form the pattern of revolution which serves as a backdrop for the actual battles which are carried on on land, on sea, and in the air.

The picture thus created is anything but simple. In fact its complexity is such that the average man, and even many leaders of public opinion, have shown a strong tendency to avoid facing decisions as long as it was humanly possible to do so. The very confusion of the situation has often served as an excuse for recommending a policy of aloofness. When it is difficult or impossible to determine whether any particular action will be advisable from the national point of view, but at the same time detrimental to the political interests of a given group, the tendency is to oppose that action. That the vertical conflicts are frequently in apparent or real opposition to the horizontal ones is a fact that cannot be denied. Few men are able to consider objectively the constant changes which take place in this multidimensional crisis and most of them have a tendency to emphasize one aspect of the problems to the detriment of the others. There are those who believe that the primary consideration is the fact that a group of aggressive nations is trying to shake off the domination of existing empires and create new ones. To them the conflict is essentially imperialistic. Another category, being more impressed by the revolutionary character of the times, believe that the fundamental struggle is a clash between different ideologies and different political, social, and economic systems. They tend to minimize or even deny the validity of the national rivalries, which assume in their eyes an artificial quality merely intended to screen or confuse the real issue.

The truth is of course that both schools of thought are biased by their own education or their own prejudices, but such a situation is not new. The same difficulty of appraisal was encountered by the contemporaries of the French Revolution and of the Napoleonic era. To this date it is hard to decide whether the most important aspect of those times is the fact that Napoleon conquered most of Europe, leaving after him new boundaries and a new balance of power, or that in doing this he spread the ideas of the French Revolution. Most historians would admit today that the two points of view cannot be separated.

The same can be said of what is happening in our times but the difficulty is that it is happening to us and that, carried away as we are by the unfolding of events, it is well-nigh impossible to ask any of us to have a historical point of view about them. The impressions we receive can be compared to those experienced when listening for the first time to a new piece of music. We grasp one, two, or three main themes and when they recur we recognize them. If we understand anything about music, we can also appreciate the skill of the composer in combining different motifs and in passing from one to the other. If we are not musical, we shall gather only a general impression which may be pleasant or disagreeable but which will escape our analysis.

Similarly the events of the day give us the sensation of something hopelessly complex unfolding under our eyes. The newspaper which we read every morning is like a single bar in a musical script. Glancing through the news, we pick up fragments of a familiar theme here and there: "Manila bombed, hundreds of people killed. . . ." This is reminiscent of something. Three days later, a columnist mentions it: "Manila, like Coventry, Rotterdam, and Guernica," says he, "will go down in history, etc. . . ." That is it: the Guernica motif.

In the same paper we read, only a while ago, of strikes in American defense plants. "While winning the war depends on American plane production, American employers and employees disagree over wages and the workers go on strike. . . ." That theme we know too. It happened in France. It is the Popular Front motif.

And these motifs in turn make us conscious of the fundamental themes: war and revolution, profoundly intermingled and real. This feeling of confusion and of inextricable complexity has been more acute in America than in Europe. The reasons for this are numerous but the main one is that all European nations have been inexorably involved in the war for a long time. They are dominated by the events, and the necessities of the daily struggle charter their course. But it is only recently that America has lost the belief that she had a choice. Up to Pearl Harbor, the Americans were made to think not only that they could decide between peace and war, but that they could decide how much war they would accept.

This capacity of choice was an illusion, as demonstrated by events. But a long habit of being able to debate more or less freely while the rest of the world was gagged by war censorship, or by the fear of the conqueror, has left its mark on the mind of the average American. Although he is fully at war now, he cannot forget overnight the point of view of the spectator which he so recently was. He still believes that it is his peculiar privilege, and also his duty, to discuss from a more impersonal angle than can the other belligerents, the social, political, and economic future which will come out of this war.

And in thinking this he may not be wrong.

The impression entertained by many Americans that this war is not their war, that they have been dragged step by step into quarrels which are not of their own making, is still perceptible as an undercurrent.

The problems which were left over by the last war and which are intensified by this one seemed to them "foreign." They have felt that these problems were foisted upon them. They believed that if it were not for the outside world, and particularly Europe, they could have solved their own dilemmas in their own way and pursued their course in peace. They still have the profound impression that America has a destiny but that the fulfillment of it is being jeopardized by the malevolence or foolishness of other nations. Their instinct has always been to consider America as a land set apart—possibly by God—in which natural resources are more plentiful than anywhere else and whose citizens, if left alone, would have the energy, the intelligence, and the wisdom to create a better life, more justice, and to maintain peace forever between themselves and their neighbors. Even the tremendous impact of the Axis aggression has not quite shattered this dream.

America, which is ready to live on friendly terms with the whole world, is constantly surprised, pained, and irritated to find that other continents and other nations are not animated by the same spirit of good will. The American dream of constant progress and "more abundant life for all" may be endangered in America itself. To many Americans it appears as a mirage at times. But the national instinct is to cling to this dream and to blame the outside world for past, present, and future disillusions.

There is no point in arguing here whether the policy of isolation followed by the United States during the post-1919 period was wise or even unavoidable. From a broader point of view it was probably unfortunate. The League of Nations might have survived as an instrument of continuous readjustments if the United States had joined it. On the other hand, the United States by remaining aloof had fewer problems to solve for itself. Its foreign policy was simplified and world issues were practically eliminated from the realm of discussion.

This enabled the United States to pursue an internal policy which, in appearance at least, was independent of external factors. Under the protective flag of isolationism, the United States went through the boom years and the depression very much as if they were local phenomena, unrelated, in the people's minds, to the general evolution of the outside world.

Up to a recent past, the impression prevailed that the internal policies of the United States as expressed through the New Deal have been progressive enough to meet the economic and social conditions which will prevail in the kind of world now in the making. By and large, public opinion had been led to think, up to Pearl Harbor, that the reforms accomplished during the first years of President Roosevelt's administration were sufficient for the time being. Since the middle of 1937 approximately, a definite movement of reaction had set in—or to be more accurate, the resistance to social reform hardened to such a point that practically no New Deal legislation had passed and the general demand had been to consolidate what had been done but not to go any further.

If the United States were really operating as an independent political, social, and economic unit on this planet, the swing to conservatism which has taken place since 1937 would be perfectly normal. The pendulum movement from Right to Left and from Left to Right has been characteristic of all democracies during the nineteenth century and up to a few years ago. A period of consolidation and sometimes of reaction has normally followed a period of social reform. This has been the norm for England, for France, for the United States, and for all countries in fact during the era of capitalist democracy. It can be argued that this cyclical behavior assured the stability of democratic institutions during the times when only a few extremist groups challenged the advantages of democracy over any other form of government.

But this easy and regular pulsation of democratic organisms has been violently disturbed ever since the last war. The Communist revolution to begin with and later on the Fascist and Nazi enterprises introduced elements of disturbance in the democratic circulatory system which tended to disrupt it even before the war dislocated it altogether.

Communism and Fascism, being both established on the principle of dictatorship, have eliminated the cyclic movement from Left to Right and vice versa in their own spheres of influence. They are both avowedly "dynamic," which means that they deny the validity of any "breathing spell" for consolidation. They are on the march continuously and can never pause, much less retrace their steps. To use a familiar image, Communism and especially Fascism are like bicyclists who cannot stop without falling.

The introduction of these movements in the world had as a first consequence on the democratic countries to pervert and distort the normal swing rhythm. One of the slogans of the French Republic—"always to the Left but never further"—became suddenly less humorous. The democratic pendulum, instead of swinging smoothly in the grandfather's clock of established institutions, became erratic. Two new poles of attraction governed its movements: whenever it went to the Left, the specter of Communism reared its bloody head. Whenever it swung to the Right, the alarm of Fascism sounded.

In France the disrupting effect of the two poles of attraction, Communism and Fascism, became so acute from 1934 on that it can be seen now that normal democracy ceased to exist in that country from that date. The disaster of June 1940 merely sanctioned that obvious fact. Although the authoritarian government of Marshal Pétain disclaims its Fascist tendency, there is no doubt that it is not only anti-Communist with a vengeance, but also anti-democratic.

In England the polar attraction of Communism and Fascism was less clearly perceptible, though no less real and no less dangerous. But the fact that opposition to democracy—with the exception of the Mosley movement— did not take a militant form, maintained the faith of the English electorate in the possibility of continuing to express their will through their established institutions. The British Parliament remained active and powerful long after Daladier had closed the doors of the *Chambre des Députés*.

Nevertheless, the advent of Winston Churchill in May, 1940, marks a definite turning point, in the sense that from then on, as far as England is concerned, democracy ceases to follow the traditional and approved pattern of the last one hundred and fifty years. It ceases to be "cyclic," and there are definite signs that it is becoming as "dynamic" as Communism or Fascism. The possibility that there is to be a new democratic solution to world problems, both nationally and internationally, finds no greater justification than in the unity made necessary by the British war effort.

In America, the disturbances caused by the impact of the Fascist and Communist movements on the normal tempo of democratic behavior have been no less real than elsewhere, but American conservatism is a powerful shock absorber, so that violent changes are rare. Very often, these changes are only noticeable by their indirect consequences.

It can be said, for instance, that those who felt that the re-election of President Roosevelt to a third term violated a tradition were right, but for more profound reasons than those put forward at the time. The elections of 1940 were significant not because the same man was to remain President of the United States for twelve consecutive years, but because the majority of the electorate was compelled—more or less consciously—to recognize, by this break with tradition, its interdependence with the outside world.

Viewed in that light, the re-election of Franklin Roosevelt had two important consequences: on the vertical plane —that is, nationally—the American electorate expressed its willingness to play a part, at least temporarily, in world affairs commensurate with the real power of the United States; on the horizontal plane it recognized the implications of the revolutionary forces and their possible effect on the evolution of American democracy. The fact that these necessities were accepted with so much reluctance and with so many reservations merely emphasizes their urgency.

Now that America is at war, it may seem that such considerations as to the meaning of past events are uselessly subtle. War is a great simplifier, and the entry of the United States into the war has given to the problems studied in this book what may appear to some as a sufficient solution. It is true that all the conflicts of our times have seemed suddenly to resolve themselves, on December 7, 1941, into one great single purpose: the defeat of the Axis powers. What the American people may have meant when they re-elected President Roosevelt to a third term and to what extent this was an indication of the profound change that had already taken place in the outlook of this country, seems now immaterial. The signs that precede the storm are forgotten when the storm comes.

But if the Americans have been forced, very much against their wishes, to take up the challenge of the Axis powers, and if, for the sake of their own salvation and of ultimate victory, they have put aside temporarily their freedom and their right to debate, one must not forget that the purpose of this war is precisely to re-establish in America and in the whole world the rights which have been voluntarily given up.

There is no doubt that the allies of America and the conquered countries hailed as a sign of victory and liberation the entrance of the United States into the war. But the reason for this is not merely because it means that the immense resources of America in men and supplies of all sorts will be used to secure victory, but because the outside world turns toward America for an inspiration that can come from nowhere else.

The Americans may complain that Europe betrayed the ideals of America in 1919. The Europeans, on their side, feel that America abandoned them after having offered them a great promise.

Today there is no way of telling how this war will end. By force of habit we think in terms of a peace conference, which may never take place for the mere reason that there may be nobody on the other side to make peace with. There may be a period of many years during which the people who have let themselves be used as the instrument of this world devastation, the Germans, the Japanese, and the Italians, will have to be maintained in a condition of tutelage. This will have to be done by force. President

Roosevelt and Mr. Churchill in drafting the Atlantic Charter seem to have been aware of this eventuality.

In any event there will be a need for American leadership, and there is not the slightest doubt that the world at large counts on it already. In fact, it is strange to have to admit that it counts on nothing else, because from no other quarter is there even a ray of light.

Whether the American people will be willing or able to do what is expected of them is unpredictable at the moment. The task will require many favorable conditions, only one of which can be set down here as indispensable and foreseeable. In spite of the discipline of thought made necessary by the war and national unity, it is going to be the business of the Americans to exert their intelligence more perhaps than any other faculty. The reason for this is that they are still in the privileged position of being able to do so. They are in this war and in this revolution, but they can still look at both and, probably, determine their course.

*   *   *   *   *   *

If one visualizes the present war as merely one form of a much broader crisis expanding both in time and in scope far beyond such events as the conquests by the Axis powers of several independent countries, the abolition of the Third Republic in France, the transformation of the loose-jointed British social system into a concentrated fighting unit, the awakening of America after the Japanese attack, it becomes necessary to attempt an analysis of the main forces which brought about these events. There is nothing local or episodic in this war and what is happening to each of us on account of it cannot be understood if we concentrate our attention on certain aspects of it and exclude the others. I would even say that it is impossible to explain the times we are living in if we adhere to any particular point of view, be it national or political. I know of course that no one can divest himself of all preconceived ideas and prejudices and that there is no such thing as objectivity. I know too that one of the characteristics of this century's crisis is the apparent breaking down of all familiar values. The common denominators which in previous periods of history seemed to survive in spite of wars and even revolutions are today invalid. There is no religious creed strong enough to preserve any spiritual unity. There is no universal morality. The ordinary laws of humanitarianism are not accepted by all and there is disagreement concerning the purpose and value of life itself. It is superfluous to state that there is no political concept universally accepted. Economic forces which are supposed to be stronger than the changing will of men can certainly be challenged—and are effectively challenged. Even the power of money has become dubious as a universal lever.

But this disintegration and shattering of all familiar values, however real it may be, should not blind us to the fact that there exist certain forces acting on all nations and all individuals, whether they be Americans or Germans, French or Japanese. These forces are in fact so strong and we are so used to being activated by them that we take them for granted and forget to give them much thought.

We lament because we have no spiritual guidance while in fact we are immersed in the myth of nationalism—a myth so strong and so commanding that it has become practically impossible to question it.

We are convinced that between the Fascists and the democrats or between the Communists and the democrats there is no political common tie. But in fact there is one: they are bound together by the trend they all follow, a trend which for convenience' sake I shall call collectivism.

There is a third force which is more difficult to perceive perhaps and not at all easy to demonstrate: it is the con-

stant growth of a kind of absolute pacifism, the manifestations of which are as clear in the aggressor countries as in
their victims—in spite of all evidence to the contrary.

These three forces, nationalism, collectivism, and pacifism, are not the only ones that motivate the actions of
men and nations today. Self-interest, greed, as well as compassion and love, are still alive in this world. But the kind
of world we live in cannot be made intelligible if one
limits himself to the use of a vocabulary so restrictive as to
eliminate the complexity of reality. The average man of
today is neither purely economic nor purely moral. A
Marxian interpretation of history has become as unsatis-
factory as that offered by any religion. There is a certain
amount of practical relativity in everything we do or
think. We know that it is impossible to practice Christian
virtues in a vacuum. Prayers or philosophical thoughts sit
badly on an empty stomach. On the other hand we know
by personal experience that it is impossible to rid ourselves completely of all thoughts. It is as impossible not
to think as not to eat.

The three forces which I have mentioned above seem to
me to be the three fundamental elements of these modern
times. They run, like threads of three different colors,
through the conscious or unconscious thoughts of millions
of men whenever they consider the world around them
and their relation to it. They unite in a strange way the
men who lead us. They can be combined or opposed, and
out of their combination or opposition wars and revolutions are born.

Part I

NATIONALISM

CHAPTER I

A Modern Imperative

IT CAN hardly be questioned that of the three forces—nationalism, collectivism, and pacifism—the most important and most potent is nationalism. Whenever there is a conflict between dissimilar philosophies or contradictory political doctrines, whichever one can assert itself as talking in the name of nationalism is bound to win out.

The power of absorption of nationalism is such that it can disintegrate or turn to its own use even those doctrines and movements whose fundamental objective is to eliminate nationalism.

Two familiar instances will be enough to demonstrate this rule:

Most churches, and in particular the Christian ones, teach the brotherhood of man regardless of racial or national distinction. Theoretically the churches are committed to promoting spiritual internationalism. In spite of this, the last war showed that in a time of crisis the leaders of the churches are very quick to uphold the nationalist point of view. The same trend is noticeable now, and there is no reason to believe that the religious leaders will resist the pressure of modern nationalism any more than they did twenty-five years ago.

Another instance is the evolution of the U.S.S.R. The

country in which Communism was first established has apparently renounced all dreams of world revolution for the moment. Stalin is as nationalistic as Hitler and mostly concerned, for the time being, in playing Russian power politics.

This primacy of nationalism over all other forces has historical and psychological causes. Historically, it is bound with some of the oldest and most deeply rooted human instincts. Psychologically, it occupied the vacuum left by the inability of religion, philosophy, or the faith in science to satisfy certain aspirations. The modern man turns to nationalism—and usually to the most extreme form of it—because the promises of religion as well as those of rationalism have failed him. Some imperative is needed for the individual as well as for the community.

The only belief common to all men today, wherever they live and whatever may be their condition, is that obedience, service, and honor are due to one's country. The allegiance to a flag is morally compulsory. When an individual or a group of individuals is obliged, for some reason or another, to renounce its native flag, it is expected either to invent a new flag or to rally under the flag of some other community. To refuse such allegiance is considered a crime. This crime is usually punishable by law, but even when it is not, the moral reprobation that surrounds the man who refuses such allegiance is sufficiently great to make the choice compulsory.

Each of us is supposed to love his country to the point of sacrificing his life for it. When we do not, we must love another country and sacrifice our life for it. The Oxford students who some years ago pledged themselves *not* to die for their King and country provoked great indignation all over the world, but even they did not pretend that they were not good Englishmen. Similarly, American conscientious objectors do not repudiate America. Quite the contrary: they believe that their refusal to take up arms against other men is the best way of showing that they are good Americans.

Conscientious objectors, however, are merely tolerated; they are exempted, on religious grounds, from killing other men. They are not exempted from serving their country. Moreover, as proved during the war of 1917-1918, they were rather badly treated in America, as Oswald Garrison Villard and many others have frequently testified.

1. The sense of destiny

Besides agreeing to serve, obey, and honor their country, men believe that the country to which they belong has what is called a *destiny*.

The word *destiny* corresponds to a set of human instincts and aspirations, the origin and nature of which are very complex. In the religious sense, it implies that God or some superior abstraction preordained the future. The Ancients thought that there were two kinds of destinies, the good and the bad, *Fas* and *Nefas*. If one happened to be on the *Fas* track, everything came out right in the end, whatever one did. If one got on the *Nefas* side, disaster and tragedy were unavoidable.

The Christians maintained the general opposition of *Fas* and *Nefas* with the concept of Heaven and Hell but introduced a new factor in the combination: individual free will. It became possible, through one's actions and disposition of soul, to alter the course of destiny. The possibility of choosing to go to Heaven or to Hell was like the opening of a new frontier. Later on, however, in modern times, and through the acquisition of a new concept— that of continuous progress—the tendency to eliminate Hell became manifest. To survive against the onslaughts of science and positive thinking, organized religions have had to become as optimistic as the worshipers of progress. Hell is definitely toned down in modern religious thinking, and the idea of frightening human beings into being good has been abandoned. They are, instead, encouraged in the belief that, with a small effort on their part, their risk of being damned is practically negligible. In spite of Pascal and Schopenhauer, Henry Adams and Oswald Spengler, the philosophical and religious outlook of the modern man (in the Western World at least) is not pessimistic. All the new creeds which have developed during the last fifty years, such as Christian Science, the Oxford group, or Buchmanism, are definitely bent on glossing over the ugly sides of human nature and on restricting the domain of Evil to very narrow limits. In fact the general modern tendency is to believe that the future *must* be better than the past or the present. And that applies to the material as well as to the spiritual world. In other words, we are inclined to think that the destiny of the human race, considered collectively or in separate groups, is pretty promising on the whole.

On a lower plane, destiny bears another name. It is called luck. Most people *know* that there is no such thing as luck, but it is difficult to find anyone who does not *believe* in it. The laws of chance are very simple and anybody with an average intelligence can understand them. Unfortunately they are nearly unbearable from the individual point of view, and each one of us much prefers to believe that what happens to him is somehow or other preordained by more or less supernatural forces. Superstition is as alive today as it was in the most primitive societies.

For instance, the man who walking in the street receives a brick on his head must struggle very hard with his own reason to accept the fact that this is a mere accident and that he was not *destined* to suffer this inconvenience. His instinct is to believe that this conjunction between his head and a brick has a meaning. What that meaning is will depend on the type of person who is hit by that brick. One will consider it a good omen. If the brick has not killed him, he will be inclined to think that he has paid the price to the powers of evil which will keep him in luck for quite some time. Another, on the contrary, will conclude that this is a sign that demonic forces are really after him this time and that the brick is only one more proof that he is set on the path of tragedy and disaster. Somehow, and whichever way one may choose to interpret it, the accident will appear as sufficiently remarkable to dull the faculty of rationalization and to allow many ancestral superstitions to come to the surface. Each man, however rational he may be, must indulge in a good deal of mystification whenever he thinks of himself. What we call our good or bad luck or our destiny is merely our personal interpretation of the laws of chance. It does not, however, make these laws less true.

This digression about destiny considered from the personal point of view is intended only to throw some light on the more general concept of national destiny. The fact that we believe that our country has a mission to fulfill explains, in part, our allegiance to it and our acceptance of all sacrifices, including that of our own lives. As long as the community to which we belong believes that its collective behavior and its actions are not the result of mere hazard but the preordained unfolding of its destiny, it is obvious that no individual can be allowed to deny the validity of the common creed.

The result of this attitude is that the link which binds together the members of a nation is considered by them as supernatural. It is the strongest that can be imagined. Although all other forms of worship have a definite tendency to disintegrate and wane, nationalism has become in-

creasingly stronger and, as a universal myth, it is well on
the way to dislodging all others. The assumption that some
sort of international controls must eventually be established is an intellectual deduction which does not affect in
any way the elemental force of nationalism.

It may be said that there is nothing new in this phenomenon. The most primitive savages have a tribal instinct. Totems and taboos are as old as man himself. This
is true, but the interesting fact is that after so many centuries of liberation from ancestral irrationalism, the modern man should find himself so close to the starting point
and so profoundly immersed in the primitiveness of national fetishism. It would appear as if all attempts to destroy our superstitions, our mythology, and even our
religiosity had had but one result: to divert them and pack
them into one channel—nationalism.

There are few martyrs to the faith these days. Christians
are not made to enter the arena to be devoured by lions.
There are few victims every year that can be attributed
directly to religious intolerance. Protestants and Catholics
live side by side in peace. If the Jews are persecuted and
killed, it is not on account of their religious views but on
account of their race. And that in itself—the violent resurgence of anti-Semitism in the contemporary world—is a sign
of the fanatical intensity of modern nationalism. It is because the Jews are supposed not to belong to any nation,
because they are said to lack in national sense, that they are
hounded from one country to the other, held in suspicion
everywhere, and treated as outcasts. They are accused of
working toward a destiny distinct from or in opposition
to the destiny of the country where they are established.

That this cannot be proved satisfactorily and that no
one has ever been able to give a clear definition of what
may be the destiny of the Jews in contrast with any other
particular ethnological group makes no difference. Na-

tionalism has its roots in human nature itself and there is no doubt that those who believe that humanity cannot progress so long as men insist on defending their homeland and their particular cultural inheritance, are pursuing an impossible chimera. But modern nationalism tends to depart more and more from this natural and normal human feeling and to exploit more and more the irrational aspects of nationalism. Anti-Semitism is totally irrational, which is one of the reasons why it has become the most effective weapon of modern nationalism in all countries.

There is, of course, an aspect of nationalism which is in no way irrational, and that is that nations must be united to survive. A weakening of the national sense entails a weakening of the whole community. A citizen who is not prepared to cooperate fully for the welfare and security of his country is therefore a danger to all. Treason is the greatest conceivable crime because it does not affect a limited number of persons but a whole community. Loyalty to one's country is therefore the primary duty of the citizen. The obvious principle that unity makes strength is the logical defense of the existence of nations, but there is a far cry between this rational justification of the organized community and the mystical cult of nationalism as an end in itself.

This is why, in nearly every country, so much of the education is directed toward bolstering up the rudimentary attachment to the place where one is born, in order to magnify it and transform it into an overpowering and indisputable sense of obligation. The modern man, when he thinks of himself as an American, a German, or a Frenchman, is not merely conscious of the geographical accident of his birth. When he says France, America, or Germany he does not recall merely certain landscapes, certain habits and customs familiar to him. He does not think merely of his friends and associations and of the bonds of his native language. There is much more to it than that: America, Germany, France, are made to appear to him as entities, the character of which is neither wholly human nor wholly divine but which exerts over the individual a sovereignty without limit. The nation to which one belongs appears at once lovable like a mother and strangely awful like Baal Moloch. We are never allowed to forget that we are not merely individuals, but part of a vast conglomeration of other individuals to whom we are bound by some very material common interests, and also by a series of taboos, symbols, more or less verified legends, and a considerable quantity of sacred falsehoods.

2. Evolution of nationalism

The tendency to consider that everything national must be good and all the rest bad or dangerous is fairly new in the history of our civilization. It did not and could not exist before the modern concept of the nation was established, and that did not really take place much before the American and French Revolutions at the end of the eighteenth century.

Before that epoch the people of Europe were seldom conscious of their "nationality" in the modern sense of the word. The policy of each country was determined by the aristocracy and the King. The effect of public opinion was negligible. Wars were made and treaties were signed without any thought of consulting the common man. It happened from time to time that what we now call public opinion did manifest itself violently. Serfs and peasants revolted in France, in Germany, and in England on many occasions. The people of England obtained certain liberties earlier than any other and maintained these liberties whenever they were threatened. But these manifestations of the popular will were fewer than we are inclined to think nowadays.

It is true that in a curious way the Middle Ages, that is, the period between the tenth and fifteenth centuries, were considerably more "democratic" than the centuries that followed, during which the system of monarchy was at its height. Christianity was effectively ruling the world. The standards of values that it had established were undisputed even by the most powerful princes. Europe was united by faith in a way that it has never been united since. This unity of faith had the effect of enhancing the power of the masses. Such enterprises as the Crusades, the construction of cathedrals, were truly democratic in the sense that they emanated directly from the people. Art and culture were popular. Between the rulers and the people, between the artists and their public, there was not as yet an unbridgeable chasm. The universal acceptance of the Christian order, as yet unchallenged either by rationalism or by temporal powers, gave the common man a relative standing which he was soon to lose.

In fact the people of Europe never behaved less as "nations" than during the three or four centuries when the monarchist principle grew and flourished. There seldom was a time when the masses made themselves heard less. The hierarchy of aristocratic power, culminating in the King, concentrated all the power in the hands of the aristocrats. Wars were declared and treaties were signed by that aristocracy, acting as such. Provinces and territories were exchanged or sold with the minimum of concern for the desires of the inhabitants.

In the realm of art and science the break between the elite and the masses was even more profound, and there are not many signs that it is in the process of being bridged even today in spite of the Soviet, Nazi, and Fascist attempts to recreate a popular art.

The communion of spirit between the people and their artists which was possible as long as Christianity was an effective force in Europe and as long as its standards of values were unquestioned—that communion of spirit has never been replaced. From the Renaissance on, a split between the artists and the masses became apparent. Art became more and more a matter of cultural distinction, less and less "comprehensible" to the average man. Painters painted for the courtiers and the amateurs. Poetry, drama, and literature in general were written for a narrow public. Even architecture became "exclusive." Versailles was not built for the anonymous people by anonymous artists, as was the Cathedral of Chartres, but for Louis XIV and his court. Not until the middle of the last century was there a rejuvenation of popular literature (through journalism) and not until our own time, an attempt at popular architecture (sports stadiums, parkways, public building on a grand scale, etc.).

The industrial revolution which began in the nineteenth century produced remarkable disturbances in the concept of nationalism. The mere fact that new inventions such as the railroad, the steamship, the telegraph, the newspapers, the radio, reduced distances in relation to the individual, changed also the conception that each man has of his own country. Although the instinctive attachment to a fairly limited area of ground (the village, the town, or the part of the town where one was born) remained real, the possibilities of rapid traveling and of knowing quickly what was happening elsewhere, increased the sentiment of mass unity and growing interdependence among individuals which is implied in the word *nation*. The nation became more than an abstraction. The people were visible, tangible, everywhere. The crowd, this characteristic phenomenon of our time, was constantly present, assembling more and more often for one reason or another, or being simply there in the streets and squares of cities, or working together in factories. Nations became conscious of their number. "We are a nation of thirty million, of forty million, of one hundred million, and in ten years we shall be more numerous still." This habit of counting oneself as part of a large number is relatively new, but the effect of statistical thinking on the modern concept of nationalism cannot be overemphasized. In previous periods of history, men appeared to be quite indifferent to the numerical strength of their country in relation to others. The fact that France was the most populous country in Europe up to the beginning of the last century no doubt accounts in part for the long history of its supremacy, but it was far from being the only or even the major factor. Other countries, such as England, with a numerically very inferior population, played a role relatively much more important. The modern emphasis on sheer numbers is obviously due to practical reasons. A greater population means more labor and larger armies and therefore more potential power. But there is more to it than that: Nations want to grow numerically because this concept of growth is mystically connected with the concept of national destiny. It is a revival of the herd instinct. No such idea ever entered the heads of the Greeks at the time of their splendor nor of the Italians of the Renaissance.

3. Nationalism and class struggle

The industrial revolution had another effect on the concept of the nation. By establishing an opposition between capital and labor it gave rise to a series of class alliances and combinations exerting their action internationally. The Marx-Engels manifesto inviting the workers of the world to unite encouraged capital to unite also. But whereas socialism tended—at least in theory—to combat nationalism, the capitalists established their lines of defense on nationalist grounds. The reasons for this were obvious: it assured them of the control of the army and armaments; it enabled them to appeal to the middle classes, who are always the most rooted element of the population and the most anxious for protection against any outside danger, real or imaginary; finally, nationalism was the only excuse of the privileged classes for justifying their hold on the government. Whereas the people enjoyed political democracy, they were deprived of economic equality. This could be achieved only, up to recent years, by the maintenance of the idea that the national interest should pre-empt all other considerations and that this national interest could be safeguarded only if the privileged classes could control, directly or indirectly, the policy of the nation.

Thus, up to the advent of Fascism and especially of National Socialism, the privileged classes, including the bourgeoisie, conceived of themselves as being the true representatives of the nation because they were its most stable and (in their own eyes) worthy element; while labor, whose armies are "permanently encamped in our midst," as Auguste Comte said, sought support outside the national frame. Socialism under its various forms and Communism as understood by Lenin were antinationalistic by definition. The class struggles of the nineteenth century and up to our time pivoted on this fundamental opposition of nationalism (identified with the interests of the privileged groups) and internationalism (identified with the aspirations of the workers).

The fact that there developed through the nineteenth century a powerful internationalism of wealth does not make any difference, because that particular internationalism could not assert itself as working for peace. On the contrary, it was always found to support in each country the most extreme forms of nationalism and imperialism. It is untrue to say that it had an inclination for wars, but it seldom did anything active to prevent them. Its affinities with the nationalist parties in each country made that impossible.

There has also developed in recent years a social internationalism, which could be called the Internationale of Café Society. It is closely linked with the internationalism of wealth although its methods of operation are quite different. They are a caricature of those of the French salons of the eighteenth century where the influence of ambitious and clever women exerted itself on an equal footing with that of clever and ambitious men. The difference between the salons of the eighteenth century and those of today is that whereas the former were dedicated to enlightenment, and inspired by a spirit of philosophical and political adventure, the latter cultivate nostalgia for the past, obtuseness, and ignorance, and if they have any inspiration at all, it is hard to say that it has any other name but fear. Like the internationalism of wealth, however, the Internationale of Café Society can hardly be counted as a constructive force on the side of peace.

In other words, the Western mind has been dimly conscious for over one hundred years of having to choose between two destinies, or to find a formula to combine both. The first one is national destiny, a composite product of ancestral instincts, cultural expansionism, and power politics. The second is what might be called a social destiny, another composite product of aspirations toward more humanity, more justice, a better distribution of labor and its products, and continuous progress.

The coexistence of these two concepts of human destiny has produced a state of chronic tension during the last one hundred years. Revolutionary upheavals such as those of 1830, 1848, and 1917 in Europe, and the American Civil War, are milestones on the road which has led to the present crisis. During this same period several wars have taken

place. Some of them were colonial wars, such as the Boer
War and the conquests of African territories by the European powers. Others were purely national, or considered
as such. All of them, however, were partial or localized
wars in the sense that they involved only a few nations at
a time. The general structure established at Vienna in
1815 was often badly shaken, but on the whole it held.
Similarly the broad lines of capitalist democracy were
maintained and extended over nearly all the civilized
world.

The war of 1914-1918, which was fought with the belief
that it should be the last (the war to end all wars), turned
out in fact to be the first episode in a new era of violence.
Looked at retrospectively, it followed a fairly simple pattern, the main features of which can be summarized as
follows:

1. It was a world-wide war, the first of that kind since
Napoleon's time.

2. It was fought by nations as such and strengthened
their fanatical belief in nationalism. The Versailles Treaty
and the League of Nations consecrated the idea that ethnological entities had a transcendent right to independence and absolute sovereignty, regardless of whether they
were powerful or weak, civilized or backward, economically viable or not.

3. Although the privileged classes managed successfully
to see the war through without losing control of the
masses, they found increasing difficulty in maintaining
that control after the war.

4. The middle classes or bourgeoisie which everywhere
formed the backbone of classical or capitalist democracy
developed, after the war of 1914-1918, a sense of chronic
insecurity. In some countries, like Germany, they collapsed completely. In others, like France, they showed
strong tendencies to desert the traditional middle-of-the-

road course. In America, the normal processes of capitalist democracy were maintained in spite of the great depression that followed. The United States is the only Western country which has withstood with no fundamental deterioration the economic, social, and political shocks of the post-1919 period up to the present. There is no way of telling whether this sturdiness is fundamental or whether merely apparent. It may be due to the usual lag in the evolution of America in relation to Europe. And there is more than a possibility that the dislocation produced by the full war effort will change the whole structure in a permanent way. But the United States still finds itself today in the exceptional position of preserving alone the general political concepts inherited from the eighteenth and nineteenth centuries. The United States alone is still in a position to identify what is national with a certain political regime—capitalist democracy—and with a certain number of ideas which in other countries are either abolished or in the process of revision.

CHAPTER II

Diversity of National Concepts

THE religious and irrational quality of nationalism is apparent in many ways. Each of us, thinking of his own nation, is inclined to believe that the peculiar kind of ideas that form its culture would be beneficial to the rest of the world if they were universally adopted. That is why conquering people have great difficulty in imagining that they are not doing more good than harm to the conquered. That is why anything can be expected from a conqueror—be he called Caesar, Charles XII, Napoleon, or Hitler—except repentance. Conquerors can regret only one thing: to have been prevented from dominating the whole world. By that way, they think, their personal destiny and that of their people would have been fulfilled. Peace would have become permanent. The millennium would be achieved.

It so happens that no conqueror and no single people every really established peace over the whole world, as far as history can record. *Pax Romana,* which is so much admired by some people and often proposed as a model, was never so perfect as we imagine at this distance. It is true that the Romans managed to eliminate all their most important rivals, but they were constantly engaged in repressing rebellions and in keeping away the Barbarians. There is not a single year of the history of Rome which is not marked by wars, revolts, and punitive operations.

In contemporary times, with the national instinct of each people so alive and so aggressive, the chances of any nation or combination of nations maintaining peace permanently are very small. The last attempt to organize Europe by force was made by Napoleon. It failed because it stimulated everywhere intense local nationalism. Napoleon never quite understood, apparently, why he failed. In his scheme of things, Europe was what he called a "molehill" and he wasted a lot of time dreaming of conquering the Orient. Like all conquerors he was blinded by a romantic view of history which prevented him from gauging the real forces that were opposed to him. Because his own mind could easily conceive of organizing not only Europe, but the world, he overlooked the fact that even the small and weak people that he had conquered were permeated with the ideas of national independence which he himself had brought them.

He overlooked also what might be called the "diversity factor," that is to say, the will of each people of Europe to preserve their characteristics—such as language, customs, and individual culture—even if this meant sacrificing order and going to war.

This diversity factor, so important for the understanding of Europe, is as difficult to explain today as it was one hundred and fifty years ago. To the Americans, in particular, there is something really devilish in this refusal of the European nations to organize themselves and unite. But that this factor is vital to Europe cannot be questioned. In fact the very essence of European culture rests on its diversity. This diversity cannot be eliminated without destroying Europe itself as the source of Western civilization. If Europe should ever be unified under one master —whoever it may be—it would soon lose its identity and become nothing more than what it is geographically: a promontory of Asia.

Only a short time ago, before the United States went to war, I heard it often said that in spite of the American opposition to Hitler and what he represents, some good might come out of his conquest of Europe, because he might achieve its unity. In the view of some Americans, the experiment of the New Order proposed by Hitler should be tried, not because it is good, but because it means some sort of unity in the chaos.

It may be that Hitler will succeed in establishing this New Order in Europe, but it will not endure more than a few years or a few months, because there is already ample proof that Hitler and his associates have less understanding of the diversity of Europe than had Napoleon. In fact, the Nazi Order is based on the presumption that all nations are inferior to the German race and that it is the destiny of the German *Herrenvolk* to rule the world. This principle, which is the cornerstone of the structure which the Nazis are attempting to build, has never been accepted by Europe since the conglomerate of people who occupy this peninsula of Asia developed a civilization of their own. There is in fact an antithesis between the conception of the nation, as it is understood in the West, and German racialism.

To make this clear, it is necessary to explain that although modern nationalism is the greatest universal force that we know of, it does not manifest itself everywhere in the same manner. The truth is that the national consciousness assumes different aspects in different people, and a good deal of misunderstanding might be avoided if it were possible for statesmen and leaders of opinion to keep in mind the fact that a German, for instance, does not think of himself as a German in the same way as a Spaniard, a Frenchman, or an American thinks of himself as a member of his nation. What differentiates a German from an Italian is not the mere accident of being born north or south of the Brenner Pass. They are equally patriotic, equally conscious of being part of a nation, but the history of their respective countries and their cultures have given the word *nation* a different connotation in their minds.

Although one of the major causes of the present crisis is a clash between rival nationalisms—and by that I mean not only a clash between imperialisms in the ordinary sense of the word, but also the conflict between opposing conceptions on nearly all conceivable subjects—it should be noted that the principal nations of Europe, America, and Asia have very different conceptions of their respective destinies. But there is usually a tendency in each country to minimize these differences.

For instance, the Germans are inclined to believe that their racial doctrine is self-evident and susceptible of a universal application. The fact that Negroes in America do not enjoy real equality with the whites and that the Jews are socially discriminated against to a certain extent encourages the Germans to think that the principle of tolerance and equality proclaimed by the Americans is a sham. They believe that the United States is not a real nation because it is composed of such a variety of races all treated on an equal footing—at least by the laws of the land. They believe that the Americans would willingly accept the German doctrine of the master race if they were not perverted by the Jews and by democracy.

On the other hand, many Americans think that the mass of the German people are corrupted and led astray by their present masters and that if these could be removed, it would not be very difficult to bring the Germans back to thinking in the right way—that is, in the democratic way.

Neither the Americans nor the Germans can quite accept the fact that there is something fundamentally different in their whole conception of themselves as a people or a nation. The Germans minimize the historical truth that the United States is a nation precisely for the reasons that make the Germans deny that they are such a thing. The Americans cannot accept the unpleasant fact that Hitler and Alfred Rosenberg have expressed ideas that are characteristically German.

1. Confusion in Vichy

The same misunderstanding, or optical illusion, exists between the United States and England, between the United States and France, between France and England. It explains why, in times like these, it is so difficult to interpret correctly the behavior of a foreign country, even when that country is considered "friendly" or in the same cultural and ideological group.

An interesting illustration of this phenomenon was furnished by the attitude of the Vichy government in France toward America and of the American attitude toward the "men of Vichy." During the period following the Armistice, the policy of Marshal Pétain and his associates was to assure the Americans that the fundamental principles upon which Franco-American friendship had been established at the time of Lafayette were unchanged in spite of the fact that the Vichy government had abolished the Third Republic, suppressed all mechanism by which public opinion could express itself, and established an authoritarian government under the personal leadership of Marshal Pétain.

The American public, and possibly the State Department, were puzzled, to say the least, when they heard Laval declare that democracy had proved a failure the world over and when Pétain himself made so many state-

ments indicating his abhorrence for all democratic forms
and ideas, while at the same time the official or unofficial
representatives of Vichy in America were so active in
assuring everyone who would listen that all this did not
mean that the French were less attached to their traditional individualism and love of freedom.

That the Vichy government was led into this ambiguous
policy by necessity cannot be disputed. Day to day oppor-
tunism inspired the men who assumed the responsibility
of pretending to govern France under the German heel
after the Armistice. But leaving that important qualifica-
tion aside, it is none the less significant that the Vichy
government was candid enough to believe that the Americans could accept the proposition that nothing fundamental was changed in the general French viewpoint in
spite of the fact that the new regime repudiates not only
the institutions of the Third Republic but the whole set
of values based on what was called the "principles of
1789."

The reason for this miscalculation of the American
reaction to such a paradoxical policy on the part of the
Vichy government is to be found in the fact that whereas
the American conception of the nation is founded on an
ideology—democracy—French nationalism is, or has become, eminently territorial. The collapse of democracy in
France is evidently of secondary importance to the average Frenchman in comparison with the desire of getting
the Germans out of the country. How many times have
I heard Frenchmen exclaim before and during the war:
"Democracy go hang! What matters is France." This does
not necessarily mean that these Frenchmen were Fascists,
Communists, Monarchists, or what not. It means, however, that they conceived France independently of its
political complexion. Such a point of view is difficult to

imagine in an American for whom democracy is really synonymous with America itself.

In an analogous way, the Americans have a tendency to suspect the English people of being more preoccupied in saving their Empire than in maintaining the principles and the code of international ethics upon which British civilization claims to be founded. It is difficult for a nation established astride of a whole continent like the United States, to imagine the point of view of the British islander whose security does not depend on a continuous system of defense but on a network of strong points spread all over the world. The British Isles are not only very small in area but totally unable to sustain their population, either materially or culturally. Whereas the history of French political and cultural development can be considered within the frame of the French borders, and whereas the French Empire has always been an annex to metropolitan France—both in fact and in the consciousness of the average Frenchman—the political and cultural history of England is inseparable from that of the British Empire.

These variations in the national consciousness of different countries are determined therefore by the geographical location of these countries, by their economy, and also by certain particularities in their historical development.

For instance, racial discrimination has always been a major preoccupation of the Anglo-Saxon people whether they live in England, America, Australia, or India. It is much less pronounced and often nonexistent among the Latins. The contrast in point of view is striking when one compares the attitude of the North and South Americans toward the native Indians or the black. There is practically no color discrimination in most South and Central American countries. Brazil, in fact, offers the perfect example of racial equality, and in Mexico the tendency of the last few years seems to be toward a restoration of the supremacy of the native Mexican (whether pure Indian or mixed) over the pure white.

It is true that the general trend of Anglo-Saxon development has been directed against racial discrimination. The American Civil War may have been motivated by an economic conflict between an area of slave labor and an area of hired labor. But it could not have taken place without the incentive of a genuine moral inspiration. The crusade to establish some equality between white men and black men because "all of them were born equal" was sincere.

Normally race discrimination was on the wane all over the world until Hitler gave it a new impetus with his theory of the master race and his avowed ambition to organize the world on the basis of a new form of slavery. In so doing, the Nazis have revived on a world plane some of the conflicts which were settled in America nearly eighty years ago.

The above examples may help to show the diversity of meaning that can be attached to the concept of nation and the amount of misunderstanding that arises from the fact that each nation imagines other nations to be animated by comparable motives. The truth is that there are many categories of nations which can be classified according to the emphasis placed on one or the other major factors that contribute to the existence of the national sentiment.

In so far as modern nationalism has become the most dynamic force in the world today, its various manifestations can be classified under the following categories:

2. *Geographical nationalism*

France is a typical example of a country preoccupied for centuries with the protection of what it considers to be its natural frontiers. Many German historians think that Richelieu is the originator of a system of French foreign policy which has been steadfastly pursued by the Kings of France from Louis XIII onward, as well as by the Revolution, the Empire, the diplomacy of Talleyrand, the Second Empire, and all the succeeding Cabinets of the Third Republic. This policy, from the German point of view, has tended consistently to establish French hegemony over Europe. To achieve this end, France has constantly waged war to prevent the rise of any other great power on the Continent. As the only serious contender, since the decadence of Spain, was the German people (whether grouped under Austrian or Prussian leadership) it is understandable that all German rulers should have tried to destroy the power of France. When Hitler writes in *Mein Kampf* that France's account must be settled once and for all, he is merely the echo of a long tradition.

But if one looks at the question from the French point of view, what seems to predominate in French consciousness through many centuries is the desire to stabilize the frontiers of the country. The fact that France possesses "natural frontiers" on all sides except the east and northeast accounts, more than any other factor, for the continuity of French foreign policy. The grandeur and the weakness of France lies in the fact that on a front of some two hundred miles, between the Ardennes and the sea, it is wide open to invasion. These invasions have created France, but they can also destroy it. It is because there is this vast passage between France and Central Europe that France has always been and still is the most active "melting pot" in Europe, a country whose people are deeply conscious of being a nation but not a race. Its unity is essentially geographic and its nationalism strictly spacial.

All nationalist movements in France—at least in modern times—have been definitely limited on the map of Europe. They may be aggressive in their indirect consequences (the fostering of alliances in Eastern Europe, the Russian involvements, etc.) but the most ambitious of them do not aim at anything more than ensuring the physical security of the country within its "normal" boundaries.

It can be said that since Waterloo, France has renounced her mission as an originator of universal ideas. This does not mean that no ideas came out of France after the fall of Napoleon. Indeed the French nineteenth century was one of the most creative in the history of that country, but there was a marked decline in the impulse to universalize French culture and French concepts. With the brief interlude of Napoleon III, French nationalism was essentially defensive. Even the tremendous expansion of the French Colonial Empire which took place mostly after the war of 1870 failed to stimulate the imagination of the public. Although the French acquired the second largest Empire in the world, they did not become Empire-conscious. For the great majority of French political leaders, the French Empire was definitely a secondary preoccupation. Their real concern stopped at the borders of France proper. When Pierre Laval, at Bordeaux, in June 1940, persuaded the French government to remain a prisoner in France rather than carry on the fight in Africa, he illustrated tragically the force of French parochialism.

3. Empire nationalism

The British people may be the only ones in the world who cannot, by any stretch of the imagination, ever be self-sufficient. Their power and their very existence cannot be sustained more than a few weeks if they cannot communicate with their Dominions and colonies. Practically all other countries can conceive isolation, either as a dream or as a dire necessity. Survival for some of them might be difficult but it could be achieved. For England, isolation means death.

This reality is ever present in the mind of every Britisher. Whether he be a shopkeeper in Birmingham, a miner in Wales, or a broker in the City, he cannot forget it. To him the maintenance of the life lines of the Empire is not a political abstraction. It is a vital necessity.

The result of this condition is that, in the mind of the Britisher, there is no definite sense of frontier. There is no fixed line drawn anywhere on the map of the world to mark the precise limit of his dominion or of his security. His Empire occupies a vast area of land on the globe, but however vast this territorial expansion may be, it would be of no value without the few strong points and the ships which permit the British to circulate freely on the seas.

It should be noted too that the British Empire could not be held by force under present circumstances. The peculiar phenomenon of the allegiance to the Crown is the only link among such diversified communities as India, Canada, and Australia. The British fleet, however powerful, could not fight successfully any real rebellion in its Dominions today. Everybody admits that if Canada chose to secede and join the United States of America, for instance, London would be powerless to stop it. But the fact is that neither Canada nor any other member of the British Empire has found it advantageous to ask for total independence. The British Empire has tended more and more to become a federation of states, linked together by certain communities of interests, by loyalty to certain cultural and political concepts which are now being put to the test more than ever before in history.

To countries whose national sentiment is founded on fairly simple and tangible notions like the geographical realism of France, or on powerful inspirations like the racial concept of the Germans, or the faith of the Americans in democracy, the whole concept of the British Empire is at once fearful and wonderful. Here is a nation of some forty-six million people, set off on an island that could not by itself support more than a tenth of that number, separated by a narrow body of water—not much wider than a large American river—from a continent which has always been able, and is still able, to raise immense armies and whose periodic outbursts of aggressiveness have caused innumerable invasions of one continental power by another. France has been invaded over thirty times in her history. What now constitutes Germany and Italy has been invaded at least as often. England alone, in the same period of time, has been invaded successfully only once, some nine hundred years ago. Even America has seen foreign armies land on her soil more often than has England.

This single fact of the practical inviolability of the British Isles has been an important factor in the shaping of the peculiar brand of nationalism which flourishes in England. To other nations—be they the French under Louis XIV or Napoleon, or the Germans under Wilhelm II or Hitler—there is something profoundly incomprehensible and often irritating in the complexion of an Empire which is at once so powerful and so rich and at the same time so vulnerable and so precarious.

In a speech made in Berlin on December 10, 1940, Hitler expressed his indignation over the fact that "46 million rule and govern a total territory of roughly 40,000,000 square kilometers," while "85 million Germans have a living space of hardly 600,000 square kilometers."

Without discussing here the fallacies of the *Lebensraum* theory, this speech of Hitler like so many other pronouncements of the same kind is interesting for the light it throws on the incompatibility between the concepts of German nationalism and those which support the far-flung and discontinuous structure of the British Empire. When Hitler tries to show by statistics the injustice of the German position, he naturally conveys the idea that forty-six million English are actually "governing and ruling" over 40,000,-000 square kilometers in the same way as eighty-five million Germans are governing and ruling their 600,000 square kilometers of territory. He purposely confuses the notion of *Lebensraum* which implies a ratio between a certain physical area and the number of inhabitants that can or could live on it, and the notion of Commonwealth. If Hitler means what he says, which is a dismemberment and a redistribution of the area now ruled by the British Crown, one wonders how he could combine the German notion of racial nationalism with the loose and flexible order necessary for the maintenance of a world empire. He also omits to say that the forty-six million Englishmen are not the only inhabitants of their Empire, which supports in fact several hundred million people.

The very condition of the survival of the British Empire is precisely a certain indefiniteness in the relation between the various components of that Empire. Overorganization and overcentralization on totalitarian lines would most certainly destroy it. If Hitler should defeat England, he could not inherit the British Empire, or perhaps any portion of it. He would have to reconquer it piece by piece.

Thus British nationalism is inseparable from the concept of Empire. The question of the survival of England is not dependent on whether forty-six million British will continue to "rule and govern" 40,000,000 square kilometers of the earth or 20,000,000. What matters for England is the maintenance of the infinitely complex system called the British Empire. This system is founded on economic and political agreement between the various members of the Empire, as well as on many imponderables, such as historical prestige and cultural affinities. It is perfectly possible to break up this Empire, but there is no way of doing so without destroying England as a national entity.

The anomalous position of the British Isles themselves, which are so totally dependent on their Empire for existence, and on peaceful relations with the world at large, accounts for the difficulty experienced by other people when they try to appraise the English point of view. No other people is thus committed by the nature of things to act and think in terms so difficult for non-Britishers to understand, because no other people is so entirely dependent on forces and resources which are outside of its own territorial limits. No other country is vulnerable on so many points, separated by such distances, and in the present crisis, none is less free, in a certain sense, to change the course of what its people think is their destiny. If the British should be defeated in this struggle—either through capitulation or a compromise peace—there would be no power strong enough, not even the German master race, to preserve any continuity between the past and the future.

British imperial nationalism is the result of a long history of world responsibility. It may not be just that forty-six million people living on a small island should have assumed the role of breaking any attempt at world domination by any other people. But that these people conceive that such is their mission explains the paradoxical fact that they exist at all.

4. Political nationalism

The American people are, like all other people, attached to their homeland. They admire their country on account of the beauty of its scenery and the richness of its resources. They are conscious of being privileged and they sometimes believe that God was exceptionally kind to them in allocating to them this particular part of the surface of the earth. They have always believed and they still believe that it is their peculiar destiny to establish on this land a society which would be more just, more prosperous, and in all ways better than anything that can be done anywhere else. They believe that their mission is to set an example for other people. They hope that, in spite of many tribulations, the march of progress is constant, that it cannot be stopped, and that it is their peculiar duty to demonstrate that the American dream is not a fallacy.

The American people are not united by blood nor by any legend of a common origin. They have a culture, but most of it is not indigenous: its origins are traceable to various European influences.

In spite of the attachment to the homeland, the average American is not particularly sensitive to the mysticism of the soil. His country is too large to stimulate the kind of feeling for the ancestral plot of ground that is so characteristic of the European peasant. A large percentage of the Americans are seminomadic. For reasons of either business, convenience, or pleasure, they like to move from one town to another, from one farm to another farm. Few of them die where they were born, or care to.

The American people speak English, but it is not necessary to speak English to be an American. There is no great reverence for the language as a symbol of unity. It is a convenience more than a sacred inheritance.

Thus the usual factors which make for the unity of a

people are less prominent in the American national consciousness than they are with other people. Yet there are few people more conscious of being a nation and whose sense of destiny is more vigorous. There are no people— not excluding the Germans—who are more unanimous in their anxiety to shape their future and, possibly, that of the rest of the world. There is no nation more firmly convinced that, if it has not solved all the problems, it has at least laid down certain foundations which are meant to endure through centuries to come. Hitler pretends that the National-Socialist order will live one thousand years. The Americans do not make such boasts about American democracy, but there are not many among them who doubt that the principles upon which their nation is founded will outlive National Socialism.

To be an American is to express an act of faith. This faith is composed of many elements which are not always easy to dissociate because they are all intricately bound with the concept of being an American.

One of the main features of this faith is optimism. There is a general belief that human nature is indefinitely perfectible. There is confidence in progress and in the ever-expanding beneficence of education and science. Although the average American is a pretty good logician, he would not accept the proposition that a gain in one field might be compensated by a loss in another. The ascetic who sacrifices the material aspect of life for the good of his soul has no place in the American scheme of life. It may be that the Americans are not able to demonstrate that man's intellectual and moral progress through centuries is as conclusive as his progress in the material field, but there is a general tendency to trust that both go hand in hand. It is assumed that the improvement of physical conditions for all has an uplifting effect on the soul and on the intelligence. The expression *American standard of living* does not mean only more and better food, more motor cars, and more radios. It also means more culture, better morals.

An American bigot is rare but a really irreligious American is rarer still. Since religious persecutions have died down in the last thirty or forty years to a considerable extent, the word *Christian* has taken a wider though hazier meaning. In many public utterances of the last years, the Jews have been included among the people who follow Christian precepts, and there is little doubt that the Mohammedans would be incorporated also if there were any number of them in the United States. The Christian morality has shown a growing tendency to be identified, in America, with the idea of democracy. President Roosevelt went so far as to say that the survival of one depended on the survival of the other. The opposition between state and church so frequent in Europe is not and never has been an American problem. The people are at once too religious and too a-dogmatic to have permitted such conflicts.

Curiously enough, Christianity, in its American conceptions, is called in to bolster up a series of notions which were originally born from the rationalist philosophy of the eighteenth century. Christian teaching in America blends itself harmoniously with the prevalent pragmatism, and in times when nationalism is becoming more acute, it supports it with all its authority.

During the last four or five years, the American people have become more conscious of their interdependence with the rest of the world than they have ever been in their history. The Japanese attack and the declaration of war by Germany and Italy have given to that interdependence a character of vital urgency. For the duration of the war at least, isolationist doctrines have lost all meaning. Pearl Harbor and the series of reverses which have taken place in the South Pacific may not have had quite so deep an effect on the American people as Dunkirk had on the English. But they have served at least to dispel a good deal of complacency and discredit those who preached the comforting gospel that America was out of danger.

The principal effect of America's becoming totally involved in the Second World War has been to accentuate the peculiar character of American nationalism. Democracy is challenged by the National Socialist attempt at world domination with the result that America is identifying itself more than it ever has with democracy. It is now clear that the survival of American unity is dependent on the preservation of the principles, the institutions, and the general political structure of the United States.

It is interesting to note that there is no regime in the world today which is less challenged by the people who live under it than the American system. The Americans criticize the methods of their Administration and the men in power. They do not question the fundamental fact that the American system is intrinsically good and capable of enduring forever. The American system of government is sacred to the Americans and there is no suggestion of changing it. The rebellion against Franklin Roosevelt when he tried to modify the composition of the Supreme Court revealed the intensity of the national feeling on such matters. The respect for the Law, that is, the Constitution, has never been so intense and widespread.

At a time when democracy is supposed to be in a condition of decadence, the mere fact that there exists a nation of one hundred and thirty million people who cannot conceive that they could exist under any other political regime than democracy, is too often overlooked. It is true that there are some who believe that Fascism will conquer even America, and that the people of the United States could adapt themselves to totalitarianism. But those who hold these views either do not understand the implications of the Fascist-Nazi revolution or consider merely certain *methods* of the totalitarian state and refuse to face the fact that what is important in the present situation is not the methods used by the totalitarians but the doctrines which enable them to use these methods.

The strength of democratic ideas in America is of course relative and I am attempting only to appraise it in relation to other countries. It is perfectly possible to destroy democracy in America as it has been destroyed in France. But it should be remembered that the general attitude of the French toward the Republic was very different from that of the Americans toward their own system of government. For many years before the fall of the Third Republic, it was not only the men in power who were attacked and discredited, but the institutions and the very principles of democracy. Nobody wants to overthrow the form of government which exists in the United States. But a large section of French opinion had lost confidence in the Republican institutions and wanted them abolished. The military defeat brought about the end of a regime which a large section of the population had ceased to believe in.

The same thing can happen in America, but at the moment there are no signs that the Americans have lost any of their faith in the kind of system which has endured since the birth of the American nation and which, in the popular consciousness, is inseparable from the very existence of America itself.

Considered from this angle, America is now the only political strength capable of opposing the National Socialist revolution. American nationalism still expresses itself best through the word *Democracy.*

5. Racial nationalism

The tribe is the most primitive form of human society and the tribal instincts the most deeply rooted in the obscurity of the subconscious. The tribe is bound together by fetishism, by magic symbols and rites, by the system of totems and taboos, and by the worship of tribal gods.

The evolution of man from the tribal stage to the conception of a modern nation has been slow and the task of discarding primitive concepts which are as old as man himself is far from being completed. In every form of nationalism there is a tremendous residue of superstition and we continue to use symbols and magic formulas and to worship certain men who have been transfigured into heroes or gods.

A few examples will help to illustrate this point:

Every nation has its flag. A flag in itself is obviously nothing but an object the value of which is purely symbolical. It happens, however, to be the only valueless object that is surrounded with sufficiently strong taboos to be considered properly sacred. A certain ritual accompanies the handling of the flag. To "insult the flag" is everywhere a grave offense.

Even in countries where the national consciousness expresses itself more or less abstractly, there are curious survivals of the times when special gods and goddesses were supposed to be the protectors or mythical forebears of the nation. We do not worship Pallas Athena, but our cartoonists keep alive the allegorical figures of Uncle Sam, John Bull, Marianne, etc. Curiously enough these representations of national entities tend to become fixed in their lines and somewhat hieratic. Marianne has not discovered high-heeled shoes and silk stockings as yet; she still wears her sabots and the short striped skirt of the guillotine days. John Bull has not changed a detail of his aspect since Pickwick's times and Uncle Sam's coat and hat are definitely dated. Thus the cartoonists respond unconsciously to one essential rule of fetishism: the symbols should be as immutable as possible.

Mystic or magic formulas are more potent than ever. *"Liberté, Egalité, Fraternité,"* "Workers of the World, Unite!" "Make the World Safe for Democracy," etc., are invocations or battle cries which have greatly contributed to the solution of the problem of making men believe they are dying for noble causes.

We have also preserved the cult of the animal totems. The cock is the totem of France, the lion of England. The bear (though not officially) incarnates Russia, and there are enough eagles, with one or more heads, to fill an aviary.

These examples are intended to show only that even among the most civilized people very ancient tribal concepts survive, at least in a mild and sometimes comic form. But in the course of time the tendency of society has been to disentangle itself from the irrational and from inherited superstition. Practical politics superseded the art of the medicine man. Men tried to organize their government according to certain rational rules. The relation between the citizen and the state was gradually established on the basis of some sort of written or unwritten contract. The idea that nations have a supernatural origin has usually given place to a more sober view of their history. All modern peoples have accepted the elimination of the fabulous in their political conceptions.

There is one exception—Germany—which in our time has boldly reversed its course and decided to restore beliefs and standards of value in complete opposition to what has been the trend of Western civilization for some two thousand years. The residues of tribal instincts which survive in a mild form elsewhere have been given a new life in Germany. Symbols and rites have regained their full value. Fetishism, superstition, collective myths have become fundamental dogmas. The irrational in the individuals and in the masses is exploited or glorified, or both, and any corrective criticism is banished as corrosive.

Germany still produces scientists and thinkers—at least one can presume so—but the spirit of research is not free. Science must work for a definite end, preferably war at the moment. Artists are in the same predicament. The result is that one of the most distinctive traits of Western culture, the spirit of free investigation, has disappeared from Germany. Science, in fact, has been reduced to the improvement of existing technology. If a German scientist made a discovery which, for some reason or other, contradicted the official dogma, he would have a good chance of going to a concentration camp. Scientific criticism and rationalism have been formally and effectively subordinated to the new mystical imperatives of "blood and soil."

This is not the place to give a full description of the doctrine which supports the Nazi movement. It has been done many times and very thoroughly. But for the purpose of this argument the following points can be emphasized:

Hitler did not invent the "racial state" nor the *Führerprinzip,* nor most of the ideas that support the conception of National Socialism. Pan-Germanism, anti-Semitism, the theory of the superiority of the Nordic race, had given rise to an abundant literature long before Hitler was born. Similarly the study of old German legends and the somewhat grotesque metaphysical vaticinations of Wagner had been a fad, but they were beginning to be considered as so much quaint junk by the time I ran around the Bois de Boulogne with my hoop.

It is quite curious to find, in fact, that the super-modern ideology of Hitlerian Germany should have its immediate origins in such pseudoscientific theories as those of Gobineau, Houston Stewart Chamberlain, Richard Wagner. These fanciful prophets had a certain vogue around 1880-

1900 but they were rapidly submerged and forgotten for the simple reason that their theories could not stand up against the findings of verifiable science which was progressing in a very different direction.

Out of their writings, however, Hitler and his disciples evolved the racial myth which is the cornerstone of National Socialism.

It is useless to repeat here what everyone knows: that the concept of "race" as used by the doctors of Nazidom does not correspond to any scientific fact. According to them, the Germans are a blend of several "races" in which the so-called Nordic, although constituting only 8 per cent of the population, is nevertheless the really valuable one from the biological point of view. This Nordic blood is creative, energetic, and the vehicle of all virtues that tend to make the Superman. The Germans are not the only people to have Nordic blood. It would seem that the Egyptians, for instance, the Greeks, and today the Japanese must have a strain of it. Thanks to this theory, one can infer also that Dante, Marco Polo, St. Francis, Giotto, Michelangelo, Bacon, Lavoisier, Louis XIV, and Napoleon owe their genius to the presence in their blood of a good proportion of Nordic blood.

The trouble about Nordic blood, according to German theorists, is that those in whose veins it flows are more exposed to extinction than races of an inferior quality. Being a warrior *par excellence,* the Nordic man has been decimated in countless battles through the ages. Being a great adventurer, he has emigrated and lost his original purity. He is also particularly sensitive to tuberculosis. But in spite of all these handicaps, the Nordic man is still the superior man and the Germans—being the only people really conscious of what the real problem of humanity on this earth is all about—must see to it that, through them, a race as pure as hygiene, eugenics, war, and deportations can make it eventually dominates and rules over this planet.

If one reads *Mein Kampf* straight through, which is not amusing, one cannot help being struck by the recurrence of expressions such as purity, purification, pollution, corruption. Most of the time Hitler accuses the Jews of being responsible for polluting the purity of the German blood, but the account he gives of his days in Vienna, in his early youth, shows that his hatred of "impurity" extended much further. The Austro-Hungarian Empire was to him the archmonstrosity of all times because it was such a hodge-podge of races to which nothing is comparable except the United States. The Jews became the most constant object of his persecutions for many psychological and political reasons, but if they are the symbol of all impurity and of all evil, one must not forget that the racial myth extends much further. It embraces in fact any nation or any part of a nation deemed inferior from the point of view of the Nazi blood-hierarchy.

The *Führerprinzip*, which is the natural outgrowth of the racial state, is somewhat difficult for a non-German mind to understand. That a whole nation should abandon all its liberties to a man who promised it a kind of apocalyptic redemption and accept the absolute infallibility of this man in all conceivable matters appears more as the result of a mass neurosis than the normal behavior of a people in search of a liberator. The truth is that such a phenomenon could probably not have happened anywhere except in Germany and at that particular time. The origins of Hitlerism must be traced much farther back than the years covered by Hitler's life, as I will try to show in a later chapter. But the conditions existing after the First World War created a perfect setting for the successful rise to power of this prophet of German nationalism in its most extreme form.

The last war had left the Germans totally humiliated. They could not accept and did not accept the simple fact that their armies had been defeated. They preferred to think that they had been betrayed. In the years of chaos and misery that followed the war and later on the inflation, the sense of frustration deepened. The small bourgeoisie were more badly hit than any other class and they developed a condition of chronic anxiety which ended in a sort of collective nervous breakdown. Millions of Germans, young or old, felt degraded by the prospect of having to become proletarians—a fear of which there is none greater in the mind of the small bourgeois. As a remedy to their frustrations and fears they were offered "reasonable" solutions: the intellectual panaceas of the Liberals and the Social Democrats. In the state of collective infantilism in which the people found themselves they could be appealed to only by forces which moved their subconscious. Being very weak physically they had to be told of heroism and power. Being spiritually disintegrated they had to be fed with hallucinations and myths.

Instead of Hitler they could have chosen a political psychoanalyst, if there is such a thing. But politics are not rational. If ever there was a man who fitted a situation, it was Hitler. Rebellious, obsessed by dreams of revenge and hatred, totally irrational, he was the Forgotten Man gone haywire. If future generations manage to regain certain standards of values which were considered normal only twenty-five years ago and which are now disintegrating, they will probably be at a loss to account for the fact that the man of destiny of our time, Adolf Hitler, should have none of the attributes by which the greatness of man is generally recognized. The physical appearance of Hitler is in itself a puzzling phenomenon. The man is neither handsome nor repulsive. His features are remarkable by the fact that they are in no way striking. His face is not

forceful and when the Führer is portrayed as a conqueror, one is led to the inescapable suspicion that he is
posing for the camera. Although Hitler has been described
more than any man alive, by both his worshipers and his
enemies, one retains only a hazy impression of the man.[1]
There is no record that he is either kind, cruel, or in any
way more gifted than the average individual. There is no
evidence that he is a good organizer, a creative genius, or
a sound thinker. His book, *Mein Kampf,* and his speeches
give the impression of an unorganized mind, very often
confused and always awkward in expression. No man has
shaken the world with his eloquence as often and as violently as Adolf Hitler. No human voice has been listened
to with more awe. And yet there is not one single sentence
of Hitler that can be quoted as reflecting exceptional
wisdom or insight, beauty or originality.

In spite of the legend built around him, he conveys a
strange impression of impersonality or anonymity. Some
like to compare him to Napoleon, but the comparison
cannot be sustained. The striking feature of Napoleon
was the incisive outline of his personality, his capacity to
give a recognizable stamp to everything he did. Hitler's
mark, on the other hand, is always blurred. His actions

---

[1] In his book *Is Tomorrow Hitler's?* H. R. Knickerbocker has listed the
following contradictory opinions on Hitler's eyes:

"They are small, greenish brown and almost poetically introspective
eyes" (Otto Tolischus).

". . . faded blue eyes between colorless brows and puffy sallow cheeks"
(William D. Bayes).

"The fanaticism in his eyes was the most commanding thing about
him . . . they possess a hypnotic quality that can easily persuade his followers to do anything the mind behind the eyes desires" (John Mc-
Cutcheon Raleigh).

"The eyes alone were notable. Dark grey and hyperthyroid, they have
the peculiar shine which often distinguishes geniuses, alcoholics and hys-
terics" (Dorothy Thompson).

"His eyes are very dark blue" (Lothrop Stoddard).

"He fixed his flat, non-magnetic, China-blue eyes on me. . . ." (H. R.
Knickerbocker himself).

do not appear to spring from any conscious plan but to be the product of irrational and mostly emotional outbursts. And yet there is a definite consistency in his method, in his systematic disregard for all rules and precedents which had hitherto been accepted as the fundamental code of governing the relations between "civilized states."

Everyone admits that the man has cunning, that he can be adroit to the point of being uncanny, that his instinct of timing and his understanding of the weakness of his opponents is far beyond that of any other leader now alive. But the process by which he arrives at his decisions escapes ordinary intellectual analysis and can seldom be explained logically. He is disconcertingly feminine in his behavior toward reality and, like a woman, senses the limits of what is possible with greater accuracy and much more imagination than a man.

From all standards he is mediocre, uncharacteristic, and colorless. The best that is said about him is that he is a "political genius," which implies a pejorative opinion of politics.

But that man is god, or the nearest thing to it that has been seen in many centuries.

He is god, for the Germans at least, in the sense that he incarnates for them what, under the Führer's spell, they have accepted as their destiny. This means in practice that the cult inspired by Hitler, the belief in his infallibility and his mesmeric influence over his people, justifies the irrational aspects of the National Socialist world revolution. Hitler is essentially the mass man of our time. The very fact that he is mediocre explains his demagogic appeal. Millions of average Germans have found in him the supreme incarnation of their own secret aspirations. His education, his tastes, his prejudices are those of the half-educated and the conventional small bourgeois all over the world. He has accomplished what it seemed impossible for the mass man ever to accomplish: he has broken down all inhibitions; he has challenged all the values of twenty centuries of civilization and restored as sublime truths the most primitive instincts and the most regressive superstitions.

Rauschning in his book *The Revolution of Nihilism* advances the theory that National Socialism is not a movement inspired by any doctrine. It is according to him totally opportunist, the only aim of the Nazi leaders being the maintenance of their power and the extension of their domination. In view of this fact National Socialism can only destroy, it can never create. The doctrine of racialism, like the anticapitalist crusade, would be mere subterfuge, useful at the moment to further National-Socialist aims but which can be discarded or changed at a moment's notice.

Rauschning is only partly right in his diagnosis. The cynicism of the Nazi leaders is boundless, but even if they do not believe in the doctrines they preach, these doctrines exist and are accepted at their face value by millions of men. In other words, one cannot accept the thesis that Hitler and his associates are mere gangsters or modern condottieri who have seized power through sheer trickery and have fooled sixty million innocent Germans with their fanciful quackery. The truth is that the National-Socialist revolution is real and its dominant feature is the assertion that the German people have the divine right to dominate and rule the world because they are racially superior to others.

Innumerable pseudoscientific volumes have been written in Germany to prove this theory, but the real justification of it is the fundamental idea that force and violence are the *ultima ratio* of human worth. This notion, of course, was not invented by Hitler and his associates. It is as old as the caveman. But the fact remains that the best test by which we can recognize civilization is precisely the long and painful effort of hundreds of generations to eliminate violence from human intercourse and replace it by either religion, morality, law, or some sort of universally recognized concept.

By establishing the doctrine that a certain race is superior to others, the Germans have, by that very fact, denied the validity of civilization itself. If it is admitted that a race is superior to others, it follows that that particular race has a *right* to impose its will on others either by force, by threat of force, or by any method which will make that right manifest.

Racial nationalism as preached and practiced by modern Germany is the most dangerous form of all nationalisms. The very fact that it is irrational and that its roots go deep into the most barbaric instincts of man ensures its vitality. It cannot be combated by reason because it has the force of ancestral primitiveness to sustain it. It is eminently contagious in a world where masses have an overwhelming power and where there is everywhere a curious reverence for the infallibility of the mass. Racial nationalism tends to destroy all remnants of humanism that still subsist in this suffocating world. The fact that it breeds war is only one of its evils—and not the worst: it also engenders the crudest forms of obscurantism and brutality. It is the straight road to a new form of barbarism in which Western civilization can easily perish.

CHAPTER III

Nationalism as a Force of Destruction

THE division of the various brands of nationalism outlined in the preceding pages should not be taken too rigidly. The characteristics of one type have a tendency to permeate the others. The political nationalism of the United States, for instance, does not exclude the geographical nor the imperial nor the racial influences. But the universal tendency is toward the most extreme form of nationalism as it exists in the totalitarian states.

It is true that in England and in the United States there are strong moderating forces—the remnants of classical liberalism—which tend to keep in check the worst manifestations of chauvinism. But there is no doubt that, under the pressure of war, these forces are becoming every day less able to stem the universal tide. Each nation shows a growing inclination to distrust any form of internationalism and to seek security or salvation in an intensification of the national spirit. Each nation too is experiencing an attack of xenophobia, and it is needless to emphasize the progress of anti-Semitism, even in the countries where it never existed before.

On the whole it can be asserted that the forces of nationalism are everywhere on the ascendant, and that concerted efforts to establish any valid alternative are as yet very embryonic.

The most interesting ideas in this line have been the suggestions of some sort of Anglo-American union after the war, the dual purpose of which would be to create an overwhelming force against the recurrence of aggression and possibly guide the world in the paths of peace and democracy. These ideas have found a good deal of response in both England and America. The main objections to them are that they do not really propose a new form of internationalism and that other countries would remain suspicious of what would appear to them as an Anglo-American attempt to dominate the world permanently. Furthermore, these plans are easier to talk about than to apply. The unfortunate accumulation of distrust which exists between the Americans and the English has been but slightly affected by the war, and a great deal of traditional touchiness and foolish chauvinism on each side would have to be overcome before the indispensable limitation of sovereignties could even be talked about.

More promising perhaps because less concrete and more general are the ideas embodied in the Declaration of the United Nations which was signed by twenty-six countries in Washington on January 1, 1942. There is not much to say for the moment about this instrument except to remark on the name "United Nations," which was carefully chosen, it would seem, by President Roosevelt and Winston Churchill. United Nations is reminiscent of United States. It is a better expression than "associated powers," which is too vague, or "the allies," which implies purely coordination for war purposes. United Nations offers a better promise. It is a happier thought. If it presupposes a change in the usual concepts of nationalism, this has not been mentioned as yet.

All these plans however will probably prove to be very inadequate when the time comes to try to apply them. The prodigious expansion of Japan in Asia, for instance,

raises a series of questions which are covered neither by
the Atlantic Charter nor by the Declaration of the United
Nations. As the war expands and evolves, ideas concerning
the organization of the peace change, and will change still
more. The only denominator common to the people fighting the Axis is the will to save themselves from slavery.
More constructive programs will have to wait.

It may be argued that it is difficult to differentiate exactly what is good and bad in nationalism. It is a matter of
standards, and we live in a time when there are no universal standards to go by. Nevertheless for those who have
not lost hope of organizing the world on a basis which
would reduce the use of violence to a tolerable minimum,
nationalism under its modern form appears as an insurmountable obstacle.

It is difficult really to appreciate how "national" each of
us has become because the process, although rapid, has
been gradual and also because we take nationalism so
much for granted.

The only way to measure the growth of nationalism as
a world force is to remember the conditions of the world
as they existed twenty-five or even twenty years ago.

Even judging by the relatively short experience of my
own lifetime, I cannot help but be conscious that I have
lived in several "worlds," or periods, as distinct from one
another as the great periods of history which I was taught
at school. I do not know whether all men of my generation
could subdivide these periods in the same manner. Personal accidents of life undoubtedly modify the perspective
for each of us. But, *looking back* on the last forty years, I
see a division of these four decades more or less as follows:

1. 1900-1914: The fabulous world of peace, security,
order, stability. This period appears to me now as curiously static. In Europe nothing seemed to move. The only
changes were those affecting the individual life. Each man

lived against a motionless background of stable institutions, fixed standards, and permanent laws. The notion of violence had been practically eliminated. Wars and revolutions were things of the past or relegated to distant lands. Only the Russians had passports, which was considered a very queer and archaic custom. There were no quotas for immigrants, no working permits. One could travel anywhere in the world with no other "papers" than a steamship or a railroad ticket. A dollar was worth five francs and nobody thought that it could be worth anything else until the Day of Judgment. People carried gold pieces in their pockets and they were called "Louis" in France although they bore the effigy of Napoleon III or of the Republic. Nobody talked of "confidence" because the whole world had forgotten fear and danger. Nationalism was represented by such quaint figures as Paul Déroulède, the rabble-rousing patriot, who clamored, in a wilderness of polite indifference, for a war of "revenge" and the return of Alsace-Lorraine.

2. 1914-1918: Four years of cataclysm. The World War appeared so terrible, so destructive, and so vast that most men of those times were sure of only one thing: that nothing worse had ever happened to humanity and that nothing worse could ever happen in the future. It was therefore assumed that in any event, this would be the "war to end all wars" and that eternal peace would follow. This hope was so real and so strong that millions of men were willing to die for it and millions of others faced incredible danger and suffering to see it fulfilled. It was only much later—several years after the war—that men began to wonder why they had fought, and whether the dead had not died in vain.

3. 1919-1929: For most of the world, a wild and intoxicating scramble to become rich quick and—under the impact of the American boom—the universal conviction that

the "American system" worked and that the secret of endless prosperity had been found at last. Wall Street became the center of the world. The fact that the Versailles Treaty and the League of Nations did not solve all the problems of peace was obvious, but it did not destroy the belief that the last war had been the last one indeed. When victors and vanquished hated war so intensely, how could there ever be another war? And treaties were still manufactured by diplomats, signatures were exchanged, and governments still "honored their words." But passports were maintained and immigration laws tightened.

4. 1930-1934: The stock-market crash and the great American depression. The brutal awakening from the dream of eternal prosperity and the sudden revelation that the "American system" had failed shook the world. The Economic Man entered into the throes of his painful agony. The allegiance between democracy and capitalism weakened and men all over turned to other remedies. Ideologies began to undermine one another and to prepare the way for the great rebellion of Nazi Germany.

5. 1934-1939: The rise of Hitlerism. The great lesson of this period was the gradual revelation that the spiritual values upon which the Western democracies had lived—or forgotten to live—had been so thoroughly eroded during the last twenty-five years that they could no longer serve as unifying factors. In front of the new threat of Nazism, the war of 1914-1918 appeared, in retrospect, not as the Armageddon which it was thought to be, but as a conflict limited to purely military, imperialistic, or economic antagonism. The new Total War forced such a thorough and universal revision of all concepts that no sensible man was able to formulate any program for the future. The men who fought the war of 1914-1918 *believed* in the possibility of a permanent peace, which Wilson tried to establish through the League of Nations. The men of this

era are dimly conscious that the Second World War may
mark a complete break in the continuity of Western civilization. The democracies are on the defensive, militarily
and morally. The possibility that they may succumb is not
excluded. The possibility of such an outcome did not exist
in 1914-1918, or was not thought of. The absence of any
common denominator between National Socialism and
the Western World is an insurmountable obstacle to the
prefiguration of any stable future order.

1. The decadence of freedom

From the point of view of the individual, taking myself
as an example, for instance, and a fortunate one, the trend
of events from 1914 to today has had as a practical effect
the gradual loss of the sense of stability and security which
were taken for granted in my youth. Like everyone else,
during the period of 1919-1929 I was carried by the wave of
illusion, in the sense that I made no clear distinction between pure speculation and constructive expansion either
for the world in general or for myself in particular.

Nevertheless I was quite conscious that the twenties
were thoroughly unstable, uncreative, and moronic, although I would have been hard put at the time to explain
why I had such an impression.

During that period, nationalism was at a relatively low
ebb in Western Europe as well as in America, but it is
interesting to note that although the world was at peace,
the freedom of peace as it existed before 1914 was never
restored in practice. Passports, registrations, and regulations of all kinds were maintained everywhere. Travel
appeared easier, more comfortable and more rapid, but
it was not sufficiently noticed that only a small and
relatively rich minority was allowed to move about freely.
Masses were condemned to live, work, and die where they

were born. Migration, the natural safety valve of the past, was made all but impossible. True enough, Italians, Poles, Belgians, and Spaniards were allowed to come to France in great numbers, but they came as hired laborers. They seldom were allowed to become French or to settle in France permanently. An even stricter policy of the same kind was applied in the Americas.

Thus, in spite of an impression of peace, of prosperity, and of freedom, restrictive forces applying both to economics and to individuals were on the increase. The fact that the "people who mattered" enjoyed growing facilities to move about from one corner of the earth to the other for business or pleasure made one overlook the restrictions imposed on those that "do not matter"—that is, the millions of men and women all over the world for whom immigration to a better or different land had become all but impossible.

It was not merely economic necessity that forced millions of men to work and live on the spot where they found themselves. The general tendency to consider labor as a product to be bought and sold had been operating for a long while. Labor was therefore subject to restrictive regulations of all kinds. But if this practice was not new it was certainly applied with increasing effectiveness and justified by the world-wide movement away from the liberal economy of the nineteenth century. High tariff barriers and the various systems of quotas made it necessary to tighten immigration laws, while the restrictions imposed on the natural movements of surplus population reinforced everywhere the nationalist and imperialist forces. This in turn led to wars.

For instance, there is reason to doubt, given the temperament of the Italians, whether Mussolini's ridiculous dream of creating a new Roman Imperium could ever have taken shape if the Italians had been allowed to emigrate freely and peacefully to America, where they wanted to go, instead of being compelled to conquer Ethiopia at the cost of much sacrifice and bloodshed.

The transition from the kind of world which existed in my childhood, before 1914, to the world of today, has been gradual. For the individual, it has usually been imperceptible, but there are probably few periods in history where such profound and world-wide changes have taken place in the space of a lifetime. The expression *laissez faire* has been applied to the pre-1914 era. It is well chosen. The dominating impression which remains in the memory of those who have known those times is probably one of a greater freedom of movement and of thought than has ever been known since.

That a certain familiar world had died forever in 1914 and that no new world had been born in 1919 was not apparent until Hitler came to demonstrate the reality of the vacuum in which we have lived for the last twenty years.

2. *Bonaparte and Wilson*

It is a strange thing to consider that the ideas of Woodrow Wilson concerning people's right of self-determination should have been hailed as an unmitigated improvement over the pre-1914 concepts. The high idealism of Wilson, and the fact that he represented some sort of promise of world salvation, blinded the Allies, the Central Powers, and the Americans alike to the fact that Wilson's ideals were typically American, drawn from the lessons of American history and not necessarily applicable to the rest of the world, and in particular to Europe.

Woodrow Wilson, like all Americans, was imbued with the quasi-religious conviction that democracy, as conceived in America, was the most perfect form of government that could possibly be achieved. The manner in which the

American nation was born—by a war of liberation from the "tyranny" of the English Crown—was ever present in the mind of the President of the United States. He took it for granted that the highest aim of civilization was to free all people from the arbitrary rule of nondemocratic governments. Wilson and the great majority of his compatriots were undoubtedly sincere in their belief that the removal of the Kaiser in Germany and of the Emperor of Austria would eliminate war, on the presumption that the people, left to themselves, would always prefer the pursuit of peaceful progress. The crusade to make "the world safe for democracy" was identified with the crusade to eliminate war.

The failure in Wilson's reasoning and the great disillusion of the American people after the Treaty of Versailles cannot be wholly attributed, however, to the failure of the statesmen of Europe to establish democracy in the whole world. Democracy, as it was known then, and the values that sustain it, were already undermined when Wilson went to Paris. The emergence of Communism and, a little later on, of Fascism were sufficient proof that new forces were present in Europe at the time of Versailles and that all attempts to build a new peaceful society on liveral democratic lines were bound to fail.

In proclaiming the right of national self-determination, Wilson did not prepare the way for the liberation of the people from tyranny: he gave a stimulus to nationalism and, quite unwittingly, paved the road for the extreme revolutionary claims of Hitler and Mussolini. It is a strange paradox that the racial myth of the Nazis, the Roman imperialism of Mussolini, the *Lebensraum* theory, and other totalitarian ambitions should find some sort of justification in the Wilsonian philosophy. Of course the Nazis, in seeking such a justification, are perverting the idealism of Wilson, who never dreamed that his wish to free the people of Europe could be used as an argument to create new forms of oppression beside which the despotism of William II, Francis Joseph, or even the Czar of Russia appear retrospectively as very mild paternalism.

Wilson and those who so fervently accepted his theories were reformers. As such they visualized pre-1914 Europe as fundamentaly bad. They condemned the imperialism of the European governments (not excluding those of the Allies) and the whole principle of the balance of power. Obsessed by the vision of a better world in which the peace-loving people would really govern themselves, these reformers were not aware that everything was not altogether bad in the kind of Europe which had emerged from the Congress of Vienna in 1815.

This Congress, under the inspiration of Talleyrand, was evidently a reaction against the French Revolution. It tried to reconstruct Europe on the principle of "legitimacy." However artificial this construction may have been, it did have one good effect: it moderated for nearly a century the extremist tendencies of nationalism. It enabled the nineteenth century to be one of the most enlightened and really civilized eras that the world has known.

Woodrow Wilson, being an American, was profoundly traditional in the sense that he molded his understanding of human history on the pattern of the history of the United States. Quite unconsciously, he conceived his mission as the continuation of the American and French Revolutions of the eighteenth century. It could be said that he undertook to pursue the mission of Bonaparte, who set off to conquer Europe under the pretense of spreading the ideas of the French Revolution and liberating the enslaved people from the tyranny of the kings, emperors, and autocrats.

But in the same way as Napoleon was defeated because

the doctrine of national independence which he spread gave birth to a series of coalitions against him, similarly we see now that the Wilsonian doctrine of self-determination and freedom of the peoples of Europe has led directly to the radicalism of modern nationalism, which is now proposed not only as an absolute but as *the* only absolute to which men still adhere.

No one can pretend of course that Wilsonism is responsible for the emergence of Nazism. But the fact remains that the philosophical concepts upon which the men of 1919-1930 tried to build the peace of the world were already potentially invalid before the First World War started. Wilson was a man of the nineteenth century, the history of which can be summed up as follows: During those hundred years Western civilization achieved a good measure of political democracy, not only in Europe but also in America, and thus the promise of the French and American Revolutions was fulfilled. But economic democracy was established nowhere. The last attempt—the Communist revolution of 1917—was a failure and ended in the bureaucratic despotism of the Stalin regime.

The war of 1914-1918 appeared senseless and appears still more senseless now because it produced not a single new moral or spiritual value. It was fought in appearance, and in appearance only, for a set of ideas already outmoded. Neither the Treaty of Versailles, nor the League of Nations, nor the "prosperity" of the twenties, succeeded in solving the inherent conflict of democracy such as we know it: the paradox of economic and social inequality within the framework of political equality.

If the United States had not taken part in the war of 1914-1918 and if, especially, Wilson had not enjoyed such a messianic prestige due to the fact that the whole of Europe was spiritually and economically bankrupt, it is probable that the disintegrating process of Western democracy would have become apparent there and then. We would not have had to wait for the failure of the Communist revolution and the advent of Nazism to discover that what we called democracy was nothing but an empty shell in postwar Europe. The fact that the United States—up to 1930 at least—remained as a living demonstration of the vitality of capitalist democracy sustained the illusion that this system could still be saved by the classical method of peaceful evolution and reform.

No doubt this idea is still alive in many American circles today, and that in spite of the dislocation produced by the war, there are many who believe that capitalist democracy can be preserved in America very much as it has stood up to now, even if it is doomed in Europe. This problem, although it interests America primarily, is in fact world-wide. The isolationists, who are now silenced by necessity, may feel that they will have another chance to make their voice heard and see their point of view triumph after the war, on the basis that the insulation of America from the chaos of Europe will be even more imperative than in 1919. Those who hold this belief can probably conceive of America functioning under one system—capitalist democracy—while the rest of the world is so thoroughly bankrupt that the notion of individually acquired wealth will cease to have any practical meaning.

This may be so. But it seems more probable that the evolution of democracy in America will not be very different from what we already see happening in England. It is true that, relatively speaking, the American people may not have to change so thoroughly nor so abruptly their economic and financial conceptions. But the fact that over 50 per cent of American production and income is to be devoted to war, that the national debt will be over 110 billion dollars in 1943 while it did not exceed 25 billion dollars in the First World War, is sufficient to give an idea of the magnitude of the dislocation which this war is bound to produce in the relations between private capital and the state. There was much alarm during the depression, caused by the system of deficit financing adopted by the Administration. It seemed unorthodox and it was feared that it would eventually destroy the capitalist system, or at any rate limit its field of action and influence. But if this could be said about the depression, what should be said now that the war is forcing the United States into a process of deficit financing the limits of which are beyond anybody's vision?

The truth is that the war has tied the fate of America to that of the rest of the world not only strategically and morally, but also economically. The isolationists may hope for a natural reaction in favor of their theory when the war is over. But there is little likelihood that this will be practical, even if the American people wish it. It will be extremely difficult for America to disentangle itself from the consequences of this war because its participation in it is so much greater than its participation in the war of twenty-five years ago. Already in fact, America is fully engaged on a road which must necessarily lead to a profound revision of the financial and economic structure of democracy. That revision is well advanced in England. It is overdue everywhere and one of the causes of the present world convulsion is to be found in the fact that no attempt at a real readjustment of the traditional concepts of finance and economics was made when the Western democracies made the Versailles Treaty.

3. Failure of self-sufficiency

The real causes of the failure of the League of Nations have not been eradicated and there is very little indication at the moment that popular opinion anywhere in the world is ready to accept the indispensable remedy. That remedy lies in the direction of a new internationalism, founded on the recognition that we have now reached a point where progress cannot go forward as long as the various nations try to advance it within the frame of nationalism.

The principle of self-sufficiency, which cannot be justified except as a means of waging war, is self-defeating, as already demonstrated by the lowering of the standard of living in the whole of Europe. America may hope to maintain its own present standards for a while on account of its favored position, but this can be only of short duration, and in any event no real progress in the future can be foreseen under the present system.

The reasons for this are so obvious that it is strange that the advocate of autarchy or isolationism under the American form cannot see them: the normal development of technology tends to make the exploitation of the resources of the whole planet easier and more accessible to all men wherever they are. It does not much matter that oil should be found in only a few places on the earth and that rubber should grow only in certain climates. The important point is that, theoretically, oil and rubber are transportable everywhere and accessible to all men. Yet the accessibility of such and many other products is becoming more difficult, and in many cases impossible, under the doctrine of self-sufficiency—be it justified by the necessity of building a war economy, as in the totalitarian states, or of saving democracy and the capitalist system as was advocated by the American isolationists.

However different the motives of the American protectionists and the Nazi revolutionaries, the policies followed are sustained by the same chauvinistic impulses. The Nazis must eventually impose their rule over the whole world to make their system work, an impossible undertaking,

while the American isolationists, in wanting to save capitalist democracy, were denying the very principles upon
which it can function by trying to limit it to a definite
area: the American continent.

Cordell Hull has been consistently clairvoyant in saying that an expansion of international trade and a liberali-
zation of commercial treaties between nations were indispensable for the maintenance and expansion of human
welfare in America itself. But Hull has failed in his efforts,
and his theories, even if they are sound, have only an
academic interest now that America itself is at war.

Moreover, it may be that Cordell Hull has put the cart
before the horse. Like so many statesmen of this generation, he believes implicitly that if it were possible to regu-
late economic forces, everything else would follow. Justice,
good will, happiness, and peace are—in his estimation—the
natural products of satisfactory economic conditions.

But the truth is that modern masses have lost faith in
the democratic ideal that the material improvement of
their living conditions entails automatically more freedom
and more happiness. That the Economic Man is dead, as
Peter Drucker has tried to demonstrate, may not be literally true. But the fact is that men have become willing to
abandon the promise of a "more abundant life" for the
minimum security that is offered to them under the totalitarian or semitotalitarian systems.

This has been proved not only by the German people,
who for eight years have accepted the sacrifices necessary
to prepare for war, but among the conquered nations in
Europe. When they submit to their conquerors it is not
due to impotence alone, but to a secret acceptance of a
modern state of slavery which ensures a minimum of
security for the price of freedom.

An intelligent Frenchman told me that one of the most
curious phenomena of postarmistice France was the rela-

tive ease with which the French accepted even the hardest privations to which they were subjected. "We discovered," he said, "that one can live without butter, soap, and other commodities and that to suffer constantly from the cold was not so unbearable as one would have thought."

This may not be literally true but the fact remains that the modern European is showing a distinct tendency to rebel against the idea that material welfare is an aim in itself. He is willing to give up progress—that is, a faith which has inspired the Western man for the last century and a half—and to turn his hope (or his despair) toward other aspirations.

What these aspirations are cannot be described precisely for the simple reason that the spiritual values of the Western World, such as they were proposed by the philosophers of the eighteenth century and the economists of the nineteenth, are temporarily bankrupt or have become unintelligible. The modern masses of Europe have lost faith in freedom and equality in the sense that these words have become mere empty abstractions and that they bring up reminiscences of the dual failure of Communism and capitalist democracy to achieve freedom and equality. It is for this reason that National Socialism and Fascism, in spite of their negativeness and their inability to propose any other *credo* than power for the sake of power, have made such headway. Even if the people of Europe are deprived of liberty, even if they have to suffer extreme privations, they have nothing to oppose to the destructive efficiency of Nazism. In the despair and the emptiness of their souls, they turn to whatever has the appearance of order and authority—which means preferably some military figure like Franco or Pétain.

The only spiritual force left is some blind faith in nationalism under its most extreme and irrational form.

France under Pétain is a remarkable example of this

phenomenon. The prestige of the Marshal rests on nothing but the psychopathic yearning for authority of a people who, through defeat, have lost faith in all rational values. Like the Germans after the war of 1914-1918, the French find themselves in a state of infantilism. They repudiate all traditional concepts, especially those of liberalism and democracy. The regime instituted by Pétain is nameless. Certainly it cannot be described as democratic, but it is not frankly Fascist either. The authority of Pétain seeks no justification. It cannot be said to be either legitimate or illegitimate, because there is no spiritual or legal or ideological frame of reference into which it can be integrated. In so far as it has principles, they are borrowed from all sorts of systems or regimes, some of which are French and others foreign. It is a hodgepodge of feudal, monarchistic, bourgeois reactionary Fascist ideas and even of Daladierism. Fundamentally it is sustained by the most primitive form of nationalism: the tribal submission to the elder, the father.

It may be that this strange state of affairs will have ceased to exist in France when this is published, but the fact that it could exist at all in a country as politically evolved as France was, shows the profound decadence of the traditional concepts which we have been accustomed to associate with Western civilization under its modern form. The authority of Marshal Pétain is as negative in its essence as National Socialism, and as it cannot even claim the dynamism which comes from the Nazi cult of power and conquest, we find the strange paradox of an authority founded on the acceptance of defeat, humiliation, and weakness.[1]

[1] "But there is a new form of Fascism abroad now. It is the Fascism of Defeat, or Colonial Fascism. It consists of persuading people to accept Fascism and become economic and political colonies of Germany in order to avoid danger. It is not the Fascism of a Leader calling the nation to awaken. It is the Fascism of leaders begging the nation to go to sleep. It

The very slogan adopted by the Pétain regime is indicative of a spiritual renunciation verging on nihilism. "Work, Family, Fatherland" are not words that can be connected with any philosophy like "Liberty, Equality, Fraternity"—moral abstractions all. Work, Family, Fatherland propose very limited aims. They create no new spiritual value and deny in fact the validity of any ideological thinking. The individual is invited to concentrate on such concrete matters as his own work, his own family, and his own soil and is discouraged from looking beyond his immediate daily existence.

Whether the implications of this new formula were felt or not by those who invented it—or paraphrased it from the Facist and Nazi terminology—nothing is more symptomatic of the spiritual abdication of the leaders of France under the crushing forces of destruction let loose by the Nazi revolution.

4. Selfishness as a national ideal

As I have indicated before, the spiritual forces that support the structure of democracy are still very alive in America. The poison of destruction is present but the antidotes are strong and the will to survive is real. Because it is the last line of defense, and because it has never known any other form of government than democracy, America can not only save itself through a genuine faith in the values upon which it is founded, but also cooperate effectively at some sort of Western renaissance which has become as imperative as the one of the sixteenth century.

Although I am absolutely unable to foresee how this can be achieved because solutions of the present conflicts are positively *unthinkable* at the present stage of these

does not awaken a desire for strength; it spreads a miasma of fear." (Dorothy Thompson)

conflicts, I do believe that no synthesis of our contradictions can be found so long as nationalism stands in the way and is accepted by all as a transcendental absolute.

Most Americans, from the President of the United States down, proclaim loudly that peace cannot be established in the world and that civilization will be in jeopardy as long as nations are ruled by violence, intolerance, greed, and other "undemocratic" and "unchristian" methods. Most Americans are pursuing the dream of a world in which wars, as well as class conflicts and other troubles, will be eliminated.

But at the same time the doctrine of the priority of the national interest over all other considerations is asserted with increasing vigor. All things foreign and all international doctrines are denounced as un-American. A Congressional committee—the Dies Committee—though looked upon with a certain amount of apprehension by the liberals when it first began to function, gradually gained recognition as a kind of guardian of patriotism. Although it would be very difficult to establish the philosophical justification of this Committee and to lay down the standards under which it operates, its general purpose is to ferret out any foreign infiltration that might undermine pure Americanism as conceived by the members of the Committee themselves. It uncovers and denounces Fifth Column activities, which is undoubtedly a wholesome purpose. But it is easy to see that it could readily transform itself into an instrument of repression of all ideas not specifically American.

In its present form the Dies Committee is neither very effective nor very firm in its doctrine. As a symptom of the progress of doctrinary nationalism in America, it is interesting.

The tendency of America to consider itself not as an heir to or an extension of European civilization, but as an opposition to it, is on the increase. In spite of the fact that isolationism as a practical policy is condemned, one wonders how many Americans would be disposed to renounce forever the provincialism so fervently adhered to by Congress. That provincialism which finds its traditional justification in a narrow understanding of the doctrine of "no foreign entanglements" advocated by George Washington is potentially as strong today as it was when Congress refused to ratify the Covenant of the League of Nations after the last war. It required the attack on Pearl Harbor really to put an end to it, at least for the duration of the war.

The conflict between the American ideal of universal peace founded on the good-neighbor policy, and the brotherhood of man, and the practical nationalism of America was clearly shown in all the discussions concerning the problem of aiding Britain and other countries in this war.

President Roosevelt and his supporters were constantly obliged to deny that the support of England was motivated by any other reason than the most selfish American national interest. Although the American people condemn "power politics" as immoral and destructive of international order, they would not accept cooperation with England or other nations in the mutual defense against the Nazi peril unless it could be proved to them that they were not aiding anybody but themselves.

It is true that from the practical point of view, it did not matter much whether in helping Britain the United States citizens thought they were defending only themselves and that mere circumstance had placed England in the position of being their bulwark in the Atlantic. What is interesting is that the idea of aiding Britain could be sold to the American people only on the basis of national selfishness openly advocated and proclaimed.

In his message to Congress of January 1941, President

Roosevelt expressed two ideas very reminiscent of the Wilsonian era. He said that the United States would not accept a peace imposed by the dictators or by the appeasers and that he could not conceive of a world at peace as long as men "all over the world" were not free to think, free to express themselves, and free to worship. In other words President Roosevelt, following closely in the footsteps of his predecessor, Woodrow Wilson, implied that the real aim of American foreign policy was to defeat tyranny everywhere in the world (represented this time not by the Kaiser, but by Hitler) and to restore everywhere in the world freedom and democracy.

But whereas Woodrow Wilson in proclaiming his objective of "making the world safe for democracy" instilled in the American people a spirit of crusade and enthusiasm, the same thing said by President Roosevelt in 1941 found a very cold response in public opinion and caused a good deal of criticism in the ranks of Congress at the time.

This part of his speech, although the most important, was in fact ignored for a long while and the discussion centered on the insoluble dilemma of whether it was possible to devise a policy by which the American people could be convinced that in aiding Britain they were not showing the slightest generosity or idealism, but acting strictly in their own selfish national interest.

Only the most incorrigible idealists have dared to assert that the essence of this world conflict was moral and spiritual and that its other aspects—the political and economic—were in fact subsidiary and absolutely insoluble as such. Like the most narrow-minded and provincial isolationists, they have had to campaign on the basis of national interest alone, because it is believed that this is nowadays the only way to stir the people out of their apathy and negativeness.

Innumerable speeches have been delivered and articles
written to prove that the European nations, whether the
French, the English, or the German, have never acted for
any other motive than pure self-interest. It is generally
considered axiomatic that this is one of the fundamental
causes of the present war. But although the Americans
condemn Europe for its selfishness, in the name of their
own morals and ideals, there is not the slightest indication that their leaders believe in following another course
themselves. Quite the contrary: the selfishness of European
nationalisms is used to justify and glorify American selfishness and American nationalism.

Thus the United States, right up to the great awakening of December 7, 1941, in spite of its relative immunity
to European political defeatism and in spite of its sincere
desire to preserve the fundamental creeds of Western civilization, had nevertheless become sufficiently skeptical of
their validity to repudiate them openly as motives for its
actions. These creeds were still proclaimed as true in
words and in writing, but they were not true enough any
more to stimulate action and justify sacrifice.

Up to Pearl Harbor, the United States, like every other
nation in the world, was taking refuge in the last blind
alley of a decadent civilization: nationalism and self-defense. It wanted to save itself and itself alone because,
like the other democracies of Europe, it believed in the
theory of the minimum risk and of the minimum immediate effort. Even today, after so many disasters and at a
time when it is clear that the United States needs all its
allies to win the war, campaigns are carried on quite
openly to throw suspicion on either the British or the Russians or both. Back of the minds of those who spread these
ideas is the persistent conviction that America's first duty
is to preserve her traditional aloofness.

I know of course that many Americans sincerely believed

that in saving America they would also save the world. That dream was not wholly selfish. It sprang from an excess of faith, so to speak, in the power of America to redeem the world. But that dream today is really a dream, the nostalgic reflection of a past ambition. In reality the mood of the American people was not very different from that of the French or the English when they finally had to face the necessity of this war. Even if the Japanese had not put an end to the American dilemma, that dilemma would have ended in the same manner. Many months before Pearl Harbor, the Americans, like the English and the French before them, had accepted this war because it was the only "reasonable" thing to do. It is true that reason alone has never been enough to induce men to act and especially to fight. The example of France shows that one cannot win a war with pure realism, because pure realism is self-destructive. France having refused to take "unreasonable" risks at the time of the invasion of the Rhineland, at Munich, and at Bordeaux, now finds itself condemned to a course of subjection and slavery.

England, on the other hand, after having followed a similar course up to the defeat of France, suddenly and miraculously shook off the disastrous chains of Chamberlain "realism." When Churchill said that he had nothing to offer his countrymen but "blood, toil, tears and sweat," he brought to the surface something which cannot be measured in terms of "reasonableness" and which, up to now, has saved England.

5. The case of Lindbergh

America before it entered the war stood halfway between these two attitudes. The people knew that according to their own standards, Right must be upheld all over the world, that there is a transcendental difference between Right and Wrong, and that a world that recognizes power and violence alone is doomed. But these instincts had become too weak and the forces of skepticism too great to permit American opinion to accept ancient truths without qualms. Charles Lindbergh was able, in the name of true patriotism and even of humanity, to combine in one doctrine all the ideas which brought about the suicidal collapse of democracy in Europe with those that are properly indigenous to America. He was at once an appeaser, a defeatist, a "realist," and the advocate of a ruthless form of imperialism to be applied by the United States all over the American continent. In assuming to be above ordinary emotions and professing a historical impartiality which prevented his passing a moral judgment on the responsibilities of this war, Lindbergh became a perfect example of the ethical and intellectual bankruptcy of the modern elite all over the civilized world.

In wanting to be thoroughly scientific, rational, and realistic, he restricted the scope of "reason" to a mere fatalism. The French High Command, miscalculating the moral power of resistance of England, asked for an armistice because it was obvious that, on paper at least, England could not hold up more than a few weeks against the German might. Similarly Lindbergh was unable to take into account any event or any force which did not fit into his mechanistic and limited vision of the facts.

On the other hand, by refusing—in the name of a superior and impartial Ethos—to pass any judgment on the conflict between Nazism and the rest of the world, he admitted that the "civilized" man had become unable to distinguish between Right and Wrong and that therefore his whole system of ethics was a fallacy.

The only positive imperative recognized by Lindbergh

was the necessity for the United States to defend itself if physically attacked by any foe, and if necessary to occupy other American nations by force in order to *protect* them.

His reluctance to aid Britain in her defense offered an exact parallel to the campaign launched in France just before the war by the Deputy Marcel Déat under the slogan: "Why die for Dantzig?"—a campaign which put Marcel Déat in the limelight after the defeat as an advocate of "collaboration" with Nazi Germany.

The extreme views of Lindbergh did not prevail in America and the Japanese have most effectively put an end to all debates on such matters. But from the point of view of this discussion these views are worth recording: they show how a sort of blind and irrational nationalism can emerge out of the decadence of all reason and all spiritual values.

This kind of nationalism is the final product of intellectual and moral nihilism.

Part II

THE TREND TOWARD COLLECTIVISM

CHAPTER I

Collectivism and Total War

IF NATIONALISM is the greatest single force in the world of today and accepted as the one categorical imperative that cannot be disputed, the trend toward collectivism can be considered as no less irresistible and no less universal.

I use *collectivism,* for want of a better term, to designate in the most general way the tendency to integrate the individual into the complex organization of our modern industrial society in such a manner as to obtain more efficiency from and—if possible—more security for that individual.

If this definition is accepted, it will be seen that the practical aims of such varied political doctrines or systems as those of Capitalism, Socialism, Communism, Fascism, and Social Democracy are the same. They all tend to obtain maximum production from the concerted and organized efforts of large masses of men and to keep these masses of men either sufficiently satisfied or disciplined to avoid starvation, rebellion, or any form of violent upheaval that might cause a breakdown of whatever political system has been adopted.

Nationalism is the great *vertical* force that tends to level down and unify social and economic groups within a country in order to strengthen it as a whole against an actual or potential enemy.

Collectivism, with the problems that it presents, cuts *horizontally* across boundaries and national allegiances.

Whatever these problems may be and whatever the solutions proposed, the trend toward collectivism tends to group men according to political affinities, social and economic interests. It segregates them into rival ideologies which are often in opposition to the tenets and exigencies of nationalism.

There is thus produced a series of conflicts which, for the sake of simplification, can be classified as intra-national on the one hand and political on the other, but which in practice are so deeply interwoven that it is difficult for those who live in a time of such crisis—which is the case of all of us—to make a clear distinction between the sets of motives that animate any particular group, or even any particular individual.

This is all the more difficult in that each group of men and even each individual express themselves in good faith as loyal defenders of the philosophical or political doctrine in which they believe, even in cases when their actions have ceased to fit within the limits of that doctrine.

As an example, the Communists, wherever they are and whatever may be the circumstances of the moment, continue to assert that they are furthering the cause of the world revolution. The fact that Stalin is pursuing a nationalist policy for the benefit of Russia does not deter the Communists in other countries from obeying the orders from Moscow, which remains for them the capital of a world founded on the concept of international Communism. This is why, be it said in passing, the German-Soviet pact of August 1939 produced fewer desertions in the ranks of Communism than could have been expected. The fact that Stalin has been playing power politics with the same intensity as Hitler has had little effect on those of his adherents who believe that the purpose of Communism is to establish social justice through the international dictatorship of the proletariat. With that belief firmly implanted in their soul, it does not matter what Moscow does. It must somehow be explained in terms of the Marxian gospel and be made to serve the cause of the proletariat.

Similarly the conservatives and big business interests who in the democracies favored the policy of appeasement even if it meant, as it did in Chamberlain's England and in France, a series of catastrophic capitulations, were convinced that they were acting not for political or class motives but through real patriotism. They were not traitors to the nation to which they belonged, because they identified their own particular ideology and their own particular salvation with that of the nation as a whole. If the majority of the citizens in that nation did not share their opinion, they merely concluded that the majority was wrong and—usually with the help of the foreign enemy—tried to impose their own view on all.

Since the present world conflict is taking place in several dimensions, it is always possible for any particular group or any particular individual to justify his apparent betrayal by stepping from one dimension into the other. General Weygand is reported to have insisted on asking for an armistice because among other reasons he had heard, while the French Government was debating at Tours, that the Communists were rioting in Paris and that one of their leaders was already occupying the Presidential Palace of the Elysée. General Weygand decided that the *horizontal* conflict (that is, the possibility of internal revolution) was becoming more dangerous than the *vertical* one (the pursuit of the war against Germany). This does not mean that General Weygand was a bad patriot. He merely tried to reconcile his patriotism with his political ideology.

The multidimensional character of the present world conflict is not an exception in history. In fact there are many precedents in which the ideological or class conflict is superimposed upon national wars.

During the long-drawn-out war between Sparta and Athens in the fifth century B.C., for instance, there occurred an interesting situation which Will Durant, in his book *The Life of Greece,* describes as follows:

> "It was a proof of Athenian courage and of the vitality of Athenian democracy, that Athens stood off her enemies for ten years more. The government was put upon an economical footing, taxes and capital levies were collected to build a new fleet, and within a year of the defeat at Syracuse Athens was ready to contest Sparta's new mastery of the sea. Just as recovery seemed assured, the oligarchic faction, which had never favored the war, and indeed looked to a Spartan victory to revive Aristocracy in Athens, organized a revolt, seized the organs of government, and set up a Supreme Council of Four Hundred (411). The Assembly, cowed by the assassination of many democratic leaders, voted its own abdication. The rich supported the rebellion as the only way of controlling the class war that had crossed the lines of the war between Athens and Sparta. . . . Once in power, the oligarchs sent envoys to make peace with Sparta and secretly prepared to admit the Spartan army into Athens."[1]

As can be seen by this episode, appeasers, defeatists, Fifth Columnists, and betrayers of democracy are at least as old as our civilization.

[1] Durant, W. J., *The Life of Greece,* Simon & Schuster, 1939, p. 449.

There are many other instances of such *interferences* of contradictory conflicts.

The great crisis of the seventeenth century known as the Thirty Years' War was even more complex than the one we are facing now. It was primarily a religious war but political and feudal quarrels became interwoven into it. The Protestant Union and the Catholic League soon broke up in fact. Predatory armies under ambitious or venal princes and self-appointed generals changed sides with remarkable ease. Cardinal de Richelieu was suppressing Huguenot rebellions in France while at the same time fighting Catholic Spain. Sensational reversals, comparable to the German-Soviet pact of 1939, were current, and when the Treaty of Westphalia was finally signed in 1648, its most positive result was not the settlement of the religious disputes but a redistribution of political power in Europe.

American history itself furnishes several examples of the intricacies of interests that tend to obscure and often divert the issues of major crises. Those who fought for American independence on this continent found strong support among English liberals. Similarly Karl Marx sang the praises of and sent congratulations to the first Republican President of the United States, Abraham Lincoln.

1. The price of security

That the modern social and political conflicts are conditioned by the universal trend toward collectivism needs little demonstration. The industrial revolution started over one hundred years ago and the continuous progress of technology have changed the life of each individual in such a way that practically no "civilized" man is able to subsist by his own independent effort, except at the lowest level. Each man has become so dependent on the activities of millions of other men that were he left to himself, he would regress rapidly to a condition of existence resembling that of the savage. We cannot make our clothes, we cannot heat or light our houses. We cannot even feed ourselves.

Technological progress, mass production, and the development of the innumerable services upon which we depend for our everyday existence obviously tend to improve the material comfort of our lives. But as a corollary they increase in tremendous proportions the dependence of the community on whatever power controls these means of production and the services of distribution.

Another consequence has been the growing preoccupation among civilized men with individual security, a preoccupation which has increased in direct proportion to the growing sentiment of interdependence.

This modern craving for security is often criticized by the exponents of "rugged individualism" as a sign of softness or of the decline of the enterprising spirit. But the truth is that the universal demand for security is a natural by-product of collectivism. The modern man knows that he is increasingly dependent on the community for his very existence. He knows that, unlike his forefathers, he cannot withdraw from society and subsist by himself. He knows that there can be starvation for him in the midst of plenty for the simple reason that "plenty" is the product of collectivism and that whoever is excluded from the collective system has a good chance to starve. The food, the light, the heat, and the clothes which he knows he can obtain only by working as an integral part of the collective system, he will exact as a right if he cannot give work in exchange. And it does not matter if the reason he cannot work is because he is too old, too ill, or because there is no work to be had. If he cannot obtain security through social and humanitarian considerations, he will sacrifice his independence and become a slave providing he can be persuaded that his sacrifice can be made sufficiently palatable, both in terms of practical security and in those of personal pride.

One of the secrets of the Nazi system is that the mass of the civilian population and especially the workers have been assured a minimum material security and—through the messianic appeal of the National Socialist revolution and of the glory of Germany—a moral compensation for the deprivation of individual freedom. The German worker is treated on the same footing as the German soldier. Like the soldier he is guaranteed subsistence and he is honored. Like the soldier he is asked to make sacrifices in view of achieving victory. Like the soldier he is made part of a gigantic collective effort in which individual thinking and personal aspirations would be as obstructive and out of place as would be the divagations of Hamlet in the assembly line of a Ford factory.

It should not be forgotten, however, that the validity of the Fascist or Nazi formula as a permanent solution to the problems that arise from the irresistible trend toward collectivism, has yet to be tested. This formula has been applied to the creation of a war machine and to conquest. As soon as Mussolini and Hitler came to power they made it perfectly clear that the sacrifices exacted from their people had the primary object of increasing their military strength in preparation for the eventuality of war. There is very little reason to believe that the war efficiency of German collectivism can be redirected toward peace aims, that is, toward the improvement of the conditions of life. First of all it is certainly not for that purpose that Mussolini and Hitler built their collectivist war machines. And secondly the chances are that the internal conflicts and points of friction which they have eliminated would reappear as soon as the discipline imposed by the war aims was lifted and as soon as men began once more

to think in terms of personal freedom and political liberties. All Hitler's political, social, and economic conceptions are subordinated to one single objective: war. The
whole system falls apart if one tries to think of it in terms
of peace.

Nevertheless, as the efficiency of the National Socialist
state has been not only demonstrated but often admired
and contrasted with the inefficiency of the democracies, it
may be worth while to consider briefly how these results
have been achieved.

2. *The Nazi solution*

It must be remembered first that Hitler did not create
out of whole cloth the economic theories or the industrial
machinery which have enabled him to transform the whole
of Germany into a huge centralized power plant. The idea
of organizing the industrial production and the distribution of goods regardless of such things as cost, profit, free
competition, and other financial considerations was put
forward by such men as Thorstein Veblen in America and
Walter Rathenau in Germany—Rathenau who was mur-
dered by the Nazis. The basic idea of these analysts, and of
many others of the same school, is to liberate the technologists from the restrictions imposed upon them by the
necessity of ensuring the functioning of a financial economy. If—according to these theories—such things as the
profit motive, return on capital investment, and other
money considerations are eliminated, it is obvious that the
measuring rod for the production and the distribution of
goods will be determined (1) by the possibilities of technology, (2) by the capacity of the existing industrial plants,
and (3) by the available labor. Such a system does away
with most of the principles upon which Western capitalism
and classical business methods are founded. It eliminates

all notion of free enterprise and tends toward the creation of complete collectivism.

Veblen, who was essentially an analyst, did not propose a practical program based on his own theories that could be applicable to America, possibly because he realized the tremendous resistance that American individualism and the prevalent point of view of the average businessman would offer to his radical ideas. But he was well aware of what a state like Germany could do in this line under the centralizing rule of the Army.

Comparing American and German industrial developments in his time, he concluded: "The American achievement in this field has been notoriously less conspicuous and less substantial for example than that of Germany since the formation of the Empire."

Were he living today he could only reiterate this assertion with even greater emphasis, although he would certainly be horrified by the practical results of this achievement. There is little question—considering on the one hand the natural resources of America, the ingenuity and skill of its people, and on the other the poverty of Germany, its lack of raw material, and other handicaps—that the accomplishments of Nazi Germany are astonishing, and even admirable, provided one leaves out of consideration moral factors and the quasi-certainty that all this extraordinary effort and all this inventiveness will finally end in the general impoverishment of Europe, a lowering of the standards of living for all, and a general regression of civilization (a regression already well advanced) all over the world. The efficiency of Nazi Germany is admirable for the same reason that Frankenstein is admirable.

Besides finding theorists who had already advocated a system by which the technologists and engineers should be given a free hand, while the financiers and capitalists should be maintained only as controlled intermediaries

and servants of the monolithic state, Hitler also inherited
the remarkable industrial plant which was created during
the postwar period, with the help of foreign capital—most
of which was American.

The industrial development of Germany, which was already impressive before the war of 1914, especially when
compared with that of France and England, was inter-
rupted by the war and even more obstructed by the infla-
tionary period which followed. But when foreign powers,
and particularly America, decided to help German reconstruction by postponing reparation payments and invest-
ing money in German enterprises, German technicians
soon caught up with American standards. By 1929 when
the world depression set in, foreign loans were called, but
what they had helped to build in Germany remained
there. Germany, although suffering from the frightful
effects of the depression, like every other country, was
nevertheless equipped by that time with the most modern
machinery run by technicians who had learned everything
that America could teach—and a good deal more besides.

The German businessman never offered as much resistance to the total economic mobilization directed by the
Nazi as would have his American counterpart under similar circumstances. There are many historical and psychological reasons for this.

First, the position of the businessman in German society
has never been one of supremacy as has been the case in
the United States. Ever since the Middle Ages, the real
aristocracy of Germany has been constituted by a caste of
warriors, the princes and kings whose leaders were the
Hapsburgs and later on the Hohenzollerns. The feudal
conceptions have remained alive in Germany up to a very
recent past. When after the Napoleonic wars and—more
markedly—after 1870, Prussia asserted its predominance
over the other German states, the real leadership in the

Reich did not change hands. The Junkers and the Army personified the state. Whatever liberalism and democratic thinking had developed in Germany under the impact of the French Revolution suffered a serious setback after the unsuccessful Revolution of 1848 through the victories and conquests of Bismarck. From then on, as Gustav Stolper has pointed out in his book *German Economy,* "the real power rested exclusively with the army and the bureaucracy, whose leading ranks were still recruited from, and dominated by, a few thousand Prussian Junker families."

Although there have been big businessmen in Germany, like the Thyssens and the Krupps, their relation to the German state and to German society as a whole has always been very different from the relation of the Morgans, the Rockefellers, or the Henry Fords to the United States government and to American society. However powerful they may have been, it never occurred to them, nor to any other German, that they constituted the ruling class. The opposition between the state and big business which is so typical of American industrial development never existed in Germany. The German businessman never forgot his place, so to speak, which was that of a servant of the state. And the state, in turn, has always been personified by the only true elite recognized by the Germans from the very beginning of their history: namely the Army and the state bureaucracy.

On account of this tradition, when Hitler came to power, he appeared to the German people not as a usurper and a revolutionary but as the normal successor of the long line of military leaders who, throughout German history, have assumed that they had the right to personify the whole of Germany for the simple reason that they personified its military might. The fact that Hitler did not belong to the Junker caste but came from a very humble class only enhanced his prestige. For the first time in German history, a man of the people became the leader of the people. But it is symptomatic that this leadership immediately expressed itself in terms of militarism and conquest and that the Army and the bureaucracy rallied to the Führer with no hesitation.

Thus the often expressed surprise at the "stupidity" and "blindness" of the German capitalists and businessmen in helping Hitler to power is ill-founded, because although the German and American businessman may be superficially alike in their behavior and in their philosophy, they differ profoundly on essential points.

1. The American businessman has been considered, up to the depression at least, as the cornerstone of American civilization, embodying all the best virtues of Americanism, such as energy, inventiveness, toughness, daring, perseverance. If there is an elite in America, it has been created by those who have been successful in business enterprises. This elite has not considered itself subject to the state. Quite the contrary: the assertion of its independence and its rebellion against state control have been continuous throughout American history for the last one hundred years.

2. The German businessman on the other hand does not think of himself as the cornerstone of German civilization, nor was he ever considered as such by the community. The most energetic and enterprising elements in German society have always believed that a military career or state service offered more satisfaction to their ambition and more honor than any other form of activity. The reduction of the German Army after the last war and the consequent limitation of opportunities for a certain type of young man was once of the causes of Hitler's success. This closing up of a career which in German eyes was the most noble and worthy of all, offended the national pride, and pro-

duced the same psychological results as if, in America, the number of available jobs for business executives was suddenly curtailed to a few thousands.

Hitler therefore had no great difficulty in obtaining the support of the German businessmen and financiers. He represented authority and he had the backing of the Army. That was enough. When it was necessary to integrate them into the unified economy of the National Socialist state, they offered little resistance. All they asked was to be allowed to remain more or less nominally in charge of the various industries, and—contrary to the reaction of the American businessman if he found himself under analogous circumstances—nothing was farther from their thought than to complain of their lack of independence.

Moreover, Hitler offered the capitalists the fulfillment of one of their dreams: he suppressed the struggles between them and the workers. There are no more strikes in Germany, no more unions (the Labor Front is the state-controlled organization of all the workers). The question of adjusting wages has been removed from the hands of the employers and they are relieved of practically all responsibilities concerning the organization and distribution of the products they manufacture. All that is taken care of by the State.

True enough their profits are seriously curtailed and liable to be reinvested under one form or another by order of the state. But provided the German capitalist is willing to cooperate with the government under these limitations, he is also guaranteed sufficient security and consideration to keep him contented.

As for the workers, the liquidation of their leaders and their elevation to the same rank of dignity as the soldier has been sufficient up to now to keep them disciplined. In view of the fact that the whole national economy is geared up to maximum production and unimpeded by the restrictions of free competition and cost, unemployment has disappeared. In fact there is a labor shortage in Germany, a shortage which has no theoretical limit except the ingenuity of the state technicians and the duration of the war.

From the consumer's point of view, German war collectivism is equally efficient. This has been achieved by the simple process of depriving the consumer of all the privileges which he enjoys in a free economy, except the one of keeping alive. The German consumer cannot choose what he wants to buy nor how much he wants to buy. His connection with the national economy is not determined by his individual preference, nor by his ability to purchase. He is merely allotted his share of the available goods produced for the whole community. This share may vary according to the season of the year or the results of the last looting enterprise conducted by the Nazi Army. It is not influenced by the "price" of the goods, which has become a pure fiction in no way indicative of the real value of those goods.

To deny that this system works would be foolish. It has in fact worked so well that it has enabled Hitler—starting from scratch—to build up in six or seven years a collectivist society relatively so efficient that none of the other systems opposed to it, although possessing infinitely larger resources, has been able to compete with it as yet.

Hitler and his associates boast that they have solved all the social and economic problems which confront the modern world. The class struggle has been eliminated by suppressing completely the independence of the capitalist group and the working class and by subordinating their interest to that of the state. The problem of production and cost has also been solved by three methods: (1) calculating the cost in terms of labor instead of money (which means that prices are purely arbitrary), (2) letting the technologist organize the industrial production with the aim of maximum efficiency and coordination, regardless of profits and competition, and (3) regulating consumption according to the available goods and not according to the purchasing power of the consumers.

In other words Nazi Germany has demonstrated that it is possible to enslave men to the machines provided they are made to believe, either by persuasion or by compulsion, that these machines are the means of achieving the national aims. These aims, as expressed by the National Socialist leaders, are not very different from the traditional aims of those who, all through history, have been the real rulers of Germany—the military elite. Hitler is right when he considers himself as the heir of Bismarck and Frederick the Great. He is right too in his nostalgic obsession with medieval Germany and in his hatred for liberalism, scientific criticism, enlightenment, and any philosophical or political doctrine founded on individual freedom. He is right, because the collectivist society which he has built would break down if the complicated and totally centralized industrial economy which supports it should get out of the control of the masters of the master race.

But a collective society as solidly unified and integrated as that of Nazi Germany is possible only under war discipline. The results achieved by Hitler for the whole German nation are only an extension of the mobilization order to all citizens and with no limit in time, because under the German conception (revamped by Hitler but not invented by him) peace is only a temporary lull in the chronic biological struggle for supremacy, the practical expression of which is war.

Those who fear or admire German collectivism and its efficiency are too apt to forget that it could be achieved only through Germany's long acceptance of the belief that the state is supreme and that the state is personified by those who bear arms. Fichte and Hegel did not invent anything. They merely explained what had been a reality in Germany for a very long time.

The contribution of Hitler and his associates was merely to take note of the universal trend toward collectivism made inevitable by modern technology and industrial development and to utilize collectivism to build their war machine. In that sense, the Nazis are certainly riding the wave of the future.

But it should be noted that the success obtained by the Nazis in organizing their industry on a national basis and in obtaining the maximum of efficiency from their technologists, is not based on any secret formula of their own. Other industrial countries such as the United States, England, and even France could have done the same. The technique of mass production is known. Machines are no mystery. We know how to build them and feed them. We know too that once built and fed they will go on producing far beyond our current needs and that the only reason why we do not have two or even six motor cars in every garage and three radios in every room is simply because we cannot pay for them. The tools which have enabled the Nazis to build up their industrial war machine were lying all over the world and anybody could pick them up and use them. In other words, the possibility of creating an efficient collective society was open to any nation.

Speaking to the German workers in Berlin on December 10, 1940, Hitler had this to say:

"The German capacity for work is our gold and our capital, and with this gold I can compete successfully with any power in the world. . . . My whole economic system has been built upon the conception of work. We have solved our problems while, amazingly

COLLECTIVISM AND TOTAL WAR

enough, the capitalist countries and their currencies have suffered bankruptcy. Sterling can find no market today. . . . But our Reichsmark, which is backed by no gold, has remained stable. Why? It has no gold cover; it is backed by you and by your work. . . . German currency, with no gold coverage, is worth more today than gold itself. It signifies unceasing production. . . . The whole problem has been solved in one instant, as if by magic. . . .

"Work alone can create new work; money cannot create work. Work alone creates values, values with which to reward those who work. The work of one man makes it possible for another to live and continue to work. And when we have mobilized the working capacity of our people to its utmost, each individual worker will receive more and more of the world's goods." [1]

Meanwhile, however, it would appear that German work alone is not enough to "create the values with which to reward those who work." In another speech (August 5, 1940) in which Hitler reviewed the profits of the campaign in the Lowlands and France, and in which he stated that "I can see no reason why this war must go on," the Führer had this to say:

"In addition, there are the tremendous possibilities presented by the acquisition of inestimable spoils and the exploitation of the territories occupied by us. In the spheres of economic interests controlled by them, Germany and Italy have at their disposal 200 million persons, among whom they can draw 130 million for military man power, whilst over 70 million are engaged in purely economic activities." [2]

[1] *My New Order*, Reynal and Hitchcock, 1941, p. 883.
[2] *Ibid.*, p. 832.

Thus it would appear that the real secret of the success of Hitler in solving all the social and economic problems that confronted him—and particularly that of unemployment—has very little to do with "magic" and a great deal to do with war and conquest. There can be no unemployment when, even out of Germany, two thirds of the conquered population of Europe is considered as potential military man power and one third only as available for purely economic activities.

CHAPTER II

The Conflict between Capitalism
and Democracy

A<small>T THE</small> present moment it is not possible to predict whether the Western nations who are now fighting Nazism will be able to develop an economic society as efficient, from the point of view of organization and production, as the collectivist war machine created by Germany, without renouncing the philosophical principles upon which these nations are founded.

The general aim of the Western democracies, and more particularly of the United States, has been to ensure more social justice and "more abundant life" for the largest number of citizens. Regardless of whether the results achieved in this direction have been good or bad, or merely mediocre, the fact remains that this aim has not been disputed—and that it cannot be disputed as long as the general lines of democracy, such as we understand them, are maintained. The idea of sacrifice and restriction cannot be accepted in a democracy except as a temporary expedient, that is, in time of war. Democracy, in other words, can function and justify itself only on the presumption that peace is the normal condition of mankind, that war is an exceptional phenomenon, and that the purpose of civilization is to eliminate it.

This is in complete contradiction with the theory of

the "biological" struggle supporting the National Socialist doctrine that considers that war, not peace, is the normal condition of mankind.

But, in spite of this fundamental opposition between the democratic philosophy and the totalitarian, both forms of society are conditioned by the possibilities open to the modern man to produce goods in vast quantities. Whether the production is destined to feed a war machine for the purpose of conquest and domination, or whether it is destined to improve the material conditions of life in a peaceful community, the methods of production imply a constant improvement of the available industries, their coordination, and an efficient distribution of the goods produced. To build machines and keep them fed is not an aim in itself, but the fact that we have learned how to do these things creates the imperative urge to go on doing them.

Democratic society has constantly struggled to iron out the contradictions involved in the pursuit of its two major objectives: to obtain the maximum efficiency from industrial technology and mass production, which implies a strong centralized organization tending toward collectivism, and to safeguard the liberties of the individual.

Roughly speaking, modern democracy has oscillated between two possible solutions of the problem: the capitalist solution and the socialist solution, the former emphasizing the necessity of preserving "free enterprise" even if it means permanent inequalities, the latter recommending the repudiation of capitalism for the sake of a more even distribution of the available production.

It is obvious, however, that the capitalist doctrine and the socialist doctrine both tend toward the same general results. Henry Ford may stand for the incarnation of "rugged individualism," but the system of mass production which he has perfected and popularized has done more to destroy individual initiative among his workers and the consuming public than all the teachings of the doctrinaire socialists. The political and philosophical conceptions are antagonistic, but the practical human consequences are identical.

The proof of this is to be found in the efforts of most big industrialists to demonstrate that under the system of private ownership workers enjoy as much security and protection and as high salaries as they would under the control of the state. Neither Henry Ford nor any other big industrialist is proposing to give up the basic principle upon which he operates—which is mass production.

On the other hand, the socialists, whatever may be the particular school to which they belong (including the Communist), accept as axiomatic the extension of collectivism as the natural consequence of the technological progress of industry during the last two centuries. Modern capitalism and socialism are both products of the machine. Both claim to offer better protection to the worker and to ensure him not only decent living conditions but a guarantee that he will preserve the privileges of a free man in spite of the moral and economic restrictions which industrial production imposes on the laboring classes. Both pretend to be fulfilling the fundamental objectives of democracy, though each accuses the other of denying them. Capitalism denounces the evils of collectivism and of the socialist state, although a collectivist society could not even be conceived without the industrial and technological developments of the past century which came into being through the enterprises of the capitalists themselves. The socialists, for their part, accuse the capitalist system of retarding human progress and of preventing a more even distribution of wealth through an excessive concentration of this wealth in a few hands and through the oppression of the workers, although it has not been dem-

onstrated anywhere that state socialism would not eventually end up in a paralyzing bureaucracy. Many socialists
reject the radical formulas of Communism, but the example of Soviet Russia has not been encouraging even as
a pure socialist experiment.

The conflict between the various brands of socialism
and capitalism has been growing steadily since the beginning of the industrial era. It is now so acute and so far-
reaching that it cannot be dissociated from the other
causes of the war, and there are many who are infinitely
more concerned with the social and political outcome of
the war than with the survival of the nation to which they
belong. But it should be noted that if capitalism and
socialism are in conflict with one another, they are also—
though not consciously—in conflict with democracy. And
it is because both capitalism and socialism have failed to
solve the inner contradictions of their respective doctrines,
that Fascism and Nazism are now threatening to destroy
both and to impose on the whole world the simplified
solution of pure force.

1. The promise of capitalism

Like all systems that are based on practical experience
and are the result of a long historical evolution, capitalism cannot be reduced to a few simple definitions. The
Western World has been evolving capitalism such as we
know it today over too many centuries for us to dissociate
ourselves completely from it. We cannot take capitalism
out of our consciousness to examine it objectively the way
we can analyze a scientific theory or a form of art. The
economist or the sociologist may be able to talk of capitalism in the same manner as the physicist speaks of the
quantum theory, or the archaeologist of Persian ceramics.
But the average man can do no such thing. Capitalism to

him is a word with varying connotations according to his own status in life, his own prejudices and emotional reactions.

The man who has $1,000 in a savings bank does not consider himself a capitalist although he may recognize that his ability to save $1,000 and dispose of it more or less as he pleases is made possible by the existence of the capitalist system. Were he to invest the $1,000 in securities or bonds in the hope of receiving some interest on this "capital," he would participate in the functioning of that system in the same way as the man who invests $100,000 or $1,000,000. In fact, the theory of capitalism is that there is no reason why the man who starts with $1,000 or less should not end up with $1,000,000 or more, provided he works hard, shows ability, and encounters the right opportunities. The association between capitalism and democracy is based on this assumption. The system does not guarantee that everybody will become rich, but it guarantees that anybody *can* become rich or at least emerge out of poverty. This is why both capitalism and democracy agree on the preservation of individualism, the former on economic grounds, the latter as a matter of philosophical and political doctrine. Unfortunately the happy marriage between our economic system, capitalism, and our political philosophy, democracy, has been constantly deteriorating for the last one hundred years, and more rapidly in recent years, because neither of them has really been able to fulfill the promises inherent in its doctrine.

Democracy, by proclaiming that all men are born equal and free, is not gratuitously reasserting the "eternal truths" upon which our Western civilization is founded. Freedom and equality cannot remain philosophical abstractions as far as the ordinary man is concerned. They must be translated into positive, practical terms. That

they are applied in the political field is a fact. All men
are free to vote as they wish, to express themselves according to their conscience, and they are equal before the
law. Such at least is the theory, and the promise of democracy is that practice should correspond to it. But long
historical experience has demonstrated that minorities,
financially and economically powerful, tend to exert an
influence over the affairs of the state completely dispro-
portionate to their numerical strength. Men of great
wealth, and those who control big anonymous corporations, are politically privileged in spite of the periodical
efforts of "progressive" governments to curb their power
and reduce the abuses that stem from it.

That this should be so is no condemnation of the principles of democracy. It merely proves that there is an incompatibility between the existence of real equality, and
real freedom for all, and capitalism as it now exists and
functions.

The inability of democracy to establish equality and
freedom by purely political means might have been compensated if capitalism, on its side, had been able to fulfill
its own promises. But this has not been the case.

During the nineteenth century, and up to the war of
1914-1918, the middle classes and even the working classes
tolerated social and economic inequalities as they existed
in Europe and in America because the capitalist system
was constantly expanding. It created work, it increased
production, it improved the conditions of life of all the
community at such a speed that its inability to distribute
the products of labor equitably was not very perceptible
to the ordinary citizen. Moreover, it guaranteed fixed in-
comes to an increasing number of people. During my
youth, before 1914, no section of the population seemed
more stable and more secure than the *petit rentier*. The
general conviction then was that the number of people

who lived partly or wholly on their *rentes* would increase constantly. The small bourgeois was gradually identifying himself politically with the big capitalist.

Even as late as 1925, when I first came to America (that is, after the German and French *rentiers* had already seen their security completely or partly destroyed), I found the idea prevalent that the ultimate end of the American system was to make every man a capitalist. I was given many times the illustration that the shares of this or that big corporation were held, not by a few rich men, but by hundreds of thousands of small people who were therefore becoming capitalists themselves. The implications of the argument were that a kind of equality was thus being created among various classes of wealth. In the same way as all citizens are supposed to be equal before the law regardless of their individual differences, all stockholders were supposed to be equal before the risks of profit or loss, regardless of whether they owned one or 10,000 shares. Regardless too of whether they were in a position to have their say in the management of their investments.

As long as prosperity held out, this dream or mirage concerning the possibilities of capitalism held out too. It did seem as if the safest guarantee against insecurity was to invest one's money in private enterprises.

It would be tedious to recall how this dream collapsed after 1929 and how the small capitalists as well as many big ones suddenly found themselves reduced to a condition of insecurity from which they have not yet emerged in spite of the recovery that followed a few years later.

The psychological shock produced by the depression, both in Europe and in America, cannot be overestimated. It has not destroyed capitalism as a system, but it has certainly shaken the faith, to say the least, of millions of men, all over the world, who up to then showed an implicit confidence in an economic order founded on the principle

of equal opportunity for all. The association between capitalism and democracy, although still solid—especially in
the Anglo-Saxon countries and more particularly in the
United States—has ceased to be a smooth one. The man
with $1,000 in the savings bank has lost hope of becoming
a millionaire. The big businessman, in spite of his valiant
efforts to redeem himself from the condemnations that
have been piled upon his head after the Hoover era, has
nowhere regained his lost prestige. He is asked to cooperate; he is refused the right to lead.

2. *Vitality of the capitalist system*

This does not necessarily mean, as so many people are
inclined to think, that capitalism is at an end. It is my
belief that the vitality of capitalism is underestimated not
only in America but in Europe, and that it can still undergo many transformations and adapt itself to many
changes.

The fate of capitalism is tied to the evolution of circumstances which at the moment are beyond our power of
speculation. But there is no doubt that capitalism will
have to contend either with the extension of totalitarianism or with an intensification of the democratic process
in the field of finance and economics. In either event,
capitalist methods will have to undergo important modi-
fications, but there is no reason to suppose that the complicated system called capitalism will necessarily disappear
as such.

Therefore it is possible that the liberal and progressive
thinkers who denounce the unholy alliance between certain capitalist interests in the democracies and Fascism as
suicidal for the capitalists may be wrong. If Hitler should
achieve the conquest of Europe, it is perfectly conceivable
that he would utilize the structure of capitalism, and more

particularly the big trusts, the large corporations, and the cartels to help him in the exploitation of the natural resources outside his immediate sphere of influence. This would mean, of course, that the leaders of large interests, such as those controlling oil, steel, wheat, rubber, and shipping, would agree to "cooperate" with the new masters of the world.

In September 1940, after the fall of France, the editors of *Fortune* magazine conducted a poll among 15,000 American business executives, asking this question:

> "If cessation of hostilities leaves Germany with a large economic bloc, would you favor doing as much business with this bloc as possible, or as little as possible even if it means the sacrifice of considerable profits?"

The replies were:

	Per cent
Much as possible	33.3
All that comes our way	12.5
Depends on circumstances	37.5
Little as possible	10.6
None at all	2.6
Don't know, or no answer	3.5

As can be seen, a large percentage of American businessmen seemed strongly inclined at that time toward some form of appeasement because they were convinced that they would survive and perhaps even benefit in a Nazified world.

Later on, in May 1941, *Fortune* published another poll on the same subject, which it preceded with the following remarks:

> "From some quarters has emanated the notion that the real 'appeasers' in this country are to be found

among businessmen, who would like nothing better than a peace restored to the world—any kind of peace—that would make possible the resumption of normal business relations at home and with other continents. That this is very far from true appears in the following:

"Suppose Great Britain is defeated without our having gone formally into the war ourselves, which do you think would be the most likely consequences?"

Per cent

Germany will succeed in establishing a new order in Europe with which it will be possible for us to resume business relations following approximately pre-war methods 8.5

In the resulting peace the U.S. will be safe from attack without the need for huge armament expenses, but to protect our economic position it will be necessary for us to compete for foreign trade by matching totalitarian methods of government-controlled barter 5.3

Not only would the U.S. have to adopt methods of barter in foreign trade, but we would have to maintain a very large and costly military establishment to assure our domestic security 36.5

We would be faced with an eventual war with the new "Nazi order" for which we would have to continue to arm at top speed and regardless of price 22.6

Not only the U.S. but most surviving countries of the earth would be faced with the calamitous prospect of continuous conflict and economic chaos 25.0

No answer 2.1

It should be noted that it is difficult to establish a real basis of comparison between this poll and the one of

September 1940, because the questions were quite differently put. The direct question asked the first time: "Would
you do business with Hitler if he was left in control of a
large economic bloc?" was not asked again. However,
Fortune magazine was correct in concluding that "84.1
per cent of the Forum's panel see some degree of danger
or disaster resulting from a Hitler victory, some consequence so serious that it should, presumably, be prevented
at almost any cost. Against them is a minority of only 13.8
per cent who believe that if Germany were victorious the
world would be safe and at least economically tolerable
for the U.S. to live in without huge armaments."

Now that the United States is at war with the Axis
powers, there is no reason to believe that the minority
of businessmen who might have favored appeasement
before have much influence today. Even from the strict
business point of view, and leaving aside all political considerations, it is obvious that it is in the interest of all
industrialists to cooperate fully in the national production
of war material. They have a vested interest in victory
like everybody else on this side of the fence.

One should not forget, however, that the small minority
of business appeasers whose influence is now negligible
have not necessarily changed their fundamental point of
view on the whole situation. There are still people—even
in England, even in America—who are not convinced that
some sort of compromise with Hitler may not be possible
one of these days. The dislocation in the economic, financial, and political structure of the United States which
the all-out war renders unavoidable is for them a serious
cause of worry. They still hope that it can be stopped and
believe that a compromise peace with the Axis, however
unpleasant the prospect, would be less disastrous than the
revolutionary consequences of a long war.

3. Appeasement as a business proposition

Those who try to demonstrate that these calculations are erroneous—citing as precedent the practical annihilation of such people in Germany and Italy—may well be wrong. Hitler's purpose is to destroy democracy and the whole system of thought associated with it, and he might find that the best way to destroy it in its last stronghold, England and America, would be to maintain the mechanism of the large corporations and even guarantee their existence in exchange for an acceptance of his New Order. They might have to pay heavily for this "protection," but they might get it—for a while. Even if the survival of capitalism at such a price were only temporary, it would appear to some leaders of big business preferable to the continuation of the dangerous conflict with democracy in which they are now engaged and which can become more acute after the war.

During the time that the Popular Front was in power in France, I heard financiers and businessmen say quite openly: "We would rather have Hitler than Blum." Others, more sensitive, said: "We would rather have Mussolini than Blum." The defeat of France made their wish come true, and although the disaster that has struck that country is of such magnitude that it is difficult to foresee how anyone can profit by it, the fact remains that these same people are not offering any visible opposition to the advent of the New Nazi Order. If anyone is to profit by French collaboration with the Axis powers, it is a few big industrialists, and Hitler is bending his efforts toward utilizing them. Through them, and whether by threat or persuasion, the Nazis have already gained control of all major French industries.

If England were to be defeated, the same thing would happen there, but on a larger scale. The economic mechanism which binds together the British Empire (and with it practically all the portions of the world not under Axis domination) is a complicated affair and the National-Socialist leaders might find it expedient to preserve the City of London, and its personnel, as a clearing center and an intermediary with the Empire and with America. The experience of British financiers and merchants in the field of international trade could not be easily replaced, and provided that conquered England could be made to serve the general Nazi aims (by the imposition of a British Pétain or Laval as subdictator) British capitalism could be offered survival under the protection of Berlin.

Such an arrangement would resuscitate the American appeasers. Some American leaders of big business would find that this situation offered them also strong protection and would strengthen their hand against the persecutions of their own "democratic" government.

On the other hand, it is now becoming clear that a defeat of Nazi Germany can be achieved only if the mass of the people in the democracies—and that includes organized labor of course—can be made to understand that this war is their war and that in fighting it they are not merely trying to maintain the status quo.

France succumbed, among many other reasons, because Daladier and his government, having sought the support of the conservative, Fascist, and defeatist elements in the country, could never explain to the people and the army their war aims in terms that the common soldier and the common worker could wholeheartedly approve. These war aims were negative and uninspiring. They did not go beyond the "stop Hitler" idea and the vague notion that if Hitler was stopped things would remain pretty much as they were. In fact, Daladier and his supporters took the occasion of the war to fight democracy inside France with even more energy and consistency than they fought the

Germans. Having chosen to lay the blame for unprepared-
ness on the Popular Front alone, and repudiated without
promise of restoration all the social legislation achieved
under that government, they forgot that the Popular
Front had been elected in 1936 by 55 per cent of the
electorate, and that, in spite of the German-Soviet treaty
of August 1939, the chances were that one half of the
French population was still hoping that the war would
have another purpose than to consolidate the power of
the conservative and reactionary groups which had regained control of the French government.

Daladier was too blind to understand that one cannot
fight a total war with a divided country, one half of which
remains suspicious of the motives of its leaders while the
other half is more or less in moral and political sympathy
with the ideology of the enemy. Because so many leaders
in France were—and still are—obsessed by the Communist
peril, and because they could not forgive or forget the
Popular Front with its sit-down strikes, its 40-hour week,
its attacks on the "200 Families," and so forth, Daladier
could never bring himself to form a government of national union, as had been done in the war of 1914-1918.

The fate of England might have been the same as that
of her ally if Chamberlain had not been forced out.
Chamberlain followed the same course as Daladier. He
too could not bring himself to "share the war" with the
mass of the people. He too wanted to defeat Hitler—and
he was undeniably sincere in his purpose—but he could
neither agree to go "all out," which would have meant a
disruption of capitalist economy in England, nor promise
anything better to the English people than the return to
the Birmingham policies when and if England won the
war. In fact, Chamberlain was frank enough to express
the most undisguised fear of the kind of world that might
emerge after the war, even if England won it.

The result is known: Chamberlain lost *his* war as clearly as Daladier lost his. But, luckily for England, she found a leader in the person of Churchill who was willing to fight the total war with total means, that is, with the full co-operation of the whole population, and regardless of future consequences.

4. *The opposition to Roosevelt*

Roughly the same pattern existed in the United States right up to Pearl Harbor. In spite of the fact that Roosevelt had been re-elected for a third term, and that, according to a Gallup poll, he enjoyed at the beginning of 1941 the greatest popular support in eight years (72 per cent), in spite also of the fact that his former opponent, Wendell Willkie, had endorsed the President's foreign policy, many conservative Republicans and many representatives of big business persisted in an attitude of systematic opposition which was curiously reminiscent of the attitude of the corresponding groups in England and France between 1936 and 1940.

The alleged motives of this opposition were varied. In the matter of helping England through the Lend-Lease Act and other methods of implying a gradual mobilization of all the forces of the country, the principal arguments against extending the powers of the President could be grouped as follows:

1. More open aid would lead to war with Germany.
2. It was too late to save England anyway, and the United States should concentrate on its own defenses.
3. To increase the powers of the Executive was to prepare the advent of dictatorship in America. What was the point of fighting totalitarianism abroad if one had to appoint a dictator at home to do it?
4. Even if England should win, it would not be an un-

mixed blessing. England had already gone totalitarian, and—as Mark Sullivan suggested—one should find out whether it was the intention of the British leaders to establish "socialism" after the war. If such was the case, should America help England make the world safe for socialism? (The answer implied by Mark Sullivan being, of course, an emphatic "No.")

There were, of course, many other arguments used by the conservatives. But as far as most leaders of big business were concerned, those listed above seemed to be the most important. Naturally they revealed only in an indirect way the real motives of those who put them forward. But these real motives are easy to bring to light because the behavior of social groups all over the world is conditioned by forces which transcend frontiers and follow everywhere a recognizable pattern.

The real reasons why important leaders of American industry and business opposed the foreign policy of Roosevelt, until Japanese aggression created national unity, can be summed up as follows:

Resistance to the recognition of the now obvious fact that the defeat of Nazism can be assured only if the *masses* are persuaded that the efforts and sacrifices required from them will benefit them. Roosevelt has constantly sought the support of these masses and obstinately refused to admit that the effort required for defense might entail a permanent suspension of the social gains achieved under the New Deal.

Roosevelt has intimated clearly that he does not intend to turn over the direction of the war to the conservative minorities and to big business interests. This is what Daladier did in France and Chamberlain in England. Roosevelt seems determined to follow another course.

The accusation that Roosevelt was seeking dictatorship was merely the expression of a fear that the perennial struggle between the underprivileged majority and the vested interests would be carried on through the war and that if the President has anything to say in the reconstruction of the world after the war, he might use his enormous prestige to consolidate his New Deal ideas on a world-wide basis.

By denouncing "appeasement" as synonymous with treason, Roosevelt committed the United States to a policy that must assure the defeat of National Socialism. He has gradually but consistently cut behind him the bridges which might permit the United States to make a deal with the Nazis in the eventuality of an improbable stalemate. This, from the point of view of the "realistic" businessman, is unsound. It tends to develop a spirit of crusade, as in the last war, to the detriment of practical interests, at a moment when the odds in favor of a universal triumph of democratic ideals are not overwhelming. In other words, Roosevelt is taking a bad business risk for the sake of ideology.

Finally, unlike Mark Sullivan, Roosevelt does not seem to be perturbed by the possibility that England or even America might go "socialistic" and it would appear that his capacity for nostalgia for a less insecure world is alarmingly small.

In brief, the cleavage between capitalism and democracy has been sharpened by the increased danger which confronts America. Before the United States actually went to war the approach of the peril had accentuated an alignment analogous to the one that existed in France and in Chamberlain's England. The American conservatives did not say, like the French, that they would rather have Hitler than Roosevelt, but the propaganda carried on by a powerful organization like the America First Committee revealed the existence of similar preoccupations. To many the choice was between two solutions, both dangerous and unpleasant. The first was the formula of appeasement. The second meant increasing participation in a war that will probably be long, exhausting, and may at any moment transform itself into a series of revolutionary processes, the outcome of which it is impossible to predict.

5. A hard choice

The first solution implied the acceptance of a Nazi domination over Europe, Africa, and Asia. It meant taking the chance that Hitler would not refuse to "protect" those who control the power and the resources of the United States. It was a dangerous risk, but a certain type of businessman has difficulty in conceiving that one cannot make a mutually advantageous business deal even with the devil. Like Chamberlàin, he cannot believe that Hitler's great power is that he has effectively subordinated economics to politics. The imperatives of business were still supreme and undisputed in America only a few months ago. Businessmen tended to minimize or deny the existence of any other category of imperatives.

But the great incentive in the appeasement theory, from the capitalist and big-business point of view, was that in dealing with the Nazis one would not be troubled with such complications as labor laws, the obstructions of unions, and other "democratic" difficulties. If the Nazis were to control the world, and if America were to survive their competition and deal with them, a revision of American economy and business methods would have to be achieved. This revision could be oriented in only one way: labor would have to be disciplined and integrated in the new order of business Fascism. This, only a while ago, was not particularly displeasing, as a prospect, to many businessmen, either in America or elsewhere.

The other course meant the acceptance of the ultimate

aims of American foreign policy as they have been defined by President Roosevelt in several speeches and particularly in his message to Congress of January 6, 1941.
In that message, the President expressed himself as follows:

"Our national policy is this: First, by an impressive
expression of the public will and without regard to
partisanship, we are committed to all-inclusive national defense.

"Second, we are committed to full support of all
those resolute peoples, everywhere, who are resisting
aggression.

"Third, *we are committed to the proposition that
principles of morality and considerations for our own
security will never permit us to acquiesce in a peace
dictated by aggressors and sponsored by appeasers.*"

Further on in the same message, the President was even
more explicit when he outlined the conditions of peace
which might be acceptable to America. These conditions,
according to him, are as follows:

1. Freedom of speech and expression—*everywhere in
the world.*

2. Freedom of religious worship—*everywhere in the
world.*

3. Freedom from want, through economic understanding—*everywhere in the world.*

4. Freedom from fear, through world-wide reduction of
armaments—*everywhere in the world.*

"Freedom," concluded the President, "means the supremacy of human rights everywhere. Our support goes
to those who struggle to gain those rights or keep them.
Our strength is in our unity of purpose. To that high concept there can be no end save victory." Since then the
ideas expressed in that speech have been frequently re-
iterated by the President and have been embodied in the

Atlantic Charter. They constitute in fact the peace aims of the United Nations.

But at the time that this message was delivered, this part of it caused less comment than the more immediate recommendation for practical aid to Britain. Nevertheless it was, and still is, the most important part of the presidential declaration because it sets the ulterior objectives of American foreign policy, as President Roosevelt conceives them. If those aims are really accepted nationally, as the President assumed they are, all other problems would become means of achieving them.

By stating that *freedom* must be reinstated "everywhere in the world," President Roosevelt has indicated that he did not repudiate the inheritance of Woodrow Wilson. He did not offer a new League of Nations, but he certainly proclaimed that peace could not be established if the American concepts of freedom did not prevail universally. Democracy, according to him, is, like peace, indivisible. It must exist universally or perish. President Roosevelt has thus committed the United States to an extension of the kind of democracy which the President himself believes in, that is, one definitely founded on popular support and not on the preservation of oligarchic control.

It is because the opposition to the Administration sensed that this was the root of the conflict that the struggle against President Roosevelt remained until the war so bitter and so personal. He, like Hitler, subordinated economic imperatives to political conceptions. And if such was the point of view of the President of the United States, it followed that he had less fear of the further "socialization" of a democratic world than of the fictitious peace that might be bought through appeasing Hitler.

It followed also that, from the point of view of some businessmen, the course recommended by Franklin Roosevelt offered risks which were no less great than trying a deal with the Nazis. Moreover, the two sets of risks were difficult to weigh with the same scales. If war should end in a stalemate by which the rest of the world should be dominated by National Socialism, it is conceivable that American capitalism could deal with these new rivals in a position of relative equality, at least for a while. They would still be outside the American fortress and the American traders would remain physically out of their reach.

Business, in America as elsewhere, has a philosophy of its own. It is materialistic and apt to visualize all human problems from the angle of competition, which is another way of subscribing to the doctrine of force. This does not mean that capitalist society is run by gangsters, as the Nazis and Communists and many democrats assert. It does mean, however, that most businessmen usually experience difficulty in believing that there are other forms of power besides the control of economic forces.

6. Conflicts continue in spite of the war

The irresistible trend toward collective organization of national production, which is as real in democratic countries as in the totalitarian states, forces upon the leaders of big business a painful dilemma. In spite of the fact that the last war did not destroy their effective influence over the governments that ruled in these democracies, that influence has been constantly threatened during the last twenty years by such movements as Communism, the Popular Front, and the New Deal. In the minds of many conservatives there has thus been created a real psychosis: the growing conviction that democracy was fatally tending toward state socialism and possibly Communism. Liberal thinking and the principle of individual freedom, which had enabled capitalism to flourish, became less attractive when they were turned into arguments to justify social legislation in favor of the common man. The growing power of the labor unions, and the tendency of the workers to consider that the factories in which they worked and by which they lived were as much their "property" as that of the absentee shareholders, increased the feeling of insecurity of the wealthy classes. In Europe, and especially in France, the fear and hatred engendered by the class struggle produced a veritable condition of panic among the propertied classes, who reached the conclusion that nothing could save them except a counterrevolution. This they finally achieved in the political no-man's land left after the military defeat.

In England and in the United States the crisis which opposes capitalism to democratic processes has not developed to the point where anyone is seriously thinking of an antidemocratic revolution. But the example of France must never be forgotten. It proves that among the reactionary and propertied classes there are elements who are in a mood, given certain circumstances, to discard democratic government and democratic thinking, and that their fear of the Nazi rule is no greater than their fear of what they imagine to be the unavoidable evolution of democracy—namely, state socialism.

Now that the United States is committed to the pursuit of the war until National Socialism, Fascism, Japanese militarism, and everything connected with these systems is destroyed, the conflicts which I have tried to describe in the preceding pages appear secondary. America is in peril, and the reality of that peril has created a sentiment of national unity which is stronger than the particular interests which made themselves heard so loudly right up to the moment when the Japanese planes dropped their bombs on Pearl Harbor.

The very vast majority of businessmen, whether large or small, have put aside for the moment their grievances and their fears. The greatest conceivable danger at the moment would be a slowing up in the production of armaments necessary to win this war. Everybody agrees on that. Most of the ideas described in the foregoing pages are out of public discussion for the time being. This does not mean, however, that such ideas have totally disappeared. In France, at the beginning of the war a pretense was made during several months that internal conflicts had ceased. Capital and labor collaborated with the government in a show of national unity. This unity unfortunately was false, a mere façade. Behind it intrigues, sabotage, and even treasonable activities were carried on. The rest of the story is known.

There is no real comparison between such a situation and the one existing in the United States; the precedent of France is brought up more as a contrast than as a parallel. It should not be forgotten, however, that wherever there is a fissure in the unity of a nation, the Axis propagandist will exploit it to the limit. It is said that Pearl Harbor has had the same effect on the American mind as Dunkirk on the English. This is true, but there is a difference of gravity between the two events which should not be overlooked. The disaster of Dunkirk was about as great as anything of the kind that can be conceived. England was theoretically wide open to invasion, logically doomed. Pearl Harbor, on the other hand, was a very hard blow. It inflicted considerable damage to the system of defense of the Pacific and wounded American pride. It was not interpreted anywhere as an irreparable disaster after which there was nothing to do but to capitulate or resign oneself to annihilation. What it did was to awaken the American people and many of their leaders to some of the realities they had refused to see up to then. This created national unity, but this American unity was not born, like that of the English, out of a total sense of catastrophe.

For that reason it cannot be said that the American people have yet reached the point of complete abdication of their individual interests, as seems to be the case for the English. It would indeed be remarkable if such a point had been reached so soon.

It is for these reasons that many of the conflicts which divided this country only a few months ago cannot be said to have dissolved into thin air in one day. In many instances they have been transposed or postponed. For instance, there is a group of ex-isolationists who (at the time of writing) are preaching that America's real and unique concern is the war with Japan and that what happens in Europe does not matter.

From a long-range point of view, the question remains as to whether the former isolationists have accepted the program outlined by President Roosevelt that the United States must play an international role after the war as well as now.

"We may wonder," wrote Vice-President Wallace, "whether the long and bitter fight put up by the isolationists in the decades of the twenties to keep the United States from behaving as if it were part of the world is to be renewed when the time comes for building a new peace." [1]

Similarly one wonders whether the inherent opposition between capitalism and democracy, with all its complex ramifications, which I have tried to outline here, will be resolved or aggravated by the war.

There is obviously no way of making any prediction in this respect. The course of the war is not fixed. Nations

[1] "Foundations of the Peace," Henry A. Wallace, *Atlantic Monthly,* January 1942.

have changed sides already, some have dropped out of the war and others have come in. More events of this kind can and will happen, producing each time a shift in the emphasis of the war itself and in its revolutionary consequences.

Granting, however, that the United States will win this war, which is certain if the necessary efforts and sacrifices are made, and quite doubtful otherwise, it can be said only that the relation between capital and state enterprises will be so thoroughly changed that the language used now to talk about these problems will have no meaning.

In the article already mentioned, for instance, Vice-President Wallace outlines some of the planning which is going on now in view of the peace. Speaking of the stocking up of raw material which is already well under way, Mr. Wallace says:

"Huge surpluses of both cotton and wheat are piled up in the exporting countries, waiting to be used whenever the stricken countries are able once more to handle them. Of cotton there is stored in the United States a supply sufficient to take care of the normal needs of all Europe for at least a year. Of wheat the United States last July 1 had a carry-over about four times the normal of the '20s and it is evident that next July 1 the carry-over will be nearly seven times the normal of the '20s. In Canada the situation is somewhat similar while in Argentina and Australia large surpluses loom for the near future. Four great wheat exporting nations of the world now have a billion more bushels on hand than they did during the first half of the '20s. . . . It is enough wheat to feed the entire population of continental Europe for a large part of a year, or to cover the Continent's import requirements for nearly three years."

What this indicates is that we are continually moving toward a situation in which the responsibilities assumed by the state are becoming so vast that the part played by private capital (however large the accumulation of it in any one domain) will be dwarfed more and more. I have already mentioned the tremendous dislocation that will take place in the economic life of the United States by the very fact that the war makes it necessary to vote a budget of 59 billion dollars. If the war is to last any length of time, one can imagine a further tremendous dislocation when the time comes to transform the war economy into a peace economy once more. The studies already undertaken in this direction by groups such as the one headed by Vice-President Wallace, and others both in America and in England, indicate that in such quarters there is little illusion concerning the really revolutionary changes that the necessary planning entails. There is no reason to believe that the men charged with the study of these questions are biased against capitalism. But, if they have any sense of reality, it is obvious that the place allocated by them to capitalism in the world of tomorrow cannot possibly be one of great independence. In the future economy of the world, private capitalism may play the role of a kind of self-starter, but the real driving power back of that economy will be controlled by the governmental agencies.

Even these changes will necessitate a revision of the concepts of many individualistic leaders of big business and industry as they still exist today.

In the final report of the Temporary National Economic Committee (TNEC) published in March 1941, one can find the following lines, subscribed to by the twelve experts who worked on this laborious fact-finding survey of American economics:

"We know that most of the wealth and income of the country is owned by a few large corporations, that these corporations are owned in turn by an infinitesimally small number of people and that the profits from the operations of these corporations go to a very small group with the results that the opportunities for new enterprises, whether corporate or individual, are constantly being restricted."

Such a discovery is not new, but its recent restatement shows that the long-drawn-out conflict between capitalism and democracy cannot be evaded or camouflaged much longer. As I have indicated before, the example of France and England proves that this war cannot be waged successfully without the total support of the mass of the people. And, in turn, the support of the people cannot be obtained without the promise that if the democratic nations win the war, it will mean in fact a tangible victory for democracy.

As the same report of the TNEC points out: "Political freedom cannot survive if economic freedom is lost."

CHAPTER III

The Conflict between Socialism and Democracy

THE various schools of socialism, including Communism, accept as a fundamental proposition that international unity of the masses, and more particularly of the industrial workers, will not only improve their economic condition but prevent the recurrence of wars. Wars, according to Leftist thinking, are the consequences of imperialistic rivalries, which in turn are made possible and even unavoidable through the fact that national governments are controlled by powerful capitalist interests. If the laboring masses controlled the affairs of the state, there would be no wars.

There is no way of proving whether such a premise is true. No political system has ever been devised by which the mass of the people could actually express their will on such matters as war or peace without the interposition of practical leadership. And it can be said that as soon as such a leadership exists, whatever may be its political complexion, it becomes immediately sensitive to nationalist influences and subject, therefore, to accusations of imperialism. Stalin is a good case in point. For many years now, and especially during this war, the Living Buddha of Internationalism has behaved like a Russian, and if he thinks in terms of future world revolution it is obviously not his main preoccupation for the moment.

Socialism is a doctrine. It offers at once a program and a dream. Like all modern political creeds it has had to assume certain of the functions of religion where religion, as a social system, has ceased to operate. It must offer a promise, an earthly promise, and that promise is the elimination of war, the reign of justice, economic equality for all, order and efficiency in the production and distribution of goods—all of which is to be achieved by turning over to the laboring classes the management of their own affairs.

It should be noted that as far as the general attitude toward society is concerned, there is only a shade of difference between that of democracy as it now exists in America and that of socialism. Concerning the problem of war, for instance, progressive democrats like President Roosevelt have stated their belief that 90 per cent of the people of the earth wanted peace and that the only difficulty was to get rid of the 10 per cent of evildoers who led them astray.

American democracy and socialism also agree on the notion that the aim of government is to improve the material conditions of existence for the greatest number of citizens and to establish as much equality between men as is possible.

Democracy and socialism, in other words, both believe in the principle that the majority rule is sound because the general tendency of human nature is directed toward good more than toward evil. They are both based on an optimistic philosophy concerning the nature of man.

Where they differ is in their attitude toward the minorities who enjoy an excess of power through economic advantages. The socialist solution is to eliminate them and to transfer their power to the state. They recommend a leveling of society that would fill in the gap that now exists between the theory of political equality and the practice of economic inequality. They would do away with private capital altogether, and—under Communism—with private property. The state alone would wield economic power.

On the other hand, democracy, as it now exists, does not believe in destroying private capitalism. It wants to control it, curb it, and prevent its excesses. It certainly does not wish to destroy private property, and the present tendency of democratic government seems to be toward an increase of managerial functions rather than ownership.

There is no doubt that in the eyes of sensitive conservatives and alarmed reactionaries these differences between modern democracy and socialism are not important enough to reassure them. Private capitalism is conscious of having failed in its effort to maintain its hold on the affairs of the state. Even in America the political power has gained the upper hand, and there is no reason to believe that it will lose it, except by a revolution which would reinstate the prestige of the economic minorities through some form of business Fascism.

1. Democracy is legitimate

Nevertheless the differences between modern democracy and socialism, however slight they may appear to those whose pocketbook and prestige are more conspicuously deflated, are fundamental, because they involve some of the most vital problems which the world is facing today.

The main difference can be expressed as follows: whereas the general premises and purposes of democracy and socialism tend to coincide more and more, the methods of approach to the solution of the problems and the attitude toward nearly all aspects of life are conflicting. Socialism implies revolution, that is, a break with the existing order. Democracy clings to the principle of evolution and to the notion of continuity. Socialism can justify itself only by trying to impose a doctrine. Democracy can survive only by avoiding at all costs any drastic step that would mark a definite break with the customs, habits of thought, and the will for permanency that is the chief characteristic of a living organism, whether it be an animal, a school of art, or a form of civilization.

Democracy such as we know it at the moment is still in a position to absorb many doctrines, such as socialism, without necessarily destroying itself, because it still remains the only mode of life and the only mechanism of society sufficiently broad as far as its philosophical basis is concerned, and sufficiently vague as to its outlines, to encompass a vast number of contradictions.

If one wishes to accept the definition of Talleyrand, democracy is now the only "legitimate" form of government known in the world. Talleyrand wrote:

"A legitimate government, be it monarchical or republican, hereditary or elective, aristocratic or democratic, is always the one whose existence, form, and mode of action have been strengthened and sanctioned over a long period of years, I might even say over a period of centuries. . . . Today there is a widespread belief, which it would be impossible to shake, that governments exist only for the benefit of the people. From this it follows that a legitimate power is one which can best guarantee their peace and happiness. Therefore the only legitimate power is one which has lasted a great many years. And furthermore, strengthened by tradition and by the affection which men naturally possess for their rulers—owing them an allegiance which becomes a law in the eyes of every individual, corresponding to the laws regulating private property—this power is less likely than any other to deliver up its people to the grim horrors of revolution. In other words, it is one which people are serving their best interest by obeying." [1]

If this is accepted, it is clear that democracy is the only form of government in existence today that is strong enough and endowed with sufficient experience and prestige to avoid the "grim horrors of revolution." Or, to be more accurate, it is the only one to which the forces who are afraid of, or opposed to, revolution can still cling. Democracy has become the only refuge of the conservatives and of all those who are conscious that the real peril of the present times is the risk of a complete break in the evolution of Western civilization such as occurred between the fifth and twelfth centuries, a period of six or seven hundred years during which the vital principle of continuity in human development was suspended.

It may be argued that socialism, in its moderate form, is by no means revolutionary, that it proposes in fact nothing but an extension of the democratic process. This is quite true if one considers socialism from the angle of social reform, the emancipation of labor, the curtailment of economic privileges. . . . As I have noted before, progressive democracy, as conceived by Roosevelt, for instance, tends more and more to fulfill the aims of socialism. But when one considers the attitude of democracy and socialism toward international relations and the organization of the Western World, certain very deep conflicts become apparent. In the same manner that the war of 1914-1918 and the postwar era showed the deep cleavage that exists between capitalism and democracy, a parallel opposition has developed between the main current of democracy—which is conservative, individualistic, anti-collectivist, and fundamentally bourgeois in its general

---

[1] Ferrero, *The Reconstruction of Europe,* G. P. Putnam's Sons, 1941, pp. 53, 59.

outlook—and the fundamental trend of socialist thinking.

It is generally admitted that if democracy survives this war, it will become much more socialistic than it has ever been before. In fact, many believe that socialism is the natural heir to the capitalist democracy which we know today. This may be so, but it implies a rather profound reform or rejuvenation of the whole socialist doctrine in so far as the problems of nationalism and international relations are concerned.

Capitalist democracy and socialism have both proved their inability to cope successfully with the phenomenon of war, but the record of socialism is even more lamentable than that of democracy. If the bourgeois democrats and the liberals of England, France, and the United States have shown blindness, incoherence, and weakness from the Versailles Treaty up to the present day, and if their prestige as an elite has deteriorated constantly, they have not equaled the confusion of socialist leadership, nor have they accumulated such a record of failures.

Admitting the validity of Talleyrand's theory of "legitimacy" (as interpreted by Ferrero), one can say that every political doctrine is in the position of bidding constantly for power but that it can obtain it only if, over a long period of time, it has succeeded in gaining the confidence and the respect of large sections of the population. Judged by such standards, socialism was in a good position at the end of the nineteenth century and up to 1914 to offer its solutions to the economic, social, and political problems of the modern industrial world, because it was the only doctrine that seemed prepared to launch a frontal attack on the growing peril of extreme nationalism and to suggest an international solution to humanity's problems.

Democracy, in spite of all its errors, has not lost its claim to "legitimacy" in the future. Socialism has not acquired it. It has even lost much of the progress it had made be-

fore the opening of the cataclysmic era which began in
1914.

Wars and the present revolutionary assault against civilization have badly shaken the democratic principles but
they have not destroyed them. Doctrinaire socialism is in
a condition of chaos and, as an international force, is reduced to impotence.

2. *The betrayal of 1914*

Up to the war of 1914, the position of the socialist parties and Leftist groups was fairly clear. The conservative
and economically privileged groups in each country being
identified with nationalism, the socialist attacks were directed against militarism, capitalism, and all forms of
power politics. In Germany, in France, as well as in all
other European countries, the socialists had pledged themselves to do all in their power to prevent war, not excluding sabotage and rebellion in case of mobilization.
Socialism, in other words, appeared as the most powerful
movement for peace because it proclaimed that unified
labor, as an international force, was stronger than the
sense of national discipline which prompts men to fight.

Before Germany and France mobilized in August 1914,
there was no reason to believe that this was not so. Since
the Congress of Vienna in 1815, there had been several
wars, but they had all been localized. None had produced
the universal disruption caused by the French Revolution
and the Napoleonic wars. For one hundred years Europe
had enjoyed if not perfect peace, at least sufficient stability
to make the nineteenth century appear in retrospect as
one of the most prosperous and progressive that history
has recorded. Material comfort due to industrial development was spreading like an irresistible wave, and this in

turn increased the power of organized labor all over western Europe.

The evolution of the class struggle defined by Karl Marx seemed to be taking shape according to prophecies. The governments of the big powers were seriously pre-occupied by such things as antimilitaristic propaganda in the armies and by threats of rebellion in the war industries in case of mobilization. Many liberals and intellectuals had definitely taken sides for internationalism. There was no real assurance that the workers, and with them a considerable part of the small bourgeoisie, would not strike against war.

When the test came, however, in August 1914, nothing of the kind happened. The German Socialist party—the strongest of all at the time—immediately rallied to the call of the Kaiser, which gave the French Socialist leaders a good excuse to act likewise. The French government, which had a list of dangerous persons to be arrested in case of mobilization—called the "Carnet B"—merely filed this list. Jean Jaurès, the head of the French Socialist party, was assassinated by a fanatic on the eve of mobilization, but it had already been decided by him and his friends to support the war.

Thus the great fear of sabotage and betrayal proved groundless. The German worker acted as a German and the French worker as a Frenchman. National unity prevailed.

But if the socialists and their followers did not betray their flag, they certainly betrayed their own doctrine of resistance to war.

It matters little whether the blame for the betrayal of international socialism should be placed on the German socialists or elsewhere. It can only be said that early in August 1914, socialism, as an international movement, received its first deadly blow. It was the first tangible evi-

dence that when an international force like socialism is
in direct opposition to nationalism, the latter triumphs.

Later on, during the First World War, there were some
attempts made to revive international pacifism, such as the
Congress of Zimmerwald. The mutinies that took place in
the French Army in 1917 showed that the old doctrine of
rebellion against war was still very much alive, but such
attempts were, on the whole, abortive and the war went
on in an atmosphere of "national unity."

The first really effective revolt of socialism against nationalism took place in 1917, when Lenin, having re-
entered Russia, overthrew the "democratic" government
of Kerensky, established the Soviets, and signed the peace
of Brest-Litovsk. This peace was worse than shameful
from the nationalist point of view, but it reaffirmed one
of the fundamental aims of socialism: that peace can be
assured only by an international rebellion of the proletariat against capitalist imperialism. Although committing
Russia alone, it was an appeal to revolt intended to re-
verberate throughout the world.

The Communist revolution naturally created a state of
extreme alarm among all the Western powers, who saw in
it the greatest threat against any form of nationalism and
therefore against the bourgeois society itself. But once
again the attempt to establish internationalism from be-
low was to prove a failure. The example of Brest-Litovsk
was not followed. The world revolution did not spread.
Lenin was compelled to compromise on fundamental
points of the Marxian doctrine, even inside Russia. After
his death, whatever hopes there might have been among
intellectual idealists that Communism offered a solution
to the complex problems of the postwar world, died.
"From its very start," wrote H. G. Wells, "the Russian
Revolution failed in its ambition to lead mankind."

There were many reasons for this, but one of the most

important, in my opinion, has often been overlooked: The very fact that the attempts to achieve world revolution were directed from Moscow weakened the chances of the world proletariat in their attempt to overthrow the existing order. Geographic conditions are as important in revolutionary movements as they are in power politics. London, Paris, Berlin, can be the capitals of Europe because they are in Europe proper. Moscow is not. However great may have been the influence of the Third International on the destinies of the laboring classes, the fact that the Comintern is located in Russia has been an insuperable handicap. For the Communist revolution to succeed, it would have had to conquer one of the big Western countries. This it failed to do, with the result that, ever since the death of Lenin, Communism has tended to become subservient to Russian power politics. Its adherents in foreign countries still take their orders from Stalin, but in doing so they cannot help knowing that they are serving Russian national interests first and that world revolution has become a mere by-product of Soviet power politics.

3. Russia goes nationalist

In spite of the fact that since June 22, 1941, Russia has found herself fighting on the side of the democracies—which has rehabilitated to a certain extent the cause of the partisans of Moscow—this rehabilitation has not benefited Communism as such. In fact the net result of Stalin's policy has been to emphasize the nationalist character of the present Russian leadership. From the point of view of pure doctrine, Stalin is no better off now that he is fighting on the side of the capitalist democracies of the West than when he aligned himself against them by signing a pact with Hitler in August 1939.

It may be argued that Stalin's calculations went wrong. He may have overestimated—like everybody else—the strength of the French Army and of the Maginot Line. He may have hoped that Nazi Germany and the Allies would exhaust one another in a long drawn-out war. Perhaps his thoughts ran as follows:

"There is no righteousness in either cause. Both are motivated by the same evil impulse, which is greed. It is not the little people who are doing the fighting and the suffering who are the greedy ones. They are innocent of that. Their only guilt is idleness. Idleness has made them stupid and stupidity has made it easy for the big ones, the greedy ones, to lead them into war. If we can keep both sides fighting long enough, until they cannot fight any more, then maybe the little people will open their eyes. Then they can see that they have been the dupes of this international clique of greed. Maybe then they will revolt and free themselves from being led into destruction again as soon as they have rested and recovered for a generation or so."

This way of looking at the situation, which is not that of a Communist, nor even of a fellow traveler, but of Henry Ford, may have been that of Stalin, and he may have concluded, like the American industrialist, that "when both nations [Germany and England] finally collapse into internal dissolution, then the United States [or Soviet Russia] can play the role for which it has the strength and the ability."

If Stalin reasoned in this fashion—that is, like Henry Ford—when he signed the German-Soviet Pact, his reasoning was faulty, as proved by Hitler, who, far from exhausting himself in his fight against the Western capitalist democracies, gained enough strength through a series of victories over them to turn against Soviet Russia with the purpose of wiping Bolshevism from the earth.

It may be that by siding with the democracies Stalin will eventually save the independence of his country and his own regime. But even if he should sit among the victors, it may be more in the capacity of national leader of the Russian people than as the head of Communism and world revolution. I do not say that a joint victory of the United States, England and the U.S.S.R. will mean the disappearance of Communist rule in Russia, but if there is to be a new international order after this war (provided it is not Hitler's) the chances are that its foundations will be democratic rather than communistic. Roosevelt still has a wider appeal in the world than Stalin.

The fact that Stalin has been compelled to follow a *national* policy as did the Czars who preceded him has discredited the cause of Communism as a formula to solve the problems involved in the present crisis. There is a growing desire that the world of the future should rest on something less uninspiring and less artificial than the Marxian doctrine of the class struggle. The slogans "Workers of the world, unite!" "You have nothing to lose but your chains," etc., have proved inoperative too many times in the last twenty-five years. It is a strange irony of fate that the prestige of the Russian people has never been so high, owing to their magnificent heroism, while at the same time, the regime under which they live, far from extending its ideological influence, would seem to be losing ground and prestige. The democracies which, at the time of writing, are supporting Russia in her war effort have lost none of their hostility to Communism. In fact the tendency is to believe that the remarkable exploits of the Russians and their surprising ability to resist the German onslaught have been possible in spite of Communism. "The Russia of today's firing line is manifestly not the Russia of 1914-1918," wrote the *New York Times* editorially in October 1941. "It has progressed in industrial power and proficiency. . . . It is probably less provincial and more nationalistic. These changes could have taken place without Communism. They may have taken place in spite of Communism. . . . After the victory, the democracies will be no more tolerant than they are now of the doctrines and practices of the Communist dictatorship. But they will owe a debt of gratitude to the Russian people, whose essential qualities will outlast Communism."

There may be a good deal of wishful thinking in this attitude, but it does not destroy the essential fact that nationalism has once more proved stronger than the doctrine of international class resistance to war. The Russia of Stalin is not the Russia of Tannenberg, indeed, but it is not the Russia of Brest-Litovsk, either.

4. Socialism alone cannot fight Hitler

Thus, ever since 1914 one of the fundamental purposes of Marxism, which is to make war impossible by opposing to it the organized revolt of the world proletariat, has failed. The later failures, such as the Spanish War, the Popular Front policy, the German-Soviet pact of 1939, and now the realignment of Moscow with London and Washington, have brought clearly into light the limitations and inadequacies of the Marxian class struggle. The simple idea that the destruction of capitalism would solve all problems, including the problem of war, appears rather naive in the presence of the complex situation that now faces the world.

This does not mean that socialist thinking is condemned. Quite the contrary. But it would appear that the attempt to impose socialism by revolution, as is the purpose of the Communist, cannot succeed better than the compromise method of the now doomed Social Democrats of Europe. A reform of socialist thinking and socialist tactics seems to be under way both in England and in the United States. In the same way that the reality of the war has revealed the weakness of absolute capitalism, similarly doctrinaire socialism has also shown its fragility. The real conflict in which the world is engaged has not as yet taken shape very clearly in the eyes of the average citizen. But certain facts are plain enough. The idea that there are three main currents of force in this conflict—democracy, Fascism, and Communism—and that they can be combined and re-shuffled according to the hazards of war is an illusion. Hitler has clearly seen the truth when he said that there were two worlds (not three) opposed, and that one of the two must succumb.

Hitler, of course, does not think in terms of politics, but of demonology. His method is to throw into one inferno all his enemies—whether real or imaginary. This is why he makes no distinction between Bolshevism, democracy, socialism, capitalism, and the Jews. All these he fights regardless of subtle distinctions. But, leaving aside the propaganda effect of such a method, the fact remains that Hitler is correct in recognizing an unconscious alliance between all those whom he considers as the enemies of National Socialism. If that alliance did not exist, he would create it.

It should not be forgotten, however, that the real opposition to Hitlerism is not to be found either in Bolshevism, capitalism, socialism, or in the Jews. There is only one real peril for Hitler: democracy, and the principles upon which it is founded. If he can destroy that, he destroys all the rest. This word—so derided by some today, so meaningless to others—contains nevertheless the essential idea of continuity and evolution, of progress and permanence, without which there can be no civilization.

And it is because socialism cannot hope to fight Hitler alone that a whole reorientation of progressive thinking has taken place in the last few years, more especially in America and in England.

Credit for this reorientation must go first to Franklin Roosevelt and the New Deal—a movement that in spite of its empirical character, its vagueness, and its errors, is the only one which to date has shown enough vitality and rallied enough support to withstand all serious attacks either from the Fascist or from the Communist ideology.

It is true that the war and the urgency of national defense have suspended for the time being any new social reform in America. The United States, like England, is mostly concerned with maintaining national unity, but it should be noted that the war has not induced either the British or the American government to cancel the social reforms obtained in previous years. In contrast to what happened in France, where Daladier seized the pretext of the war to wipe out the social gains of the Popular Front government, President Roosevelt has been careful, up to now, to reassert the inviolability of the New Deal. War has brought no reaction as yet in America, and it is certainly the purpose of the present Administration to pursue its present policies through the war and after it.

In England, the participation of Labor in the government is not a mere gesture symbolic of national unity. It is a serious challenge to the ability of the conservative leaders of England not only to conduct the war successfully but to prepare the future peace. British Laborites and Liberals are growing every day more aware that, at the end of the First World War, they got "no new Britain and no new Europe," and that some attempt must be made this time to obtain both.

Many Roosevelt supporters as well as many English Liberals may object to applying the term "socialistic" to the kind of society which they are trying to foreshadow as a solution for the future. But whether this word or another is used, the basic trend remains the same. That trend is toward an increase of power of the people, and the consequent elimination of the rulers of the last twenty years. It may eventually imply the elimination of those who are now at the helm. It is a trend that points toward a more militant and more virile form of democracy, the general outlines of which can be only vaguely perceived as yet, but which is already an accomplished fact in England today. It is the natural sequence of the experiments in social democracy that were carried on before—and failed—but the inspiration is different, because it is born out of the mortal perils of the war.

As far as England is concerned, Goering and his Luftwaffe are as much responsible for this awakening of a new democratic spirit as are the new leaders of revolutionary England.

5. Marxist miscalculations

A fundamental distinction should be made in the way social-democratic experiments were conducted in Europe and in America.

In Europe, more especially on the Continent, the socialist dream of international brotherhood, of a more even distribution of wealth and of stable peace, was shattered by two perverting forces: National Socialism and Communism. The former has used socialism and distorted it into a method of enslaving people to the German war machine. The latter has bogged down into autocracy and bureaucracy.

In central and western Europe, socialist and labor leaders and all forces of the Left failed to realize that their effort to resist Fascism could not succeed if they relied on the workers alone. The great error of Karl Marx was to believe that the small bourgeoisie being gradually impoverished would finally join hands with the proletariat. But this small bourgeoisie reacted everywhere more or less as it had done in Germany. It refused to make a common front with the workers, whom it had always considered as a class socially inferior. Whenever a showdown came, as in Austria, in Spain, or in France, the small bourgeoisie balked at the idea of allying itself with the forces of organized labor—not because the economic interests of the workers were different from theirs, but because they feared that socialism or Communism meant the leveling down of all to the social status of the proletariat.

Moreover, this small bourgeoisie of Europe had remained fundamentally nationalistic, and the idea of joining hands with those who were fighting with the weapons and the slogans of the international revolution seemed sacrilegious.

On the other hand, the governments of England, France, and the other countries threatened by Fascism and Nazism, were unable to understand that the totalitarian states had effectively solved certain technological problems common to all the Western World and that a purely negative attitude toward these problems was bound to discredit and doom democracy itself.

As has been explained before, the economic solution offered by the National Socialist leaders (which is to harness to the maximum capacity the technological knowledge, the industrial plants, and the labor available) is vitiated by its ultimate purpose, which is war and destruction. But there is little doubt that the governments of the Western democracies, committed as they were to the formulas of capitalism and classical financing, made little or no effort to modify their outworn conceptions. They fought for the preservation of capitalist democracy as it had developed in the Victorian era. The obsolete and inadequate opposition between the Marxists and the anti-Marxists was emphasized. Conservative and reactionary "realists" on the one hand and befuddled Marxists, socialists, and Communists on the other, chose to fight one another to the death, not realizing that they had nothing but antiquated weapons to fight with. This is literally true when one considers the kind of armies and armaments that the capitalist democracies put into the field, and figuratively also, as is proved by the insistence on both sides that this world crisis is essentially a class struggle.

6. Social democracy in America

When one envisages the development of social democracy in America, the same general pattern is found, but there are very important differences.

The first one is the fact that in America no idea can express itself except through a system which, during one hundred and fifty years, has proved at once sufficiently solid and sufficiently flexible to absorb every new doctrine provided it did not clash too obviously with the concepts of American democracy.

The second is the existence of the two-party system, which prevents the emergence of any party based on a doctrine so rigid that it could not appeal to the majority of the whole electorate.

If one wishes, therefore, to identify the New Deal reforms with a series of experiments in social democracy, it is necessary to keep in mind that whereas political doctrines in Europe are always represented by a party bearing a recognizable label, these same doctrines when transplanted in America must find their expression through the established tradition of the two-party system. The result is that European political doctrines, in their pure form, seldom find an echo in America. They blend with

the ways of thinking and the ways of life of the Americans.
When they do not, as is the case with socialism as represented by the Socialist party of Norman Thomas, they fail
to take root or to progress.

Usually political conceptions are identified with the
name of a leader. More often than not that leader is the
President. The names of Jefferson, Lincoln, Theodore
Roosevelt, Wilson, Coolidge, Franklin Roosevelt, assume
the value of political programs considerably more precise
and informative than the Democratic or Republican plat-
forms upon which they were elected. This identification of
American trends with individuals is another reason why it
is always dangerous to look for too much correspondence
between what happens in Europe and in America, especially when the individual identified with the trend is the
President of the United States. The President, by the very
nature of his office, cannot assert his leadership if his point
of view is too sectarian and therefore too obviously in contradiction with large sections of public opinion.

It is nevertheless true that the general trend of the New
Deal has been toward socialization and centralization. But
if one envisages the accomplishments of the Roosevelt Administration as a whole it is difficult to decide whether
they are the results of a concerted effort to find a new
formula for a working democracy or merely the products
of empiricism. President Roosevelt has always given the
impression that the measures he took from time to time
were made necessary by the emergency of the moment.
If most of his social reforms have now assumed a permanent character it may not be because they were clearly
planned as such. American public opinion has been led to
accept the New Deal legislation as a temporary expedient.
This has had the advantage of depriving the opposition of
a good deal of its possible strength. But it has had the inconvenience of preventing any clear formulation of the

New Deal philosophy as a solution to the problems that confront democratic governments in the United States and elsewhere.

The fundamental trend toward collectivism has certainly been taken into account by the New Dealers but they have not faced squarely the unavoidable consequences of this trend. They have understood that capitalist methods and the folklore of business stood in the way of democratic progress. And so they have tried to curb the large corporations, the monopolies, and speculation, and they have attempted to replace the primacy of the businessman's point of view by a wider concept of human rights. But while they have acted as if they perceived the inner contradiction of capitalist democracy, they seem to have overlooked the fact that social democracy is also discredited by its own failures, its own Marxist or reformist mythology. More especially, it has not been able to solve the riddle of the man in the street, who knows that the improvement of his own status is dependent on the improvement of the status of millions of other men all over the planet, and yet finds himself drawn irresistibly into the orbit of nationalism and war.

The New Deal, in so far as it is colored with socialism, has not succeeded as yet in shaking off the liabilities attached to a doctrine which was founded on the abstract and outworn notions of internationalism, as conceived by Marx and his disciples. There is no doubt that a good deal of thought is given to the role of democracy as a new force in a new world, but the blueprints now available—such as the eight points of the Atlantic Charter—throw little light on the fundamental problems. They seem to uphold the principle of the sovereignty of states while at the same time proposing a solution of economic problems on an international basis. Once more the inherent contradiction of the Western World is put before that world but no solution is offered.

The reason for this is obvious: nothing practical or constructive can be done until the elimination of Nazism and all that it stands for is assured. Nevertheless it is already clear that even if we had victory in our hands tomorrow, there would be no ready solution for the construction of a rational and workable peace.

The future remains unpredictable.

* * * * * *

Those who feel that Western civilization has arrived at a turning point as critical as the periods of the Reformation or the French Revolution are right. But for us who are living through this crisis it is as difficult to foresee its outcome as it was difficult for the contemporaries of Martin Luther or Robespierre to predict the kind of world that they were helping to create. The Reformation broke the unity of the Christian world, but its consequences were infinitely more far-reaching than a mere religious schism. The medieval world in which the Catholic Church exerted the functions of an absolute international state came to an end. Secular power increased and nations as such began to assert their independence. Simultaneously rational thinking and scientific criticism received a tremendous impetus from the liberation of dogmatic tyranny. None of these consequences were foreseen by the Protestants, who merely believed that they were engaged in a religious dispute.

Similarly, the men of the French Revolution in attacking the privileges of the monarchy and feudalism had no inkling that they were working for the establishment of a new privileged class: the nineteenth century bourgeoisie. The smugness of the Louis Philippe era, the militarism of

Napoleon III, and the capitalist democracy of the Third Republic are strange heirs to the Jacobins.

Today we find ourselves in a comparable predicament. We are trying to preserve the framework of democracy, because we feel that we must maintain, if we can, a certain continuity in the evolution of our civilization. The Nazi revolution, if it should succeed, would mark a complete break in this continuity, and one need not be a reactionary to understand that a break, coming at this time, would entail a regression of culture which might well be fatal to the whole Western World. The rapidity with which Europe is being plunged into a state of barbarism—both materially and intellectually—is sufficiently instructive.

The question is not whether democracy can be made to work according to capitalist formulas or socialist doctrines. The imperative of collectivism disregards such subtleties. The dilemma is whether a collectivist society—that is, one founded on our real possibilities of production—can be established without destroying the essential principles upon which democracy rests.

Part III

THE OPPOSITION TO WAR

CHAPTER I

"Why Fight?"

WHAT may turn out to be the most important and characteristic trait of the times we live in is the existence of a universal and deeply rooted opposition to war.

This sentiment is so general and so new in some of its manifestations that it will take the perspective of history to analyze it fully and to appraise correctly its influence on the state of mind and on the behavior of the millions of men and women who are involved directly or indirectly in this war.

Though, as far back as one can trace the history of mankind, there have always been men to contrast the blessings of peace with the horrors of war, war in past ages was accepted as a necessity. The warrior was surrounded with an aura of respect. He was glorified by the poets and the conqueror often received the tribute reserved to a god. Men recognized the horrors of war, but they also praised its glorious and heroic aspects. They also believed it was useful and profitable because, up to a fairly recent past, there was no better way for a people to enrich itself than to make war on others and plunder them. The idea that war does not pay is a modern idea. It could not have been thought of before our time because it is only in our time that this may have become true.

Wars of the past, implying the acquisition of new territory and the subjugation of new people, were undoubtedly profitable to the victor. Wealth was directly connected with the amount of land under the control of a ruler, because under the economics of scarcity which prevailed everywhere, and in the absence of transportation, more land meant more food and the annexation of more people, more labor to cultivate the land. In other words, the ratio between the cost of a successful war and the profits it brought in were not what they are today. Our forefathers knew as much as we do about the horrors and devastation of war, but they seldom doubted that such sacrifices were worth while. Even when they fought for other motives than conquest, such as preserving their independence, there was a clear connection in their minds between obtaining victory and improving their condition. They preferred peace, no doubt, as we do ourselves, but when they plunged into war, they seldom had the moral scruples or the misgivings which characterize the modern civilized man. They did not feel that war in itself was a regression or a denial of their purposes and ideals. Quite the contrary: war in most cases appeared as a means of achieving progress, or benefiting both the conqueror and the conquered (as for example, the Roman conquests or the conquest of America by the Spaniards, the Portuguese, and other Europeans in the sixteenth and seventeenth centuries). In other cases, wars enabled a people to liberate itself from an oppressor, and that objective was usually considered sufficient in itself.

The contemporary man, however, has another conception of war. The ratio between the possible profits and the certain sacrifices has changed in his mind. The latter tend to overbalance the former. The industrial developments of the last hundred years, as well as the facilities of transportation, have destroyed the idea that more land means more wealth, more people more profitable work. The average man knows that he does not have actually to own a wheat field to eat bread or a vineyard to drink wine. He knows that the necessities of life can be produced in super-abundant quantities and transported anywhere in the world. He knows that the fundamental problem of today is not one of production but of distribution. War obviously cannot solve that problem. It can only make it more insoluble, as proved by the terrible conditions now existing in Europe due to the disorganization brought about by the war.

The contemporary man may not know how to improve his spiritual, economic, and social conditions in time of peace, but he senses that peace is the prerequisite condition for any approach to the problems which confront him. He senses, too, that the interdependence of nations and continents such as has developed in our time tends to make war not only increasingly more disruptive but obsolete as a method of settling the difficulties both of the individual and of the nation. The damages and the destruction caused by war under modern conditions are so vast, so far-reaching, and so obvious that it has become difficult, and sometimes well-nigh impossible, to persuade the modern man that it is nevertheless necessary for him to fight, even when his very existence is at stake.

1. War appears senseless

Believing that even the victor will come out of a war impoverished and generally worse off than before, he tends to obliterate in his own mind the very notion that the people who make war on him are his foe. He prefers to think that they are temporarily misguided by their leaders, and that were it possible to make them see the light, they would stop making war. The modern civilized man cannot understand why other men—presumably equally civilized—want to make war when he himself is so profoundly attached to peace. Being unable to explain this paradox, his inclination is to deny that it exists. Thus when war does come, he finds himself in the curious predicament of having to fight without even the primitive incentive of hatred or even, sometimes, the desire for victory. Each argument for war turns into an argument against war. Even the supreme reason, which is the survival of the nation and of the individual, becomes a contradiction in itself. "Why should I go to war to save my country," asks the average man, "when I know that war in itself is an unmitigated evil which will probably debase and perhaps destroy both my enemy and myself?"

Moreover, the whole logic of Western civilization cannot be justified if war is accepted as a method of settling human conflicts. The Western man believes that he is master of his own destiny, which means that he must reject the idea that war is unavoidable, for the simple reason that war, contrary to other calamities such as plagues, diseases, earthquakes, and floods, is man-made. With the increased consciousness of this fundamental distinction between natural calamities and those which he brings upon himself, the modern man's horror of war has increased, all the more so because his success in combating disease, famine, poverty, and in reducing the damages caused by the forces of nature has been very remarkable.

War—man-made war—remains the one great scourge toward the elimination of which no progress has been made. After twenty centuries of gradual emancipation from primitive and irrational barbarism, the modern man is still periodically confronted with the greatest of all absurdities: the willful and organized destruction of human life, of property, and all the self-inflicted suffering that war brings in its wake.

When war occurs, therefore, it must be justified by
motives which, from the point of view of "civilized" thinking, are somewhat artificial or, at any rate, regressive, such
as the bare instinct of self-preservation, or the renovation
of ancient myths, usually quite barbaric, like the whole set
of nonsensical dogmas (the master race and the "blood
and soil" theories, the cult of the warrior, etc.) which have
enabled Hitler to rehabilitate war and even to sanctify it.

But neither the rationalization of self-defense nor the
rejuvenation of archaic myths offers any satisfactory answer
to the average modern man, be he a German, a Frenchman, an American, or an Englishman. Whether he fights
or refuses to fight, whether he shows bravery, resignation,
or apathy, the fundamental and baffling questions remain
ever present in his mind: "Why must I make war? Why
must I destroy to avoid destruction? If it is true that we, as
well as our opponents, are our own masters, why do we
make war when we obviously prefer peace?"

It may be that some men have always asked themselves
this kind of questions, even in the most savage periods of
primitive history. But the important fact is that today
practically all men ask them. The point of view of the few
men of wisdom which expressed itself rather exceptionally
in past centuries, has now become the point of view of the
man in the street. The Western man of the twentieth century has finally learned his lesson. He does not need any
further demonstration that war is not only inhuman and
evil, but also senseless and futile. And yet, we live in a
time when this lesson has to be unlearned, when we have
to rehabilitate within our own selves instincts which our
reason has condemned as barbaric, or create new reasons
and new impulses to justify our plunging into what we
want to avoid.

Sir Nevile Henderson records that Goering told him
one day that the British had to be "brutalized" in order

to survive. There is no doubt that Goering himself has accomplished that feat with the help of his *Luftwaffe,* if what he meant was that the British should recover their fighting spirit, but both the advice and the consequent result throw a good deal of light on the fundamental dilemma of these times. The Nazis, having "brutalized" the Germans, are now forcing their opponents to "brutalize" themselves—because there is no other choice—but the accumulated teaching of twenty centuries of civilization cannot be forgotten in one day. In fact, the whole conflict in which we are engaged revolves around this question: Is it possible for the Western civilized world to stop the barbaric assault launched upon it by Germany without reverting itself to a state of barbarism?

Or, to put the problem in a more concrete form, can we demonstrate to the average man on our side of the fence these three things?

1. Although everything he knows and feels about the evilness of war is true, he must nevertheless make war now.

2. He must therefore either forget temporarily everything he has been told about the senselessness and uselessness of war, or find new reasons for having recourse to war.

3. If he cannot do these things, he must nevertheless be ready to sacrifice practically all the spiritual and material achievements of civilization on the mystic premise that the sacrifice in itself will ensure, somehow or other, the salvation of this civilization.

2. *Apathy, a modern disease*

If the problem presented in this fashion approximates the reality of the situation, I believe that one can say that it has not been solved as yet. Admitting that most of the people who oppose Germany are fighting for the defense of civilization, their behavior up to now has not demonstrated that they had as yet overcome the formidable inhibition of the antiwar feeling. They are at war no doubt, but no war, as far as history can record, has ever been fought with less enthusiasm, with less conviction as to the necessity of waging it, and with less faith in the prospect that victory will bring about a better world. The complexity of the issues involved, as I have tried to explain them in the preceding chapters, and the recognition that the world is engaged in a dual conflict of rival imperialisms and revolutionary upheavals, have greatly contributed to the confusion of mind of the individuals and of the nations who are involved in this crisis. The aims are dim, and even certain oversimplifications such as the denunciation of Hitler as a new Caesar whose intention is to dominate the world, and the efforts to rally the free people for the defense of their liberties have not been sufficient to overcome the inhibitions and the doubts of the leaders nor the apathy of the common man.

The most interesting aspect of this universal lack of enthusiasm for war is that it is but slightly affected by the varying conditions of the war itself. Neither victory nor defeat seems to influence perceptibly what might be called the potential of combativity of the modern man. A few momentous exceptions, such as Dunkirk or Pearl Harbor, both of which transformed a nation overnight, only seem to confirm this rule. There have been great feats of heroism in this war, prodigious battles and demonstrations of courage and of the spirit of sacrifice which prove that man, in his nature, remains unchanged. But the important fact is that the reaction of world consciousness to such deeds has been dulled as by some tremendous repressive force which tends to prevent the average man from being stimulated or inspired by these examples. His opposition to war remains the same, as if he had developed some sort of immunity to all the emotions, and even to the natural reflexes, which inspired his forefathers to take up arms through an instinctive impulse to fight and obtain victory.

Certain people, and first of all the British, have shown a courage and a fighting spirit which cannot be questioned. In fact, the British, and they alone among the highly civilized nations of the West, have been able to re-create within themselves the spirit of unity and resolution which has allowed them up to now to withstand against practically hopeless odds the forces of destruction launched against them. They alone today have what is called a good morale, which means that the individual citizen has sufficiently identified his own particular interests and his ideals with that of the community, so that he has, in advance, made the sacrifice of everything he owns, including his own life. Harmony has been established between the individual Britisher and the community to which he belongs. In the midst of danger, suffering, and death, many say that they have, for the first time, found a certain peace —that kind of peace which comes from the knowledge that one's existence is truly coordinated with other existences, that the individual is part of a whole, and that the nation has a common aim.

But if the English have a good morale, one must not forget what price they have had to pay, what price they are paying daily, to achieve it. Up to the capitulation of France, the English morale was no better than that of the other nations involved in this war. The unity they have now found, their dogged resolution to resist destruction, are born of a certain intensity of despair. In this sense they are singular and great, but in this sense too they show how deeply affected they are by the universal opposition to war: it is because they have no choice but war that they are now fighting with such heroism and with such peace among themselves.

The Germans too are fighting with courage, it will be said. This is true of their troops, or at least of that spearhead of fanatical young men which Hitler has specially trained, both technically and psychologically, to carry on the blitzkrieg. Among this corps, which forms an elite, the concept of man as a warrior has been developed to a supreme degree. The German aviators, the parachutists, the crews of motorized divisions, and, in general, all the specialized parts of the German Army which have actually done the fighting and assured the long list of Nazi victories are undoubtedly imbued with a combativeness and a spirit of sacrifice which cannot be questioned. But all observers agree that this high quality of morale is not universal in the German Army. It is said that France was actually conquered by 200,000 men, the elite specially trained and mentally conditioned by intensive Nazi education. But there are innumerable stories concerning the fairly low morale of the German army of occupation now quartered in conquered countries—ordinary German soldiers whose main preoccupation does not seem to be new conquests and more battles, but the desire for peace and the wish to go home.

As for the morale of the German civilian population, as good an observer as Joseph Harsch, of the *Christian Science Monitor*, writing in March 1941, at the height of Germany's triumphs, has this to say about it:

"There is almost no public or private enthusiasm for the war [in Germany].

"There is widespread cynicism about Dr. Joseph Goebbels' propaganda.

"There is no deep faith in the Nazi war cause.

"There is no general enthusiasm for the Nazi party,

or confidence in its integrity or the loftiness of its aims.

"There is intense weariness over protracted privation, rationing, and strain after living in what has amounted to a state of war for eight years. . . .

"But when all this is said, the plain fact remains that civilian morale is entirely adequate for Hitler's purposes, and there is not the slightest prospect of these moods being translated into any action against the regime or against the war effort in the measurable future. It is bad morale according to democratic standards of civilian morale. It is just as bad as the morale of the armed forces is good. But under dictatorship such as that in Germany today, such deficiencies become almost meaningless."

This diagnosis of Germany's state of mind contains many lessons. It shows that the successes of Hitler have been possible not on account of any real fighting spirit among the German population as a whole, but in spite of the absence of it. Hitler has concentrated his effort in developing a high morale and a spirit of total sacrifice in the Army and he has succeeded (in so far at least as the actual combatant units are concerned). But all his attempts to overcome the apathetic condition of the masses of the population, their fundamental antiwar attitude, have been fruitless. The fact that the German temperament is inclined to passivity and blind acceptance of discipline has helped him to carry on the most aggressive form of war against a deep current of opposition to any form of war. It has not reversed that current.

3. Men remain brave

With necessary allowances for each particular situation, the same attitude toward war has existed in all the countries opposing Hitler, but symptomatically enough, it has been much more marked in those which can be considered as highly civilized (from the point of view of Western standards) than in the more primitive.

A good morale, among both the civilians and the army, that is, a unification of national consciousness in the presence of war and a merging of individual interests into that of national consciousness, was evident in Poland when that country was invaded by Germany. It was present in Finland when Russia attacked it. The Greeks showed similar heroism, and the Serbians actually overthrew their government because it had made what they considered a humiliating treaty with Hitler. In all these cases the morale of the people and of their soldiers was what one might have called "normal." Their fighting spirit was brought up to a pitch and stayed there. There was practically no dissension among them, no hesitation as to what they should do. Even against the greatest possible odds, with practically no other prospect except defeat, they fought to the end.

The same can be said of the Russians, who have astounded the world not only by their unsuspected skill in meeting Hitler's war technique but by their courage and patriotism. This has been explained, in the complacent democracies, by saying that the Russians were fighting with so much heroism not because they were defending Communism, but because they were defending their land, Mother Russia. Be that as it may, it is interesting to note that the Western highly civilized people have been actually surprised to find that the "godless," "barbaric," or, let us say, backward Russians could fight so well. But the explanation may merely be that the Russians, like the Poles, the Finns, the Greeks, and other less highly "civilized" people have retained toward war an attitude which I would call more "normal" than that of the Western Europeans. This does not mean that they enjoy war, but merely that they are less confused than the Western people when the brutal choice between war and destruction is presented to them.

No such unity of purpose, no such acceptance of total sacrifice, no such morale existed among the people whose civilization was more complex, who had grown to depend more on the intricate mechanism of Western industrialism, and whose political life also had, during the last twenty years of the postwar period, been more directly subject to the dissolving forces of Western antiwar education.

Without minimizing the heroism and suffering of hundreds of thousands of men and women of the Western democracies, there is no doubt that the Scandinavian, the Dutch, the Belgians, and the French did not enter this war or fight it with the same disregard of individual sacrifice and of future consequences as did the less complex people of Poland, Finland, Greece, or Russia.

As for the attitude of the Americans toward the war since they have entered it, I believe that it is too soon, at the time of writing, to attempt to analyze it with any accuracy. As I have noted before, the public mind has seen a parallel between Dunkirk and Pearl Harbor as two tragic but also salutary shocks which served to shake off complacency and awaken the people to the reality of the danger. The parallel holds good, however, only if one keeps in mind the obvious fact that the disaster of Dunkirk seemed to foreshadow at the time an unavoidable and prompt end of the war and of England itself, while Pearl Harbor really meant for the American people an unpleasant way of *beginning* to fight.

There is no way of telling at the moment whether the American people are going to react to this war, now that they are in it, in the same manner as the other Western nations when they first entered it, or whether they are going to carry it on with a totally different spirit—more resolutely and more wholeheartedly. The latter seems more probable for various reasons: first, it has usually been in the American temperament to see a thing through, even if at first they encounter tremendous difficulties (the best example of this is the Civil War). Second, the long period during which the Americans were debating whether they should go to war or not may not have been wholly wasted: enough hesitancy, timorousness, complacency, fear, and defeatism were expressed publicly during that period so that one may hope that the Americans have purged their system of this sort of thing for the duration of the war. In other words, the unavoidable and dangerous phase of adaptation to war, sometimes called the "phony war," may be over for America. The poison was expelled through such means as the long debates on the Neutrality Law, on the aid to England, on the respective merits of a "shooting war" and a "non-shooting war." Finally, the chances are that the civilian population of the United States will be spared the direct and worst effects of a modern war. Contrary to the European belligerents, the American civilians will probably not suffer very much from aerial bombardments. Nor is there any serious threat, as far as one can judge now, of an invasion. Restrictions too will be relatively mild. Therefore, even if the American forces are sent abroad in great numbers, even if they should suffer heavy casualties, the morale of the nation as a whole will not be affected by such events in the same way as that of the civilian populations of Europe, who often suffer from the war more than their armies.

For all these reasons it would be unwise to try to judge the probable evolution of American opinion in relation to the war by what has happened elsewhere. Many of the manifestations of the antiwar sentiment, in its noblest and worst forms, were present in America, but the attack on Pearl Harbor has had one definite effect: it has closed the door on escapism. As far as the Americans are concerned, it cannot be doubted that they have no intention of not seeing the war through.

4. The fallacy of defense

In all other cases, and regardless of whether the war was really on or in its "phony" stage, there was the same tendency to evade it by all possible subterfuges, including some that were not particularly honorable, the same persistency of doubts as to the advisability of fighting, the same division of counsel when it came to weighing the advantages of pursuing the fight to the limit or of saving something through compromise or surrender.

Underlying such events as the surrender of the Belgian King and his army or the French capitulation in Bordeaux, one senses the profound lack of faith of millions of civilized men of the Western World in the necessity of defending not only their conceptions but even their soil by waging war. The horror of war remained stronger than war itself, even in the midst of war, and when it was proved that the whole psychological approach to war—based on defense—was a fallacy, whatever morale there was disappeared. Those who had placed their faith in "neutrality," which is a form of legal defense, succumbed when that talisman proved futile. The French, having relied on the Maginot Line, had no time to recreate for themselves a new strategy and a new morale when the Maginot system failed. All these nations had hoped that the full impact of total war upon them could either be kept away or be avoided altogether by a limited effort on their part. In the same manner as Léon Blum used to say that he wanted to introduce as much socialism in the capitalist system as that system could bear without destroying it, the Western people opposed to Hitler tried to preserve as much peace in a state of war as the phenomenon of war could stand.

The theories of Liddell Hart that defense is preferable to offense and that it assures victory were nonsensical, as amply proved in this war. But they were accepted and applied by the military leaders of the democracies because they corresponded so well to the psychology of the people. Defense and offense are two aspects of war which cannot possibly be separated if one understands war to be a conflict of forces, the purpose of which is to destroy the opponent. The use of one form of tactics or the other is determined by the changing aspect of a war. But the democracies were psychologically committed to defense because the word seemed to imply a limited effort, a sort of state of lesser war. A country which proclaims that it is compelled to *defend* itself feels itself less warlike than the country that takes the initiative of attacking. To take up arms to protect oneself appears less immoral than to invade another country. But whether true or not, it does not change the fact that, as soon as war exists, the choice between defense and offense becomes merely a military problem.

Hitler, in spite of the reluctance of his people to go to war, which was slightly less great than that of the democratic people, in spite of the bad German morale, has never been encumbered by such fine distinctions in planning his strategy. He (or his general staff) has clearly understood that the conduct of a war cannot be determined by peacetime inhibitions.

The fact that the Western democracies and the neutrals were bound to the theory of defense, both psychologically and strategically, cannot be understood fully without an analysis of the causes which made them adopt this attitude. The defensive attitude was predetermined, so to speak. Given the mentality of the Western people, their ideas of war and the education they had received during the twenty years that separated World War I and World War II, there was no possibility for them to accomplish overnight the fundamental transformation from pacifism to full war-mindedness that was necessary to meet the crisis. Still clinging to peace, they slipped into war. They behaved like a man who has fallen into the water and who struggles desperately to reach the shore, but whose frantic efforts will not prevent him from drowning if he does not know how to swim.

5. From defense to defeat

But this confinement to pure defense is only one of the manifold aspects which the antiwar feeling has assumed. Other manifestations are to be found in all fields of thought.

Leaving aside pure pacifism and various doctrines of nonresistance to force, we find that in recent years certain schools of thought of a semiphilosophical or mystical nature have grown in influence and greatly contributed to the *demoralization* of the Western people and of their leaders. Among them can be noted the Buchmanites, the partisans of the Oxford group, and the queer and equivocal fraternity of so-called Men of Good Will. In these groups—or traveling alongside them—we find the strangest assortment of people: political appeasers, such as Chamberlain in England and the Socialist leader Paul Faure in France; humanitarians like Herbert Hoover or the King of Belgium; befuddled or suspect fanatics like Rudolph Hess; and confused poets, like Anne Lindbergh.

All of them are the products of this great movement of nonacceptance of war which has developed in our world in the last twenty years. Many are sincere idealists and express some of the noblest aspirations of mankind. Others are fools, or cowards, or Quislings on the make. They are all united by one characteristic, however, which is that—willingly or not—they help to divide and demoralize. In many instances they are the apostles of sheer defeatism, which under the conditions of this war can mean only surrender to force and ultimate annihilation.

The antiwar sentiment finds another form of expression in what is called "realism." The realist is the man who having weighed all the visible factors in a given situation and having found that the odds are against him, decides that fighting is useless. He will not engage in a war if he cannot have the assurance of victory. As this assurance can never be given to him, he will always oppose war because it is always, to him, synonymous with defeat.

Georges Bonnet, in France, was a typical "realist." He felt that France, with its low birth rate, its bad morale, and its attachment to peace, was no match for the dynamism of Nazi Germany. France, in his eyes, was a sick old woman that any violent shock would kill. He saw with a realistic eye all the poisons that made France weak and vulnerable, but his "realism" was not an antidote; it was merely more poison.

There were many Georges Bonnets in America too, "realists" who although they could not argue that America was weak and sick, nevertheless feared that it could not survive the test of war. Democracy would perish, they said. America was not prepared to fight. Let us wait for the enemy. Let us die on our shores.

When the last war ended in 1918, the power of the victorious democracies was so great and so obvious that it did not seem possible that it could ever be challenged again. The belief in peace in those days was apparently justified, because it was supported by the overwhelming superiority of the victors. And these victors wanted peace. In spite of their disunity, of their inability to organize the peace they had won, there was no prospect that the world would be at war again. War was absurd and criminal. No one in his right mind wanted war. War had been eliminated.

And yet, in less than twenty years, this immense will to preserve peace deteriorated in such a way that war, once more, became a possibility—a probability, and very soon, a fact. Frightened and powerless, the "peace-loving" people clung to their illusions. As they were shattered, one by one, they felt that their own power was dwindling. They could not organize resistance. They could not unite. They had nothing to stop Hitler with except their own hatred of war, their own unwillingness to fight, and their bad morale.

And so, one by one, they entered the war—or rather were forced into it—reluctantly, without songs and without heart. They were not prepared for it, either materially or mentally. One by one they waited for the onslaught, always hoping to the last that by some miracle it would not come, that they might be spared. Whether weak or strong, they considered themselves as victims and their preoccupation was always to prove their innocence rather than to help one another. They glorified in selfishness. "Our national interest," they said, "commands us to defend ourselves and ourselves alone. Why fight for Czechoslovakia? Why fight for Danzig? Why fight for England?" And when, one after the other, they fell, those who had lost all would say: "We were wrong to fight at all. Why did we help the Czechs, and the Poles, and the English, and the Greeks? They have dragged us into defeat."

Every time a new disaster has taken place, those who were still out of immediate danger said: "Let this be a lesson to us." Hundreds of books and thousands of articles have been written describing what happened to those who thought themselves secure, and how it happened. The technique of Hitlerian aggression is, in fact, so well known by now that a precise vocabulary, brand-new, has been invented to describe it, a vocabulary which every man everywhere in the world understands. "War of nerves, Fifth Columnists, Quislings, peace offensive, infiltration, tourists, strategy of terror," these are words which we read or hear several times a day. We know what they mean. We know that they are the weapons which Hitler has created and which he himself has defined as intended to produce "mental confusion, contradiction of feeling, indecisiveness, panic."

Although we know how these weapons work, although we understand the mechanism of this war thoroughly by now, we are still vulnerable to Hitler's methods of internal dislocation. The example of Austria did not help to save the Czechs. The invasion of Denmark and Norway did not convince the Belgians and the Dutch that their own neutrality was no protection. The Americans were surprised by the Japanese "treachery," the copyright of which is to be found in Berlin.

The reason for this is not to be found in the superiority of German or Japanese arms alone, nor even in the perfection of German propaganda. In fact, the "mental confusion, contradiction of feeling, indecisiveness, panic," which Hitler refers to as his best weapons, have not been forged by him. His success in this line is due to his ability to exploit a state of mind which already existed when he came to power, but which he alone understood and appraised correctly. The confusion was there, the disunity was there, the uneasiness was there, the blindness was there. They were the conditions under which the Western World lived, and *wanted* to live, ever since the end of the First World War. They were our inheritance.

CHAPTER II

The Guilt-Complex

WHEN the Allies drafted Article 231 of the Treaty of Versailles, making Germany responsible for the damage they had suffered through the war, they had no conception of the psychological and political consequences of what they were doing.

This article reads as follows:

> "The Allied and Associated Governments affirm and Germany accepts the responsibility of Germany and her Allies for causing all the loss and damage to which the Allied and Associated Governments and their nationals have been subjected as a consequence of the war imposed upon them by the aggression of Germany and her Allies."

The real purpose of this article was not to make Germany solely guilty for the war, but to make it legally possible for the Allies to collect the war costs. The Allies and the Americans had no doubt at the time that the war was the result of a German aggression. It was also obvious that the Allies had suffered enormous damage from the war and public opinion clamored everywhere to have Germany foot the bill, or at least part of it. The only reparations disagreement among the Allies was concerned with the

amount, the mode of payment, etc. There was no disagreement as to the principle of reparations.

But Article 231 was worded in such a way that it was
immediately interpreted as a moral condemnation of Germany designed to make the whole German people solely
and collectively responsible for the war. It was called the
"War Guilt Clause" and was seized upon by liberals all
over the world as a proof of the immorality and duplicity
of those who had drafted the treaty. The German governments who succeeded one another up to the advent of
Hitler exploited this idea for all it was worth. And it
proved to be worth a great deal. As Paul Birdsall noted:
"Probably no single item of the Treaty of Versailles has
been so useful to Hitler in destroying the morale of his
democratic opponents before attacking them."[1]

The introduction of the notion of guilt in the Versailles
Treaty was indeed a boomerang. The prevalent concept of
the time was that all people were naturally peaceful (a
transposition of the Rousseau concept that all men are
born good) and it was assumed that the Germans had been
led into the war by their rulers. The whole philosophical
structure of the peace was founded on the assumption that
now that the "aggressor nations" had been liberated from
their bad rulers, the people of these nations would naturally renounce war and fall into the general conception
of a world governed by international law and democratic
good will. But when the leaders of the victorious democratic nations wrote into the treaty a clause which seemed
to pin the guilt of the war on the German people, it was
seen as a proof that they themselves were destroying one
of the fundamental principles upon which the new democratic peace was to rest. Was not this clause a clear proof
that the peacemakers, far from trusting sincerely the will
to peace of the people of the world—of all the people, vic-

[1] *Versailles Twenty Years After*, Reynal and Hitchcock, 1941, p. 255.

tors and vanquished alike—intended in fact to use the
Versailles Treaty and the League of Nations to perpetuate
national rivalries and maintain the Germans in a state of
moral inequality forever? This was certainly not the "peace
without victory" which Wilson had advocated, and although the Allies had always been reluctant to accept
such an idealistic formula, the War Guilt Clause proved
that the Clemenceaus and the Lloyd Georges, the Japanese
and the Italians, had had only one purpose: to make use
of Wilson's lofty plan of world regeneration in order to
camouflage their real purpose, which was to grab as much
of the spoils of victory as they could, and perpetuate the
system of power politics.

To make Germany solely guilty for the war was to
brand it forever as a criminal nation, unfit to become a
member of the family of nations living in peace together
and on an equal moral footing. It wrecked in advance the
whole dream of a just and enlightened world order
founded on the premise that all people are innocent, and
that their rulers alone are responsible for the crimes they
may commit. In the eyes of the liberal reformers of those
times, it made the whole war appear as senseless and the
victory a deceit.

1. America against Versailles

The condemnation of the War Guilt Clause and of the
whole Treaty of Versailles was more vocal and more passionate in the Anglo-Saxon countries, and especially in
America. Moreover this condemnation was not wholly
motivated by pure idealism. The United States having refused to ratify the Treaty of Versailles and to join the
League of Nations, it became necessary to justify this decision by painting both the Treaty and the Covenant in
the blackest colors possible. The admission that the Wil-

sonian proposal had been repudiated by a Republican majority whose real intention was to discredit a Democratic President was politically inadvisable. American public opinion wanted to be convinced that if the United States refused to subscribe to the work of Wilson, it was because the whole project was unsound, impractical, and immoral. American national consciousness—or subconsciousness—wanted to wash its hands of this international crime, but this implied the necessity of proving: (1) that the peace conference had in reality been a cutthroat party in which candid Woodrow Wilson had been duped by the ruthless cunning of the European diplomats; (2) that the result of these discussions—the Treaty of Versailles and the Covenant—in no way answered the disinterestedness and the idealism of the American people, who had joined the war to make the world better and not worse; and (3) that, by inference, the Americans had committed a formidable error in taking part in the war at all.

As the years went on these basic ideas grew in strength and were supported by an ever-increasing wealth of new arguments. The perennial tendency of America to oppose itself to Europe was accentuated. Aloofness became the true expression of America's mission in the world. The condemnation of Versailles and of the war itself buttressed the national belief that the United States was not a nation or a power comparable to others—that America was essentially a moral force and the American people a people apart whose true mission was to show the rest of the world, and more particularly Europe, that peace, prosperity, justice, and happiness were practically attainable provided one kept clear of the chronic conflicts of national rivalries, and the eternal quarrels of Europe.

The national American belief that America was founded by people who had fled Europe precisely to escape its tyrannies and its wars made the American participation in the last war appear as a denial of America's fundamental purpose. If it was true that the *raison d'être* of America was to create a new and better society for men of all nationalities and races, had not America sinned against its own destiny in sending back its sons to the inferno of wars and decadence which their forefathers had purposely abandoned to its hopeless fate?

For twenty years this concept of an American destiny antithetic to that of Europe has been the basis of the isolationist point of view. For twenty years also this conflict between the American dream of aloofness and the realities of a wicked world has sought justification in the denunciation of all attempts that were made in Europe—whether good or bad—to resist the forces of disruption or to compromise with them. For twenty years there has been a steady effort on the part of many leaders of American thought to expiate the sin of having gone to war in 1917 by trying to prove that the American people, had they been able to act freely, would never have committed that sin against themselves and their true destiny. Allied propaganda was blamed for it. Munition makers and bankers were blamed for it. . . .

2. *The war was an error*

To prove that the American people themselves were innocent—as any people must always be according to democratic philosophy—it was necessary to discredit not only the Versailles Treaty but the war itself. The vogue for a school of history which interpreted all human events in terms of economic determinism came in very handy at this point. This method, which originated in Germany but flourished fully in America immediately after the war, answered perfectly the mood of the times. After four years of war, during which the people of all countries had been submitted to the most intense passions—hope, despair, heroism, hatred—there was a normal reaction against emotivity. The war-weary public found relaxation in books, articles, movies, and plays which appeared as a return to sanity and intellectual normalcy. Even if the image of himself which the demobilized soldier saw in these new mirrors was unheroic and often sordid, it gave him some satisfaction because it proved that all the horrors he had suffered and inflicted were not of his own making. In debunking himself he was also whitewashing himself. The revulsion against war and the passionate desire to prevent its recurrence incited the debunkers to present the soldier as a victim rather than as a hero. Heroism, the spirit of sacrifice, and even courage were sentiments that it was difficult to fit into a world which had just fought the war to end all wars. They were properly warlike virtues, things of the past therefore, and of no particular use in a world yearning for normalcy.

There is no clearer expression of this attitude than the cult of the Unknown Soldier. The idea of commemorating the sacrifices of the World War by honoring the remains of an anonymous soldier originated in France, but it soon spread to all the other nations. The prestige and the mass appeal of this new cult was immense and is still alive today. It never had to be stimulated by any artificial propaganda because it responded directly and fully to the universal desire of rendering pious homage not to the heroes of the war but to its victims. The cult of the hero cannot be built up anonymously. Hero worship implies the recognition of exceptional virtues and exceptional actions. Heroism must be personified. An unknown soldier, by his very anonymity, cannot qualify for anything except the fact that he was killed in the war. The unknown soldiers who are buried in Paris, in London, in the Arlington cemetery, or elsewhere, may have been heroes indeed, but the cult which surrounds them does not stress the courage of the warrior. It expresses the communion of mankind bowing before the mystical impersonality of martyrdom.

As for the historians and teachers who undertook to demonstrate that all human motivations were economic, they had a field day. Searching into the origins of the war, they had little difficulty in proving not only that the German people were not guilty of it, contrary to what Article 231 seemed to assert, but that the responsibility of their leaders was not greater than that of the Allied statesmen. It was demonstrated that the war of 1914-1918 was merely a clash between rival imperialisms and the Versailles Treaty nothing but the consecration of the victory of one group of powers over the other. The Marxian concept which considers the imperialist state as the supreme expression of capitalism influenced greatly during those years the thought of those who believed that history could be interpreted in purely materialistic terms. The Russian revolution, which appeared as such a promise to the liberals the world over, reinforced the position of those who, in the Western democracies, were trying to show that the war had been caused by a small group of men who, in each country, controlled its wealth and were seeking to increase it. Had not Lenin discredited the whole war by taking his country out of it in order to save the Communist revolution?

The postwar historians were not all Communists. Most of them were liberals and some of them were conservatives. But they could all agree on the fact that the war had shaken to its foundations the economic, financial, and social conditions of the world existing before 1914 and that the Versailles Treaty had done nothing to remedy the chaos. The obvious shortcomings of Versailles in respect to economics turned out to be a formidable weapon in the hands of Germany and of all those who, outside Germany, were discovering that even the greatest war of history and four years of extreme suffering were not enough to teach men brotherly love, justice, and wisdom.

This disillusion on the part of the progressives and the idealists, coupled with the success of the new doctrine of economic determinism, had the curious result of destroying the last shreds of moral judgment in the minds of the victors. Having become convinced that Germany had unjustly been accused of being responsible for the war, the notion of who was guilty of what became more and more obscure. In each of the victorious countries there developed a tendency to accuse one or another or some group of interests within each country for having been unable to prevent the war and for obstructing the construction of a real peace.

Self-deprecation, cynicism, and smugness became fashionable. In the name of a narrow-minded positivist philosophy, it became quite impossible to differentiate between right and wrong. The intellectual game which consists in justifying the opponent's point of view, even if that opponent is a thief or a murderer, became an end in itself, with the result that all standards of judgment were abolished. The ordinary morality which was still applied to individuals ceased to operate in the relation between nations. Thanks to such verbal subterfuges as the distinction between the "haves" and the "have-nots," the latter were excused for breaking the law, for resorting to violence, and for committing any number of criminal or immoral actions, under the pretense that the rich man is in no position to condemn the poor because they are both actuated by a different set of economic imperatives.

The victors of 1918 felt it was their duty to observe the code of international morality, not so much because they believed in that code, but because victory had given them a queer sense of inferiority. This made them very alert to denounce any violation of morality among themselves, but it was enough for one of them to align himself with the other camp (as did Italy and Japan) to benefit immediately from the boundless indulgence of their former partners. The victors of 1918 behaved like the members of a club who will not suffer the slightest breach of etiquette on the part of other members of the club, but will consider it ungentlemanly to call for the police when a ruffian holds them up in the street and asks them for their wallets.

The effect of all this dissection was to create in world opinion what can properly be called a universal guilt-complex. The various national governments and the press that supported them spent so much time and trouble in proving their innocence and their self-righteousness, while at the same time trying to pin the blame on others, that the average citizen gradually rallied to whatever doctrine appeared most cynical, most negative, and less exacting of any moral discipline.

3. The debunking era

The destructive criticism of the historians and the economists forced the intellectuals to take refuge in an attitude either of hazy and mystical pacifism or of hard-boiled cynicism and scientific detachment. They thus helped effectively to undermine the only standards by which an elite can ever survive, that is, their proven ability to strengthen and exalt the beliefs and hopes of the common people.

In fact this elite—writers, poets, priests, educators—although it was their sincere and avowed purpose to seek the truth and help the common man to better arm himself against the deceits and machinations of those who were made responsible for the war and the disillusions of the peace, merely succeeded in creating an ever-widening chasm between themselves and the people. The philosophy of debunking may be sound when, after the debunking is done, there is something constructive to propose. But the kind of debunking that was practiced during the postwar period was gratuitous, and satisfied only the intellectual or artistic indulgence of the debunkers. The mass of the people in the democratic countries reacted as could be expected: they lost whatever faith they might have had in the principles which were still taught them in their schools and which appeared to them as nothing more than naïve fictions or quaint legends handed down from the past. They lost confidence in their political leaders because it was obvious that most of them—if not all—had themselves lost confidence in these fictions. The ideas which had given birth to democracy were lost sight of or discredited by those whose normal role was to keep them alive. Nothing remained, as far as the common man was concerned, but the everyday struggle of material existence, a vague impression that all concepts which could not be attached to an immediate "referent" were illusions or traps, and a confused but tenacious conviction that the whole system of civilization to which he belonged was an empty shell held together by nothing more real than the verbiage of the politician and the force of outworn habits.

During the first ten or fifteen years that followed the last war, it did not appear clearly that the process of debunking democracy—or whatever might be done by the governments of the countries who had fought in its name —could eventually lead to another war. Although constantly at cross-purposes in their actions, the three major powers of the West, the United States, England, and France, still felt that they had an effective control over the world. Although their elite might deplore the poor use they made of this power and denounce the wickedness or blindness of their political leadership, the selfishness of the ruling classes, or the lack of responsibility of the workers, it did not seem possible that the real peril could take the shape of this outmoded and outlawed monster called War. Public opinion had been thoroughly educated against the idea of its recurrence. The problems confronting the world were of another nature: however grave and baffling, they belonged definitely to the realm of peace. Men of good will, humanitarians, and religious leaders were fully convinced that as far as war was concerned, the task of eliminating it from men's thoughts was well advanced. It was universally recognized not only as an evil, but as a sin, and it did not seem possible that any man with a modicum of intelligence could think otherwise. True enough, everyone had been guilty of that sin in the World War, but for that very reason it also seemed that everyone was thoroughly repentant. The impenitent nations, such as France had been under the leadership of Poincaré, were obviously coming to see the light. Universal disarmament had not been achieved, but it was still believed that it could be accomplished sometime, somehow. The idea that to possess armaments was an inducement to use them was strongly rooted. To maintain large armies attached a stigma to those who had them. Nations who voted high military budgets were considered backward and potentially dangerous. Disarmed countries were glorified.

The only country which actually escaped condemnation even when it started to rearm openly was Germany. The very fact that it had been made solely responsible for the war and that the War Guilt Clause was now recognized as unjust plunged the former enemies of Germany into a frenzy of atonement for their errors. For four years, Germany had been branded as the most barbarian nation that the world had known since the Huns, as the very enemy of civilization. But a few years after its defeat, it had become the great victim of modern history, to whom much should be forgiven because it had so much been sinned against.

It so happened that the role of the great victim of human injustice fitted perfectly the German temperament— a nation whose faith in its own military genius renders it unable to accept the plain reality of defeat. Not only did the Germans succeed in convincing themselves that they were not solely responsible for the war and the defeat, but they achieved the rather remarkable feat of liberating themselves completely from the common guilt-complex. At the same time their former enemies were piling ashes upon their own heads.

It soon came to pass that Hitler could proclaim to the face of the world that Germany's own guilt was not to be attached to the notion of responsibility for the war, but merely to the fact that Germany lost that war.

"What guilt had Germany herself for the outbreak of the war?" asked Hitler as early as 1923. "Her guilt consisted in this: that at the moment when the ring closed about her existence, Germany neglected to organize her defense with such vigor that through this demonstration of her power either the others, despite their abominable purpose, would have been robbed of their will to strike or else the victory of the Reich would have been assured. The guilt of the German people lies in this: that when in 1912 a criminal Reichstag in its unfathomable baseness and folly had refused to allow the raising of three army corps the people did not create for itself those army corps in the Reichstag's despite. With these additional 120,-000 men the Battle of the Marne would have been won and the issue of the war decided." [1]

[1] *My New Order*, p. 55.

4. *Moral disarmament*

Thus the efforts of the intellectual leaders in the democracies combined with the German feeling of frustration to create a situation in which the "criminal" of the war era was moved into a position where whatever he did appeared as a justified effort to redress the wrong done to him by his victors. When Germany defaulted on the reparation payments, it was excused because the burden imposed upon it was considered unjust. World opinion turned against Poincaré and the French because they occupied the Ruhr in a vain effort to exact those payments. Whenever an attempt was made to obtain general disarmament, the blame for the failure of these attempts was heaped either on France, England, or the agents of the munition makers. The fact that, in the meanwhile, Germany was rearming appeared negligible.

It is not my purpose to whitewash Poincaré or those who, in one way or another, were accused of wrecking all efforts at organizing a peaceful world based on justice.

The important single fact is that while the democracies did not succeed in achieving their avowed aim, which was physical disarmament, they succeeded beyond all expectations in disarming themselves morally. Twenty years of self-accusation and masochistic criticism created a moral vacuum in which it became impossible ever to determine whether any particular action was just or unfair, wise or dangerous. All concerted effort between nations was rendered ineffectual because it could always be proved, by one way or another, that it might lead to a repetition of past errors, that is, to another useless war and another unfair peace treaty. The past was condemned, but the future appeared no better because it was impossible to imagine it as anything but a relapse. Such manifestations as the Briand-Kellogg pact, outlawing war, were consid-

ered as positive and constructive acts, although it was
clear that the only reason why such a pact was accepted
by all was because it was nothing more than the visible
expression of the universal desire to repudiate the past. It
satisfied the guilt-complex, for a while, or rather put it to
sleep, but was about as effective as would be the outlawing
of last year's forest fires.

It was in fact worse than that, because it outlawed fire
as a means of fighting fire and thus intensified the hopeless
dilemma in which we still find ourselves concerning the
problem of war and the use of force: how to stop war
without making war, how to prevent the use of force without the use of force. And at the bottom of this dilemma
is the guilt-complex born out of the postwar period, the
full paralyzing effect of which only became apparent when
Hitler openly proclaimed that there was only one standard
for justice, honor, and law: his own conception of them;
and that whoever denied that this was true should be
destroyed.

Those who say that Hitler and the Nazi world revolution are the consequences of the last war and of the Versailles Treaty are partially right, but not in the way they
usually think. It is because the victorious democracies did
effectively destroy any moral basis for the recourse to war
that it was possible for Hitler to reinstate the idea that
war is noble, heroic, and holy. "War," said Robert Ley,
the Labor Front leader, "is no punishment, but rather the
ultimate and most beautiful test of strength of the German people and their fitness to live." It is because the
democracies have spent twenty years in beating *mea culpa*
on one another's breast that it has been possible for Hitler
to divide and conquer by the easy method of asserting that
when all his opponents are so unsure of the righteousness
of their own cause, they must all be wrong and deserve to

be exterminated or at least brought to subservience by an avenging sword.

5. *The great heresy*

The success of Hitler is due to a very large extent to the fact that he is the only known combatant of the last war who came out of it with no sense of relief that four years of suffering were over. Quite the opposite: on the day that the war ended, he felt nothing but an immense sentiment of humiliation and revolt. On that day, too, he experienced a kind of transfiguration. An unknown soldier himself, "a nameless man in an army of eight million" as he calls himself, alone and powerless, surrounded by a people exhausted by war and longing for peace, he alone stood against the irresistible wave of opposition to war that was sweeping the world. On November 10, 1918, while he was lying in a hospital, a pastor came to tell Hitler and his comrades that the end had come, that the war was lost. The pages of *Mein Kampf* in which Hitler describes this scene are the key to the twenty years that followed and to the present war:

> "But then as the old gentleman [the pastor] tried to continue and began to tell us that now we had to end the long war, that even our fatherland would now be submitted to severe oppressions in the future, that now the War was lost and that we had to surrender to the mercy of the victors . . . that the armistice should be accepted with confidence in the generosity of our previous enemies . . . there I could stand it no more. It was impossible for me to stay any longer. While everything began to go black again before my eyes, stumbling, I groped my way back to the dormitory, threw myself on my cot and buried my burning head in the covers and pillows.

"I had not wept since the day I had stood at the grave of my mother. . . .

"Now all had been in vain. In vain all the sacrifices and deprivations, in vain the hunger and thirst of endless months, in vain the hours during which, gripped by the fear of death, we nevertheless did our duty, and in vain the death of two millions who died thereby. Would not the graves of all the hundreds of thousands open up, the graves of those who once had marched out with faith in the fatherland, never to return? . . .

"The more I tried to clarify this terrible event in that hour, the stronger burnt the shame of indignation and dishonor on my forehead. What was now all the pain of my eyes as compared with this misery?" [1]

Hitler concludes these burning pages by what might have seemed an anticlimax at the time. "I, however," writes Hitler, "resolved now to become a politician."

A politician! A politician no doubt, but more correctly speaking the prophet of the great heresy.

In the atmosphere of war which now prevails in the world, it is difficult to recapture the absoluteness of the antiwar feeling which existed at the end of the last war. The cataclysmic importance of the Hitlerian heresy can therefore only be judged in retrospect and by comparison with the kind of literature which was finding favor at the time (Remarque, Barbusse, Dos Passos, Hemingway, etc.).

We must remember that the fundamental impulse which dominated the course of the war of 1914-1918 was the quasi universal conviction that it was the last one, the "war to end all wars." The immense sacrifices which this war had entailed, the repeated holocausts of hundreds of

[1] *Mein Kampf*, Reynal and Hitchcock, 1939, p. 266.

thousands of men had been accepted because, in the last analysis, both the civilian populations and the soldiers were convinced that whatever happened, the end of the war would mark the opening of an era of eternal peace. Men died with a purpose: that their children and their children's children would not have to wage war. Those who survived were sure that they would never have to fight again.

It was universally believed, as shown by the newspapers and the books of the time, that never before in the history of the world had a war been fought on such a scale causing such widespread suffering, such massive loss of human life and such extensive material ruin. It was felt that a maximum had been reached, that those four years of war represented a kind of final paroxysm. The men who lived through this war were convinced that it had been their destiny to take part in an apocalyptic convulsion of mankind. It appeared to them as the fateful conclusive chapter of the endless series of wars which had shaken Europe and the world since the dawn of history. Because it seemed to be the biggest and most horrible war ever fought by men, it also seemed that it must be the last. Nothing worse could be imagined. Therefore nothing worse could ever happen again.

Such slogans as "to make the world safe for democracy" were merely a transposition in political or ideological terms of that feeling. But as far as the common soldier and the average citizen were concerned their aim and hope were expressed more simply. They believed that they had fought for the last time.

The unique prestige of Woodrow Wilson and the godlike worship which surrounded him when he first came to Europe after the war had their roots in this sentiment. Wilson was the long-awaited messiah, the living incarnation of the supreme dream of Western civilization which for so many centuries had striven to eliminate violence through the process of law and rational morality. Wilson was a professor and he was usually considered as a slightly frigid and somewhat unrealistic intellectual. But the truth is that he was closer to the soul of the common man of 1919—that man who had just come out of the trenches— than any other leader of the time. He, too, firmly believed that the war just ended was to be the last and that it was his mission to inaugurate an era of eternal peace. A pure product of the nineteenth century, Wilson had put all his faith in the fundamental goodness of man and in the power of reason.

In fact the brief period during which Wilson seemed to have in his hands the destiny of the world may go down in history as the culminating point of Western classical civilization (then called democracy) in its prolonged effort to establish peace and order by mutual consent and toler-ance. No one came nearer to fulfilling the dream of per-manent peace. He was so close to the goal indeed that for nearly twenty years afterward, the Western World lived with the illusion that he had succeeded in reaching it. Wilson was the symbol of the universal renunciation of war which even today survives in the midst of a new war.

Even during the ten or fifteen years that followed the armistice of November 1918, and in spite of the innu-merable disappointments brought about by the malad-justments and errors of the postwar period, the whole Western World could not let go the dream which had carried it through four years of unprecedented sacrifice. That the equilibrium of Europe and the world was de-teriorating was obvious, but it still seemed impossible that this deterioration should finally lead to another war. All the political and intellectual leaders of the Western na-tions belonged to the "war generation." Whatever their differences, they were united in a sort of transcendental mandate: to avoid and even to deny the recurrence of war as an actual possibility. All their notions concerning the phenomenon of war were centered on the one great experience which they had lived through themselves: the great war, the last war, the war to end all other wars. War was a thing of the past, of that at least they were sure. To admit that it could recur in the future appeared as a betrayal of the millions that had died. However precarious the peace, however ominous the future, that peace, any peace—anything that was not called war—must be preserved. When Aristide Briand said: "As long as I live, there will be no war," he expressed the mystical pledge which millions of men of the war generation had dedicated themselves to keep.

But the reason why the dream of Wilson, which was the dream of nearly all men alive at that time, did not come to pass, should not be sought in the incidental errors of the postwar period. The truth is that Wilson was not so much a prophet of the future, the inaugurator of a new era of peace, as the last exponent of a rational and humane philosophy which, at the very moment of its apparent triumph, was being repudiated and challenged by the cries of rebellion of an unknown Austrian soldier who, on the very day that the war ceased, resolved to devote his life to revenge. While Wilson was driving down the Champs-Elysées in an atmosphere of delirious fervor because he had brought peace, Adolf Hitler, in the gloom of a military hospital, was dedicating all his frenzy and his despair to the great heresy of war which, once again, was to pit Germany against the whole world.

6. From Clemenceau to Pétain

The guilt-complex which is still pestering us today has made it fashionable to discuss endlessly the mistakes of the past.

For twenty years, the great majority of the liberal elite

of Europe and America has seen in the Versailles Treaty
the cause of all evils. Many find in it the explanation, if
not the excuse, for the advent of Hitler and National
Socialism, as if this latest rebellion of Germanic barbarism
against classical Western civilization—a rebellion which
has happened several times before in European history—
had no deeper cause than a treaty, the most drastic clauses
of which were never applied. The habit of considering
Versailles as the original sin of our time has been so thoroughly cultivated by the modern educators, especially in
America, that the youth in the democracies actually judge
the events of the recent past and of the present as if the
history of the world had begun in 1919. Nothing that
can possibly bear on the present seems to have happened
before. Versailles is the cornerstone of the contemporary
world, the one narrow and distorting prism through
which all is seen and judged.

There are those of course who now think that the
trouble with Versailles is that it was not harsh enough.
They regret that Clemenceau and Foch did not have their
way. Others again blame the present calamity on the weakness or blindness of the English and French during the
postwar period. They argue that sanctions should have
been ruthlessly applied to Italy when it invaded Ethiopia. The French should have mobilized when Hitler
reoccupied the Rhineland. The Fascist powers should
never have been allowed to establish Franco in Spain.
Czechoslovakia should not have been betrayed at Munich.

Then there are those who denounce the responsibility
of the United States in refusing to ratify the Covenant of
the League of Nations, thus condemning this institution
to impotence and finally to death. The United States, having refused to assume its share of responsibility in the
maintenance of the peace, and reverted to traditional iso-

lationism, made collective security impossible and the present war inevitable.

This kind of argumentation is too familiar to the readers to require amplification here. It is easy for us today to see the mistakes made and to speculate on what might have happened if they had not been made. But history is not and can never be an exact science. It is not the fixed record of past events, never to be changed. Quite the contrary: history, in so far as that word embraces the faculty of exerting a judgment on past human actions, is a constant creation of the present. It can even be said that history is only valid to the extent that it serves to throw light on the present. Each generation, and perhaps each man, carries within him a different version of what has happened before. Historical truth is therefore as variable as life itself, because like life it is made up of the experience of yesterday seen through the contingencies of today and the hopes or fears of tomorrow.

That is why there is little profit in denouncing the mistakes of the past twenty years as if each of them could have been avoided separately at the time. These mistakes, as we see them from our present vantage point, were not seen as such then. They are part of a pattern. They must be considered as several expressions of whatever attitude of mind prevailed at the time. They grew, naturally and irresistibly, out of the deepest convictions of men of all nations who believed, or wanted to believe, that the final payment to the frightful scourge of war had been made.

There were statesmen and some leaders of public opinion who recognized that the God of War, contrary to the Great God Pan, might not be quite dead yet. The Covenant of the League of Nations reflected this preoccupation in a few of its articles. The principle of sanctions against whoever broke the peace was introduced, but as its application implied the acceptance by all sovereign

nations of a collective decision in Geneva, it was clear—
as the future was to prove—that this timid admission that
force *might* have to be used in certain circumstances
sprang from the fond hope that even sanctions might
never have to be used.

The practical result of this wishful attitude was to direct all the pressure of the peace-loving people not against
a possible resurgence of the war spirit among the defeated
Germans—who being defeated were considered thoroughly
chastised and therefore converted to peaceful ways—but
against those who through a sense of their own insecurity
insisted on maintaining the coalition which had made
victory possible, or failing that, on refusing to disarm
completely and renounce the system of alliances.

France was the main offender in this respect. At the
peace conference, Clemenceau fought step by step to obtain for France a permanent guarantee of effective help
from its allies in case of renewed aggression. Clemenceau
was one of the rare men of the time who was unable to
forget that France had escaped defeat by what was instinc-
tively called a "miracle," the Battle of the Marne, and
twice again, in 1917 with the submarine warfare and in
1918 with the Ludendorff offensive. He could not forget
that the victory of the Allies had been achieved by a
world-wide coalition and that it had taken four years to
defeat the German armies.

But if one may consider today, in the light of present
events, that Clemenceau's fears were not unfounded, the
important fact is that they were incompatible with the
general spirit of the Peace Conference and ran against
the trend of the postwar period.

The ill-fated occupation of the Ruhr was the last attempt to try force against Germany. The experiment was
condemned by the whole world as a senseless abuse of
power against a defenseless victim. After that, the whole

evolution of French policy conformed, more or less reluctantly, to the general pattern of compromises and suc-
cessive retreats which led ultimately to the doctrine of
appeasement, to the present war, and as far as France is
concerned, to complete defeat.

Looking back on the twenty years of French history,
which led from Clemenceau to Daladier and Bonnet, and
finally to Pétain, one is tempted to see in this prodigious
degradation a proof that France has lost its ancient stam-
ina, its lucidity, and perhaps even its very will to survive. In the defeat of France one may see also the defeat
of one of the most vital elements in the secular fight of
Western civilization against the ever-recurring rebellion
of barbarism.

No one can deny the magnitude of the disaster represented by the downfall of France, and it may be that no
one today can as yet imagine what would be the consequences of this catastrophe, from the point of view of the
survival of Western civilization, if France was to disappear as a living entity.

But one should realize that the fundamental cause of
this disaster is to be sought beyond the incidentals of
French politics, beyond the men who ruled France in these
twenty years, beyond the institutions of France with all
their imperfections, and even beyond France itself.

The defeat of France is due to the fact that the French
were part of a world which actually believed that the
oldest dream of classical civilization, the elimination of
war, had come to pass, a world which had come to deny
what it feared the most and which trusted in the mere
virtue of denial to abolish the danger.

The error of the French was to consider it impossible
that, across the Rhine, there should arise—in the midst of
the twentieth century—the apostle of a new heresy which
preaches that war is holy and that the primitive and bar-

baric instincts of the tribe are superior to the restraints and the rationale of civilization.

Adolf Hitler has subjugated France. But this is only a step. Hitler is the incarnation of forces greater than himself. The heresy he preaches is two thousand years old. It is the latest phase of the secular revolt which, every so often, turns the German people into an instrument of destruction and death and through them threatens the whole structure of the Occident.

But whatever may be the outcome of this war, there is little chance that the universal and profound opposition to war will be eradicated. It is true that men are fighting in five continents today with increasing bitterness, and sometimes with despair. They are fighting because one man, Adolf Hitler, has preached the ugly, barbaric, stupid heresy of the sanctity of war to his own people and thus forced the whole world to fight. But even should the Germans win this war with the help of the Japanese, their domination would not last. Such a victory would be followed by endless rebellions on the part of the subjugated peoples during which what is left of an orderly concept of society would very probably perish. The final outcome however could only be the downfall of Hitler and of the people who follow him.

Part IV

THE FOLKLORE OF DEMOCRACY

CHAPTER I

Democracy: an American Point of View

IN THE preceding chapters, I have used the word *democracy* as if I presumed that the readers were in agreement among themselves as to the meaning of this word, and in agreement with me. It is obvious, however, that this cannot be the case, except if the word is understood in a very vague and general sense, and more especially as a negative term to designate an opposition to doctrines and forms of government repugnant to the great majority of the Americans and actively or potentially inimical to them.

The difficulty encountered by most people in defining what democracy is—rather than what it is not—is due to the fact that up to a fairly recent past, democracy proved successful, and went practically unchallenged as a political system and a philosophy best suited to the development of civilization. In fact, if the expression "wave of the future" ever had any meaning, it can be said that up to a few years ago, there was a universal consensus that the "wave of the future" was democracy.

But today democracy finds itself on the defensive and in mortal danger of being wiped off the earth—not only because the forces pitted against the democratic nations are very great, but also because within these nations, there is uncertainty and division of council when it comes to defining precisely what it is that, in the name of democracy, they wish to preserve and what it is they will reform or sacrifice in order to survive.

It is strange to think that if the armies of the Kaiser had won the war in 1914, there might have been little change in the political complexion of the world. Imperial Germany, though rapacious enough, was not pursuing a world revolution. If it had won the World War, the chances are that the vanquished democratic countries could have retained their ways of life and their institutions. In a sense, it was the democratic leaders twenty years ago—and first of all, Woodrow Wilson—who were revolutionary enough to wish a transformation of the world, and not the Kaiser nor his generals, who were merely old-fashioned imperialists. But now, what has happened to date clearly shows that Nazi Germany is not only intent on conquering territories but in spreading everywhere the National Socialist Order. As Hitler has said, the two ways of life—the democratic one and his own—cannot coexist. One of the two must disappear.

The threat therefore is now infinitely greater and more far-reaching than it was in 1914. Defeat will mean the complete eradication of our political, philosophical, and social systems, and not merely the loss of some territory. Although we know this to be true, we find a curious difficulty in agreeing among ourselves on the meaning of a word—democracy—which, by the very nature of the attack launched against us, cannot be separated from the notion of our own existence.

It should be noted, however, that the belief that democracy is the best possible form of government, and democratic processes the only ones that can assure progress, is now essentially an American conception. Other nations, like England, France, and the Scandinavian countries, were strongly democratic, too, but none of them were fully convinced that they would actually cease to be themselves if they abandoned a democratic form of government. The history of the United States is the history of a democracy, and it is impossible to dissociate the national destiny of America from the destiny of democracy itself.

It follows that although American democracy was greatly inspired at its origin by English and French ideas, it rapidly assumed a typically American character. The extraordinary development and expansion of the United States during the one hundred and fifty years of its existence served to focus the attention of the world on the fact that the United States was not only a democracy, but *the* democracy.

It is through the growth of the United States as a people, through the spreading all over the world of American methods of mass production and of goods made in America, that the achievements of democracy—of the greatest of all democracies—received such tremendous publicity. Democracy, as a system of government, as a philosophy, as a civilizing force, reverberated through the whole world with a growing intensity. The part played by Woodrow Wilson in the last war already proved that the center of world democracy was Washington as surely as the center of the Catholic world is Rome.

Today this situation has only been accentuated and the revolutionary assault of Nazism against everything that can possibly be associated with democracy has emphasized the historical fact that the democratic ideas which originated in Europe a century and a half ago have found their complete expression on this continent.

This does not mean that democratic ideas flourish today only in the United States. They exist in England and survive also in the minds of countless Europeans now submerged by Nazi Germany. But it is significant that, although England has been completely engaged in this life and death struggle for a long time while America has just started to fight totally, the man who personifies democracy in the consciousness of the world is not Winston Churchill but Franklin Roosevelt.

This more than any other demonstration proves that the United States is not only the "arsenal of democracy" in the material sense, but also its real spiritual stronghold and its fountainhead. If democracy as a form of government and a philosophy of life is to survive the present crisis, it will have to find a new momentum in America. France cannot be counted upon for some time to act as a "democratic" force. Even if it should re-enter the war on the Anglo-Saxon side, it would do so for the sole purpose of getting rid of the German yoke, but it is more than doubtful that the French will be able for some time to overcome their present neurosis in regard to political ideologies. As for England, it will remain faithful to its democratic convictions if it wins the war, but the chances are that it will have to rely on the moral support of America to make a democratic peace, as it relies on its production to make war.

These considerations may justify the fact that in the following pages I will try to analyze certain aspects of democracy primarily from the American point of view. For the time being at least, democratic thinking has undergone a process of contraction and it is no exaggeration to say that it is for the moment essentially an American phenomenon. A new period of expansion will come if the Nazi attempt at world domination is checked. But at the present it is practically impossible to discuss democracy from any other point of view than that of America.

1. *A way of life*

It is often said that what the democratic people wish to preserve, and more particularly the Americans, is not so much a form of government, but a way of life. Democracy, they say, is a way of life.

This substitution of three words for one is, perhaps, not very illuminating. It proves, however, that for many people to preserve democracy merely means that they would like things to go on pretty much as they are. Democracy represents, for them, a state of affairs sufficiently satisfactory to make it appear that any radical change could not be for the better. It expresses the fact that, by and large, a vast number of Americans—certainly the majority—are content with their way of living. It reveals the important fact that the American people are more conservative than any other, and that the beliefs, principles, and hopes upon which the nation is founded are sufficiently vivid in their minds to be accepted without much questioning. Democratic *truths,* as understood by the American people, have not lost their dogmatic and somewhat superhuman quality.

It is true that the preservation of democracy as a way of life is dearer to the hearts of those who are, in general, contented with their lot than to those who are not. The "underprivileged third" are certainly not particularly anxious to preserve a way of life which maintains them at their present level, and it is noteworthy that "revolutionary" movements, such as those initiated by Huey Long, Father Coughlin, Dr. Townsend, and other demagogues, are usually popular with the poor. They do not make much dent on the mass of the electorate, which in the United States, more than in any other country in the world, has remained remarkably faithful to its traditions and institutions.

But if American democracy is to be considered as a way

of life, does it mean that most Americans merely want to be able to go on living as they are today? Is their real purpose the preservation of the status quo and will they oppose to the revolutionary forces now loose in the world a purely negative attitude, as did the European democracies?

If it were possible to answer these questions with any degree of certainty, one could predict whether or not democracy is going to survive the assault now launched against it. This, however, cannot be done. The examples of other democracies, and particularly France, are instructive but not conclusive, because it is now apparent that nowhere except in the United States did the national sense identify itself completely with the ideals, principles, and to a large extent the practice, of democracy.

It is true also that when the average American thinks of preserving the democratic way of life, he is keenly conscious of his privileged position in relation to other countries. He is on the whole satisfied with the facilities of education offered to his children, with his churches, his movies, his radio, the mechanism of business, and his range of opportunities. Although the achievements of American democracy could have been greater given the enormous wealth of the continent and the natural inventiveness of the people, it remains that no one but a Communist or a Nazi can assert that American democracy has been a failure. The real test may come in the future, but it has not come yet, and no sensible observer can deny that, up to now, American democracy has successfully overcome all the crises that the nation has had to face.

It is this consciousness of relative success—often exaggerated, it is true—that convinces the average American that his way of life is worth preserving, and although he may now feel the need of redefining and reasserting his objectives, there is no doubt that his belief in their validity has not been profoundly shaken. As a matter of fact there is no other nation—not excluding the English—more unable to conceive a repudiation of its fundamental and traditional *credo* than the American. To be an American remains an act of faith, founded on the universal acceptance that the principles of American democracy are as valid today as they were when the nation was founded, and that they will always remain true.

This, of course, is merely a point of view. Specifically, it is *the* American point of view. But it happens to have been a remarkably stable one. The reasons for this stability are geographical and historical. Compared with other nations the United States has known very few vital crises. Leaving aside the birth pangs of the Revolution, the only really dangerous crisis was the Civil War. This was the only time when national unity was seriously threatened. But its outcome served only to strengthen the fundamental beliefs of the Americans in the soundness of their ideals. The foreign wars in which the United States has engaged never involved the very existence of the nation; its way of life was not threatened by them. This is true even of the war of 1914-1918, which—as can now be seen in retrospect—was only the preliminary phase of the twentieth century world conflict, the complexity of which was hardly discernible then. After every crisis, large or small, America has reasserted its original convictions. Many things have changed in America and outside of it during the century and a half that this nation has been in existence, but the American point of view has not changed.

This is why the United States is the only country where the belief in democracy is sufficiently sincere and the practice of it sufficiently normal to enable one to visualize its motivations, which, in many instances, are as fresh today as they were in the minds of the eighteenth century thinkers and statesmen. Were it not for the stability of American thinking and the peculiar faithfulness to tradition which characterizes the Americans, democracy as a system of government and a way of life based on fairly well-defined philosophical concepts could be of only archaeological interest today. This does not mean that all other people would have renounced such things as freedom and the belief in progress, but these concepts would probably be detached by now from the democratic frame of reference.

In considering therefore what is meant by democracy at the present moment, it is necessary to recall the principal ideas upon which the Americans established their own conviction of what is right or wrong, true or false. These ideas are not new. Most of them are very ancient and bound with the general tradition of Western civilization. They antedate the foundation of the American nation, whose task has been to coordinate them in such a way that they have endured up to now, and preserved their quality of absolute truths.

The *truths* which justify democracy in general and American democracy in particular cannot be fully analyzed in the scope of this book. The following list is necessarily simplified.

2. *The goodness of man*

The fundamental promise of democracy is that man is naturally good. This idea came as a "revelation" to Jean Jacques Rousseau, and through him it influenced all Western thinking. But the important fact is that, although the Rousseau principle always met with a great deal of resistance in Europe—and under such various forms as the Catholic Church and the Marxian dialectics—it permeated American thinking, and still permeates it today to a remarkable degree. The characteristic optimism of the Americans concerning their own future, and that of the human race in general, is founded on faith in the natural goodness of man. Germanic philosophy, and particularly that of its present leaders, obviously contradicts this belief: the worthiness of the "biological man" is measured by his force and not by his goodness.

Faith in the natural goodness of man is necessary to any democratic process. When ten men vote "aye" and nine vote "nay," the only reason why the "ayes" should "have it" is based on the presumption that a good and right decision will *naturally* sway more men than a bad and wrong one.

There is of course no rational way of proving that this is so. To prove it one would have to define what is good or bad, right or wrong, a task which has been attempted often enough in the history of mankind, but with no permanent success. Luckily the practice of democracy has solved the dilemma in a pragmatic way. A decision adopted by the majority may not be right in the absolute, but it is made right by the fact that the majority adopts it.

3. The people express the will of God

In a democracy, the people are endowed with virtues, insight, and power which identify them as much as possible with the will of God. The word *people* in such expressions as "the will of the people," the "good of the people," the "rule of the people," is used as a metaphysical abstraction. The vitality of the democratic faith can be measured by the capacity of the citizens to believe that— as a people—they commune in some sort of supernatural unity which cannot be desecrated or destroyed whatever may be their terrestrial dissensions. When Lincoln spoke of a government "of the people, by the people, and for the people" he coined a formula which expresses fully the mystical value of the word *people* and the transcendental basis upon which democracy itself rests. This formula has the added advantage of appearing to bridge—at least verbally—the chasm that separates the people as an abstract entity and the people considered as a living aggregate of human beings.

If one needed further proof that democracy rests on a considerable amount of mystical interpretation of the people as a concept, one should try to substitute the word *masses* for the word *people* in the Gettysburg address. The immortal words of Abraham Lincoln would become ludicrous, because although the word *masses* does signify an aggregate of human beings, it has no spiritual content, except in the liturgy of Marxism.

It should be noted, however, that one of the most dangerous pitfalls of democracy, as a system of government and a philosophy, is precisely the tendency to degenerate from the high concept represented by the term *people* to the lower level of the *masses,* and finally to the *mob*.

This phenomenon of degradation or despiritualization of democracy is not peculiar to our times. In fact it happened on several occasions in the history of Ancient Greece as well as in Rome, and in every case the result has been the same: the establishment of personal power, and more usually, of tyranny.

The laws governing this process may appear mysterious because the outward circumstances are always different, but they are fairly simple if one accepts the fact that no human society can survive without the belief that it is guided, or inspired, or ordained by some supernatural entity or set of entities. It matters little whether God is identified with a man—king, Caesar, tyrant, or Führer—or with a projection of the collective faith in a set of ideas or laws—as is the case in a democracy. What is important is the existence of that belief.

Even Marx and Engels, who by the philosophy of dialectical materialism pretended to explain all historical and social phenomena in purely scientific and mechanistic terms, could not escape metaphysics. The Hegelian system of the *thesis* and the *antithesis* being automatically reconciled in the *synthesis* implies the recognition of some sort of supernatural and mystical law governing the affairs of humanity. In their vocabulary, moreover, such expressions as the *bourgeoisie,* the *proletariat,* and the *class struggle* become mythical entities. Marx and Engels and their disciples set out to destroy ancient myths with the weapons of pure reason and scientific criticism. But they succeeded only in creating new ones. The deification of Lenin and of Stalin is the proof that the tendency of all ideological systems to degenerate into personal worship is universal, and perhaps quite independent of the nature of the system itself.

American democracy, however, has given practically no indications up to now that it was threatened by this classical form of disintegration. In spite of the alarms felt in certain quarters that President Roosevelt was trying to establish his personal dictatorship, there is little to justify the fears of those who believe that democracy is at an end in America. A political regime and the philosophy that supports it show signs of decadence when they are discredited in the eyes of the people. This is what happened in France many years before the fall of the Third Republic. No such situation obtains in America, where men and groups of men may be violently criticized and even hated by some sections of public opinion, but where the institutions and the principles upon which they rest enjoy as much prestige today as in the past.

As long as the Americans believe that the people, as a concept, can be identified with divine inspiration and that their government and their institutions are best suited to translate into practical acts the will of the people, there is little danger that any man will be able to capture for his own benefit the power which is now so safely guarded by the faith in their own idea of 130 million Americans.

4. Happiness on earth

Another fundamental belief is that man can attain happiness on this earth.

When the bloodthirsty, sinister, but intellectually superior friend of Robespierre, the revolutionary Saint-Just, said: "The idea of happiness is new in the world," he threw on his own time and on the times to come one of those rare beams of light which, once in a while, seem to illuminate the course of history.

For Saint-Just to speak of happiness as a new idea—he who had sent so many to the guillotine and was to die on it himself at the same time as Robespierre at the age of twenty-seven—may seem paradoxical and even somewhat ironical. But Saint-Just, like all fanatics, had flashes of insight which were totally irrelevant to his actual behavior.

Approximately one hundred and forty years later, another fanatic was to make another remark on the same subject which helps us to appreciate the deep opposition between the French and the German revolutionary. "The era of personal happiness," said Hitler, quoted by Rauschning, "is closed."

Thus, without knowing it, Hitler replied to Saint-Just and gave him a denial as to the place of happiness in the world.

It would obviously be stretching the point to attribute to Saint-Just the discovery that the era of happiness was beginning in his time and to honor Hitler with the privilege of deciding that it is now closed. But it is true that the French Revolution did launch through the world the new notion that the aim of life was happiness, and that

Hitler is doing his best to make this aim impossible by contending that the aim of life is merely the assertion of power.

As it is always well-nigh impossible to imagine the outlook of life of men living in past centuries, we have difficulty in conceiving today that for our forefathers the notion of happiness was not connected with this earth. Up to two hundred years ago, men placed their hopes in a life hereafter. Such had been the teaching of the Church since the Middle Ages and the pursuit of happiness on this earth was neither conscious nor encouraged. The whole moral outlook of the Western man was indeed based on the fundamental precept that the purpose of life was to deserve a place in Heaven, and that earthly ambition or satisfactions were more of a handicap than an asset to those who, one day, would have to appear before their Creator. Such was the conception of our forefather—the "theological man."

The philosophical evolution that leads up to the eighteenth century and the great break of the French Revolution can naturally be traced back quite far. But the progress of rationalism was slow to penetrate the consciousness of the individuals. When Saint-Just declared that the idea of happiness was new in the world, he merely stated the fact that the reign of the theological man was at an end.

If one keeps in mind this concept of the theological man while reading the literature and memoirs of Western Europe previous to the eighteenth century, one cannot help being struck by the profound repercussions that this difference of point of view between ourselves and our forefathers had on the behavior of individuals and on their whole conception of the world in which they lived.

For them—and more especially for those living before the Renaissance—the notion of the future was meaningless in terms of progress or happiness. The grim dogma of Original Sin permeated all thinking. Man was born wicked and his only hope was for a better life after death. There was no concept that man considered as an individual, or as a succession of generations, could improve his lot on this planet. The future was not associated with any notion of betterment, except in so far as the promise of the advent of the Kingdom of God on this earth would be eventually fulfilled. Men were expecting the end of the world, sometimes in terror, sometimes in hope. They were not expecting that life on earth could ever be anything but miserable. To live was admittedly a punishment.

The Renaissance modified this pessimistic outlook to a great extent, but did not change the fundamental relation between the theological man and his environment. The discovery of the beauty, wisdom, and science of the ancient civilizations of Greece and Rome merely confirmed —on the secular plane—the religious belief in a Paradise Lost. The men of the Renaissance found a new source of inspiration in the revelation that great cultural epochs had preceded them. But their admiration for these epochs, far from inciting them to look toward their own future, merely convinced them that the limit of perfection in art, thought, and knowledge had already been reached, and that they could do no better than to try to imitate and recapture it. With their eyes fixed on the glorious and fabulous mirage of past centuries, they walked backward into the future. If, in so doing, they were themselves equaling and often surpassing their masters, they were not conscious of it.

Thus the Renaissance and the centuries that followed, in spite of the vast new fields that they opened to the curiosity and speculation of the Western mind, did not affect very rapidly nor perceptibly the outlook of the generations of men to whom the notion that humanity as a whole could become *happier* on this earth through its own efforts was still foreign. No doubt such men as Bacon and Descartes perceived that human reason could be utilized not only as an instrument of analysis of what was and what had been, but also as a means of elevating the status of mankind. But it is only in the eighteenth century that the concept of progress, such as we understand it today, became sufficiently clear to influence the course of history. The most important single fact in both the American and French Revolutions is probably the conscious will to create something *new*. For the first time in the history of the West, men deliberately turned toward the future and expressed the faith that the condition of mankind could be improved by human means.

5. *The sense of progress*

The two Revolutions opened an era in which the whole philosophical nature of the Western man was to change with extreme rapidity and in such a way that nearly all the concepts of the past were to be abandoned. Society, instead of being merely a conglomeration of individuals each intent on his own personal salvation, became the medium through which the material as well as the spiritual welfare of these individuals could be gradually improved.

It is not necessary to dwell here on the various philosophical doctrines and scientific discoveries which, all through the nineteenth century, confirmed the modern man in his belief that he was definitely set on a new road, and that step by step he was advancing toward a better future.

The prestige of science and rational thinking as a means of solving ultimately all human problems was at its height at the end of the last century. The few thinkers who were

beginning to doubt the limitless possibilities of science
and were reverting to some sort of mysticism made little
impression on the public mind. The tangible and un-
deniable progress of applied science could only reinforce
the popular faith in a philosophy of life the truth of
which every new discovery seemed to verify.

The religion of progress was universal, but nowhere did
it find a more complete and harmonious expression than
in the United States.

The philosophical and political concepts of the founders
of the American republic, inspired as they were by English and French liberalism, adapted themselves perfectly
to the expansion and growth of the American people. The
whole history of America, in fact, appeared as a practical
demonstration that these philosophical concepts were
sound. Pioneering and the frontier spirit were the physical
manifestations of the new faith of mankind in its own
ability to reach happiness—or rather to create it by its own
efforts.

That the pursuit of happiness often translated itself in
the crudest kind of materialism cannot be denied. In
America as elsewhere the tendency to identify happiness
with wealth has been constant. In a nation where success
is worshiped as a sign of superiority, and where the current measure of success is neither a title nor any distinctive honor, it is natural that wealth should be adopted as
the universal standard of value.

But the remarkable thing is that the American faith in
the principles of democracy as a means of distributing
happiness to all should have survived the innumerable
assaults of piratical groups, who all through American
history have attempted to capture power for no other purpose than their own interests.

Many Europeans, from Karl Marx to Hitler, have been
deluded by the so-called materialism of the Americans. It

seems incomprehensible to them that in a country where
there seems often to be only a difference of appreciation
between the methods of the robber barons and those of
the gangsters, the faith of the people as a whole in the
validity of democratic ideals should remain intact. It is a
fact that in no other civilized nation—and up to a very
recent past—has the power of money given more impunity
and caused more injustice than in America. But it is also a
fact that in no other nation have these abuses caused less
moral damage to the nation as a whole.

The reasons for this phenomenon are complex, but the
main one seems to me to be found in the rocklike quality
of what has been called the American dream. As long as
the Americans believe in progress, in the pursuit of happiness on this earth, in the possibility of improving themselves and the rest of the human race both physically and
spiritually by concerted efforts—as long as they believe that
democracy, both as a system of government and as a philosophy of life, offers them a means of achieving those ends—
as long as these political and moral truths are identified
with the American nation itself, such "heresies" as the
purely materialistic enterprises of some privileged individuals or minorities will be suppressed periodically.

The conviction that man as an individual and as a
species can become increasingly happy on this earth is so
deeply rooted in the American concept of life that it is
not possible to consider any aspect of American activity
without being struck by the realization that progress is
accepted as a law of nature, as rigid and as unfailing as
the law that governs the fall of Newton's apple. The possibility that progress, in the material sense, might not necessarily bring with it more happiness, is not accepted, and
the whole trend of American civilization is determined by
the belief that happiness is indeed a function of progress.

6. An American synthesis

Without going into a futile philosophical or moral discussion of what happiness means (the only word, said someone, that corresponds to nothing at all) it would appear that one of the great achievements of American civilization is to have created and kept alive the faith of the people in the practical possibility of achieving more happiness by a positive and constructive effort of the community. In so doing they have also solved effectively the embarrassing problem which for so many centuries baffled the Christian world: the moral conflict arising from the incompatibility between the enjoyment of life and the pursuit of one's own salvation. When President Hoover promised two cars in every garage, nobody accused him of immorality. What did appear immoral in fact was the failure of Mr. Hoover to make his promise come true. There is room for any type of religious or moral reformer in America except one: St. Francis of Assisi.

That the concept of happiness and that of progress have been merged into one has had as a further consequence the nearly complete elimination of the opposition between the spiritual and the material. According to the current American viewpoint, any material improvement entails automatically a spiritual one and vice versa.[1] The uncom-

---

[1] This conception has naturally resulted in extravagances which are sometimes absurd, sometimes merely funny. The following advertisement which appeared in New York papers recently is a fairly good example of this sort of thing:

"I TALKED WITH GOD (Yes I did, actually and literally . . . and so may you) and as a result of that little talk with God, a strange Power came into my life. After 42 years of horrible, dismal, sickening failure, everything took on a brighter hue. It's fascinating to talk to God, and it can be done very easily, once you learn the secret. And when you do—well—there will come into your life the same dynamic Power which came into mine. The shackles of defeat and fear which bound me for years went a-shimmering—and now?—well, I am President of the News Review Publishing Company, which corporation publishes the largest circulating af-

fortable suspicion that although man can and does improve his material surroundings and his body, but does not improve his mind, may trouble at times the sleep of the philosophically minded, but such is not, by and large, the popular belief.

There are so many manifestations of this belief in everyday life that I can give here only a few examples:

The American faith in the benefits of education as a means of collective and self-improvement is so absolute that it can be said that no other nation spends so much time per capita in trying to solve, through learning, some problems which in other times and other lands have been left to individual initiative or which have been left out of the field of education altogether. I am not referring here to the education given in the schools and colleges, but to the fabulous amount of books, magazine articles, lectures, radio talks, etc. which purport to teach the adults of both sexes such subjects as the art of being happily married, of making friends and influencing people, of becoming successful, of thinking, etc. Not that such pseudoeducational enterprises or quack advice is particularly harmful. But it is revealing of the belief of a very large public in the possibility of solving practically all conceivable human difficulties by the same methods as one gets a tooth filled or a car repaired. Extended to a larger sphere, it explains also and confirms the American faith in some political, social, and economic formula by which the ills of the world could be cured once and for all.

---

ternoon daily in North Idaho. I own the largest office-building in my city. I drive two beautiful cars, I own my own home which has a lovely pipe-organ in it, and my family are abundantly provided for after I'm gone. And all this has been made possible because, one day, about twelve years ago, I actually and literally talked with God.

"You too may experience that strange mystical Power which comes from talking with God. . . ." (From an advertisement of a religious corporation, Moscow, Idaho.)

In another field, that of health, one recognizes the same tendency to believe that the progress of the human mind is intimately dependent on the improvement of health and hygiene. The old Latin saying *mens sana in corpore sano* is certainly part of the American *credo,* but it has been extended and improved in the sense that physical health and the outward perfection of the human body have become aims in themselves on the assumption that the mind and even the soul cannot but benefit indefinitely from a progressive elimination of the ills and imperfections which affect the human species.

The Greeks showed an analogous interest in health and beauty and in the athletic aspect of man. In fact they deified the human body. But what is typical of the American point of view on this subject is that it is in no way pagan. There is no cult of human beauty nor even of health. What sustains the immense efforts made for the furtherance of medicine and the beauty parlor is not only the desire to alleviate suffering and to satisfy vanity, but the conviction of serving the future of the race as a whole. Here again we find a materialistic objective justified by and merged with a moral end.

The identification of the notion of happiness with the faith in progress has strengthened the belief that not only is happiness on earth attainable but that one can measure the advance toward this goal. Material progress can usually be computed in terms of statistics, and if it is assumed that more progress means more happiness, it follows that happiness can be weighed quantitatively. If fewer people die of pneumonia this year than last, if more people have radios this year than last, progress has been accomplished and this progress can be measured accurately. By inference the amount of happiness can also be measured, and although philosophers and moralists have argued for centuries to prove that individual happiness is totally independent of material circumstances, the American viewpoint and the American way of life formally deny their conclusions.

In regard to the present crisis and the war in particular, the American faith in constant improvement of mankind has produced many strange contradictions and insoluble mental conflicts. For instance, many spokesmen of public opinion have frequently expressed the idea, ever since the war started, that the reason why American opinion had been lethargic for so long in the presence of a recognized danger, and so hesitant to make the necessary sacrifices to ensure victory, was the fear that the peace would not offer anything much better to humanity in general, and to the United States in particular, than had already been achieved. The Americans, it was argued, could not be convinced of the validity of this war until it could be demonstrated to them that they were fighting for a *better* world.

What this better world is to be varies according to individual ideas, but there appears to be a consensus that to defeat Nazi Germany is not enough. In the same manner as Wilson, in 1917, suggested a "peace without victory," which implied the triumph of a moral concept, contemporary Americans would like some sort of guarantee that this second world war has, as its ultimate purpose, not the defeat of the enemy, but the establishment of more justice and more prosperity for all (including the enemy). War, in other words, which means the conflict of force regardless of all considerations save defeat of one side by the other, cannot be accepted by the Americans for what it is. In spite of the realization that the very existence of America as a nation is at stake in this struggle, the waging of war must be presented as a means of furthering human progress, and not as a brutal necessity. War, in fact, must be integrated in the American concept of things, which implies that everything must, somehow or other, serve the progress of humanity.

Even the fatalists who believed that Hitlerism and the rise of German imperialism should not be resisted because this is the "wave of the future" did not renounce their fundamental American optimism. Quite the contrary. In fact their "fatalism" was bolstered up and justified by a firm belief that nothing can happen which does not eventually further the good of humanity and its happiness on earth. Thus the recommendation that one should abandon oneself to the "wave of the future," far from being the expression of a philosophy of nonresistance to a possibly dangerous fate, was merely a blind act of faith in the future. Those who adopted this attitude did not believe that Hitlerism was a good thing in itself. In fact they professed to loathe it. But being imbued by American idealism, they could not accept that even evil should not, by some obscure way, finally serve the cause of good.

7. Freedom

Freedom, from the point of view of democratic thinking, is a fundamental right of man. Taken literally, this is a recognition that each man born on this earth should be allowed to think, express himself, and act without any restriction save that of his own conscience, or his own whim, or his own limitations. By stating that this is a human right, each man becomes the arbiter of his own destiny. In fact this could be taken as the definition of the "democratic man" in opposition to the "theological man," who preceded him historically.

It goes without saying that if freedom was recognized as an absolute *right*, the result would be anarchy and a fairly rapid return to primitive barbarism. In fact the philosophical contention that freedom is a right would be an absurdity and the position of the democratic man untenable were it not for the other fundamental contention of democratic faith that man besides being born free is also born good. Being born good, it can be conceived— at least in theory—that he will use his right to freedom not only for his own betterment but for the betterment of his fellow men.

Democratic society, however, like all other societies, does not rest alone on philosophical principles, and although one may believe that man is born good and that he tends toward perfection, it has been found expedient not to rely entirely on this assumption. Individual freedom therefore may be an absolute right, from the philosopher's point of view, but in practice, there is no such thing. The exercise of individual freedom is limited by custom, laws, prejudices, and in general by all the restrictions that enable a society, however primitive it may be, to exist as such.

Individual freedom, in other words, is always relative, and one of the most important problems of politics, if not the most important, is to determine how much freedom can be tolerated without detriment to the order of society.

Although this problem is as old as man himself, the general assumption has been, up to a fairly recent past, that the normal trend of history pointed toward a constant increase of individual freedom, and that the very aim of our civilization, in fact, was the liberation of man from all restrictions except those that he might impose upon himself and willingly accept as just and reasonable.

Such a point of view—which is that of the democratic man—was only possible, of course, as long as the conditions of existence were not such as to make our interdependence what it is today. Before the industrial development of the last century it was perfectly reasonable to believe that there was neither inconvenience nor danger in assuming that an infinite expansion of individual freedom was beneficial per se. Such movements as the abolition of slavery or the extension of the right to vote to those who had no property, and later to women, the right of free assembly, the freedom of the press, and innumerable other measures inspired by liberalism were accepted as progressive because they did not obviously interfere with a more effective organization of society. There was no clear sense, even as late as 1914, that the time was so near when an extension of individual freedom would jeopardize further improvements in social organization. The democratic man was not aware that he was going to clash with the collective man.

That this clash has now come in the shape of a war between Nazi Germany and the democracies of the Western World obviously complicates the analysis of the issues involved. As I have said previously, the extremely effective collective society set up by Hitler and his followers would probably not have come into being at all without the will to power and the incentive to war which made it possible. Nevertheless, I believe that the problem or reorganizing democracy in accordance with the collectivist trend would have had to be faced anyway, war or no war. It may be that the violent challenge of Hitlerism may help us to redefine more exactly and more convincingly, under duress, what we do mean by freedom and how much of it we are resolved to preserve.

8. Roosevelt's Four Freedoms

I have already indicated that the essence of the problem has been stated by President Roosevelt when he set as the objectives of the war the Four Freedoms: namely, freedom of speech and expression, freedom of religious worship, freedom from want, and freedom from fear.

It will readily be seen, however, that out of these four freedoms, two (freedom of speech and expression, and freedom of religious worship) belong to what might be called the classical inheritance of democracy. They re-assert the doctrine of individual independence. The two others (freedom from want and freedom from fear) imply the recognition of human interdependence as well as social, economic, and political organization on a world basis.

Whereas the right to speak and worship freely can be guaranteed by the mere application of tolerant legislation, the freedom from want and from fear—which means the elimination of economic inequalities and the prevention of war—requires collective organization and a revision of the place of the individual in society. The first part of the program has been achieved, not only in America but in all other countries which were, or still are, democratic. It may be said that, on the whole, it has been fairly successful. The second part of the program, however, has not been realized. We still do not know how to organize our production in such a way that all men shall be "free from want" and we certainly have failed to eliminate wars.

The Four Freedoms program of Roosevelt thus appears as a bridge linking, in a plausible formula, the inheritance of the past and the hopes of the future. But it should be noted that while freedom of speech and religious worship is directly in line with the democratic theory that emancipation of the individual is in itself a good thing, the elimination of want and of war predicates necessarily a drastic regulation of individual independence and a limitation of national sovereignty. Freedom from want cannot be assured except through a recognition that collective discipline is an imperative, and wars cannot be abolished until nations and states accept to submit themselves to some superior international order founded on force, like the Roman Empire, or on some idea, universally accepted and transcending all nationalistic interests.

It need hardly be said that the program of President Roosevelt, although revamped to fit modern preoccupations, is a call to arms which follows the long tradition toward freedom and liberation which has been expressed every time the world was threatened by some form of tyranny. Benjamin Constant, writing about Napoleon, in 1813, expressed himself as follows:

> "The world will unite against him [Napoleon]. Peace, independence and justice, these will be the rallying words: and because they have been so long proscribed, these words will take on an almost supernatural power. . . . A cry of union and liberation will resound from one end of the earth to the other. A sense of common decency will inspire the hesitating and the timid. No man will dare to remain neutral lest he be a traitor to himself." [1]

The same sort of sentiment is latent today among the people who have already been conquered by Hitler and among those who are threatened by him. But it should be noted that, although the form of tyranny imposed by Hitler is infinitely worse than that of Napoleon, and far more devastating because Hitler's aim implies a revolution in the inner nature of man, "the cry of union and liberation" is neither as loud nor as unanimous as one might expect. Benjamin Constant spoke more than one hundred and twenty-five years ago, and it seems to us today that his denunciation of Napoleon can well apply

---

[1] Constant, *Prophecy from the Past*, Reynal & Hitchcock, 1941, p. 40.

to Hitler. But the trouble is that whereas the words of
Benjamin Constant were fresh and full of meaning in
their time, they appear hollow and faded to us today.
Peace, union, justice, liberation, common decency, are
words which can still be heard in public speeches and
read in the columns of the newspapers. But the contemporary man, who lives through these years of devastation
and anguish, wonders if these ancient slogans can ever
be revitalized for him and his children. He senses their
truth but also their incompleteness.

Being a rational being and the heir to a long civilization, he knows that freedom—whether taken absolutely
or classified as in Roosevelt's message into four categories
—is the cornerstone of the world which he has built. He
knows that without freedom of thought, of expression,
and of action there can be no creation, that art and
science and all manifestations of culture will cease if the
artist and the scientist are not free to experiment and
work. He knows too that although happiness cannot be
measured quantitatively—in spite of a certain American
inclination to do so—there is a certain profound relation
between *more* freedom and *more* happiness.

The contemporary man knows these things to be true,
and yet it cannot be denied that he seems to hesitate when
he has to assert them, as if he were not certain that his
reason and his faith were showing him the right way, as
if he had lost the inner capacity to act according to his
own belief and to trust his own self.

Benjamin Constant wrote further that:

"Peace, industry, domestic happiness, private virtue, the enjoyment of all these is not enough to satisfy
man's needs; nature has endowed him with intellectual powers, if not more noble, at least more brilliant.

More than all else, these powers are endangered by arbitrary power; it first tries to bend them to its will, then, irritated by their resistance, it finally suppresses them."

And quoting Condillac, Constant concludes:

" 'There are two kinds of barbarism; the one precedes centuries of enlightenment, the other follows them.' The first is a desirable era compared to the second. But today it is toward the second that the peoples of Europe are being led; and in consequence, their deterioration is proceeding rapidly: for what degrades men, is not that they are without certain intellectual powers but that they surrender them." [1]

9. Frailty of tyranny

It may be a consolation to think that these prophecies of Benjamin Constant proved wrong. Two years after he wrote them, the tyrant whom he accused of "degrading men" and of leading Europe back to barbarism was defeated at Waterloo, and there opened an era of freedom and peace such as had seldom been seen in the history of Europe.

Those who trust in the "wave of the future" to land them safely on a happier shore, even if they are rather severely tossed by it in the process, and who like to draw a parallel between Napoleon and Hitler, could point to the exaggerated pessimism of Benjamin Constant in order to denounce the alarmist outcries of his intellectual descendants of today.

But leaving aside the falsity of the parallel between Napoleon and Hitler, I believe that even should Nazi Germany be defeated tomorrow, the fundamental prob-

[1] *Prophecy from the Past*, p. 90.

lem of adjusting our traditional concepts of freedom to
the new conditions of our lives will have to be faced. The
democratic man of today, when he faces the world of tomorrow, may indeed wonder if the necessary transition
from the present relatively laissez-faire order to efficient
collectivism can be accomplished without renouncing his
freedom and surrendering certain intellectual powers to
the tyranny of one man.

In other words, the central problem of the Western
World of today could be formulated as follows: Can our
conception of civilization, which rests finally on the principle of individual freedom, be reconciled with our
knowledge that both war and want can be eliminated only
through collective discipline? Has the time come when
we must make a choice between the preservation of freedom and the greater material security that could be obtained through a much more complete integration of the
individual in the collective centralized state?

It is not my purpose to solve these riddles, for the simple reason that I am quite conscious of belonging to that
vast multitude of men who although they may be able
to state the contradictions which confront the world they
live in, have not found the synthesis that will reconcile
them. Being a "democratic man" myself, I am aware of
the limitations that a certain culture, tradition, habit of
thought, and sense of continuity impose upon all other
democratic men. It may be that the solutions we are looking for lie in a direction that we do not now perceive.
After all, and as I have pointed out before, the men of
the French Revolution who fought to abolish the privileges of feudalism and absolute monarchial power had no
inkling that they were working for the creation of a
bourgeois world.

What I do know, however, is that the solutions offered
by Communism and National Socialism are invalid be-

cause they depend finally on the precarious power of one man: Stalin, Hitler, or Mussolini: whose fortune and that of his system are at the mercy of a battle, or an assassin, or merely of old age.

That this is a weakness and not a force, as so many people are apt to forget, is shown by the insistence of the "dictators" in assuring that they represent the people they lead and that they are the product of real "democracy." Tyranny must always prove that it is legitimate.

"The so-called National Socialist Revolution," said Hitler on January 30, 1941, "defeated 'democracy' in the days of democracy by means of democracy. It ensured power for itself by perfectly legal means. I stand before you today on the basis of the mandate entrusted to me by the German people, a mandate which is far more complete than those held at this moment by any so-called 'democratic' statesmen."

Thus one might say that the advent of Hitler and other "tyrants" to power would justify the fatalistic point of view of Aristotle, who thought that pure democracy led unavoidably to tyranny. "Democracy," said Aristotle, "is not the Government of the many but of the poor." And as the poor (read *have-nots* in our language, or *underprivileged*) are unable to govern themselves through lack of culture, intelligence, or mere lack of the proper means of transmitting their ideas, they become the prey of tyrants.[1]

---

[1] It is curious to find that one of the bitterest denunciations of democracy in modern times was launched by an American, Edgar Allan Poe, who in *Mellonta Tauta*, a conversation supposed to take place in the year 2848, expressed himself as follows:

"They started with the queerest idea conceivable, viz: that all men are free and equal—this in the very teeth of the law of *gradation* so visibly impressed upon all things both in the moral and physical universe. Every man 'voted' as they called it—that is to say meddled with public affairs—until at length it was discovered that what is everybody's business is nobody's, and that the Republic (so the absurd thing was called) was without a government at all. It is related, however, that the first circumstance which disturbed the self-complacency of the philosophers who constructed this 'republic,' was the startling discovery

The tyrants are required only to maintain the illusion that the poor or underprivileged masses govern through them. This—according to Aristotle—is always done through the same methods: by exciting the mob instincts, suppressing the intellectual elites, removing all liberties, finding an enemy, real or imaginary. The poor or have-nots want to be taken care of in their material needs, and nothing else.

To maintain himself therefore, the tyrant must keep the masses in a state of tutelage. They must feel that they depend entirely on the tyrant for their existence. They must also be deprived of all means of finding out what is going on in the rest of the world.

It should be noted that the kind of democracy that Aristotle has in mind, and which according to him leads straight to tyranny, is precisely the same that Hitler talks about. It is a system in which the majority and nothing but the majority can be heard. Hitler, when he held elections, always received some 99 per cent of the suffrage, sufficient proof that no dissenting minority is able or allowed to be heard. Under such conditions, freedom must naturally be repressed, because freedom means dissent.

that universal suffrage gave opportunity for fraudulent schemes, by means of which any desired number of votes might at any time be polled, without the possibility of prevention or even detection, by any party which should be merely villainous enough not to be afraid of the fraud. A little reflection upon this discovery suffered to render evident the consequences, which were that rascality *must* predominate—in a word that republican government *could* never be but a rascally one. While the philosophers, however, were busied in blushing at their stupidity in not having foreseen these inevitable evils, and intent upon the invention of new theories, the matter was put to an abrupt issue by a fellow of the name *Mob*, who took everything into his own hands and set up a despotism, in comparison with which those of the fabulous Zeros and Hellofagabaluses were respectable and delectable. This Mob (a foreigner, by-the-by) is said to have been the most odious of all men that ever encumbered the earth. He was a giant in stature—insolent, rapacious, filthy; had the gall of a bullock, with the heart of an hyena and the brains of a peacock. He died, at length, by dint of his own energies, which exhausted him."

Many people today are inclined to think that Aristotle is right and that democracy does inevitably lead to tyranny. But this can happen only when the institutions have become so weak or so discredited that they lose all authority. The desire for authority then becomes so great —especially in times of crisis—that it will inevitably be transferred to one man. This man is called Marshal Pétain in France today, Hitler in Germany. They may appear to be very different but the process that has brought them to power is the same: the Third Republic had ceased to operate and the Weimar Republic never had operated.

It is obvious that no such situation exists either in the United States or in England. In both these countries, men and not institutions are open to attack. Winston Churchill still depends on the Parliament and on the support of public opinion to preserve his power. President Roosevelt is still checked not only by Congress but by the varying pressure of minority groups which can, at any time, swing public opinion if it should happen that the policy of the President was in opposition to this public opinion. Those who denounce Roosevelt with the greatest vigor are not suggesting that the system of government of the United States should be changed. The mechanism of democratic government is still functioning smoothly both in England and in the United States, especially as regards the freedom of dissension.

10. Tyrants and dictators

In fact the great problem which faces both countries is how much of this freedom is compatible with the necessities of war. This introduces the question of national discipline and the often heard paradox that this war— one of the purposes of which is to preserve democratic

freedom—can be fought successfully only by relinquish-
ing this freedom. "Why fight dictatorship," it is said, "if
to defeat it one must adopt it?"

To present the problem in this form is a fallacy. Those
who formulate it in this manner are not really voicing a
fear of "dictatorship" but a fear of the effort exacted by
the war. They are also taking advantage of a confusion
of ideas made possible by an imperfect use of the word
"dictatorship."

Neither Mussolini, nor Hitler, nor even Pétain are
"dictators." They are properly tyrants, in the sense that
they have assumed limitless power for life. "Today, as
yesterday," said Marshal Pétain in a broadcast, "there is
only one France—it is that which has entrusted her hopes
and her salvation to me." This is absolute power in its
most extreme form, and the Greeks, who made a more
rational study of such matters than we have, thought that
to assassinate the tyrant was perfectly legitimate, for the
simple reason that there was no other method of getting
rid of him.

The dictator, on the other hand, is a normal phenomenon in a democracy. To him are delegated, in time
of emergency, certain powers clearly defined and for a
limited period of time. He remains at all times under the
control of the law and of the constituted bodies who represent the people.

Up to recent years, that is, up to the time that the
"tyrants" Mussolini, Hitler, and Stalin usurped the title
of "dictator," the democracies found no difficulty in time
of national emergency in delegating very great powers to
a President or a Prime Minister. In France, during the
last war, Clemenceau received dictatorial powers, and so
did Poincaré in 1926, to "save the franc." Both remained
subject to the control of the Parliament and of the elec-

torate, and were promptly deprived of these exceptional powers once the emergency was over.

In the United States, the same thing was true in the case of Wilson, whose extraordinary powers ended with the war, and it is now true of President Roosevelt. Moreover, it should be noted that under the American system of government, the Chief Executive is constitutionally a potential dictator (in the true sense of the word). In this sense he is, by the nature of his office and by the extensive powers granted to him by law, in a position to assert his leadership with greater effectiveness and greater authority than either the Prime Minister in England or the President of the Council in what used to be the Third Republic in France. The only danger of the American system, in so far as the Presidency is concerned, is that the nation should face a crisis at a moment when the man who occupies the White House lacks the personal qualities which would enable him to assume the authority and the leadership which the circumstances require.

Although the American system of government, inspired as it is by the ideas of Montesquieu and Locke, whose main preoccupation was to prevent arbitrary power, is devised to limit by all possible means the development of a strong state, it remains that the President of the United States can always, in time of crisis, establish between himself and public opinion a direct link which is usually much stronger than all the checks intended to prevent it.

As Harold J. Laski has pointed out in his book *The American Presidency:*

"Every President has an incomparable audience waiting for the pronouncement he may choose to make; to whomever else the Americans may not listen —and they are in any case a nation of listeners—they will listen to *him*. In any crisis, in the discussion of any big problem, they expect him to speak; in a very real sense, when he has spoken, they feel that the nation has spoken."[1]

This privilege of the President of the United States to speak in the name of the nation and to lead it has always existed, but it has shown a definite tendency to increase ever since the United States has become a major power in world affairs.

It is true that Congress, which has a vested interest in preventing the executive power from becoming too strong, has lost none of its traditional spirit of opposition to the Presidency. However, the lack of effective coordination between the executive and the legislative branches of the American system, which is its main defect, benefits on the whole the executive rather than the legislative branch in times when the nation senses that rapid action is necessary.

The question whether the American system of government, as it exists today, is adequate to meet the present world emergency will be answered only by events. It can be said that it is the first time in history that the Americans are really facing a peril from abroad which threatens their existence.

As far as America is concerned, it is obvious that to overcome this peril something more is needed than mere confidence in the eternal values of civilization—such as freedom, justice, the one-way march of progress. There are moments, as England has found out, when the defense of certain ethical values and certain intellectual concepts is superseded by the necessity of defending one's own existence, and that to defend one's soul one must first of all save one's skin. This is why the interesting speculations in which the Americans used to indulge so passionately, not very long ago, as to the validity of this war, the right and

[1] Laski, *The American Presidency*, Harper & Brothers, 1940.

wrong of the German or the British case, have become profoundly futile now that war for America has become a reality.

"Every world-moving idea," wrote Hitler in *Mein Kampf*, "has not only the right but the duty to avail itself of whatever means will make possible the realization of its purpose. The result is the only earthly judge of the rightness or wrongness of such an undertaking."

Civilization based on freedom, and translated as it is today into the formulae of democracy, has been a world-moving idea for many centuries and there is no particular reason to believe that it has ceased to be so now. If such is the case, it is also the right and the *duty* of those who believe in this idea to avail themselves of whatever means will make possible its realization.

Part V

GERMANY AND THE WORLD

CHAPTER I

The German Revolt

IT IS currently said that Hitlerism and, by extension, present-day Germany, constitute a threat to civilization. Through newspapers, magazines, books, and the radio, and through the speeches of the most authorized leaders of public opinion, from President Roosevelt down, this idea has been spread with increasing intensity ever since Hitler came to power in 1933, but more markedly since the beginning of the war.

In fact the whole multidimensional conflict which forms the background of the present world crisis tends to resolve itself in the broad opposition of what Hitler himself has called "two worlds," the German National Socialist world against the non-German world.

And this non-German and non-Nazi world which is our own we identify with the concept of civilization. It is to save civilization that we fight. It is to assure its survival that England has overcome the powerful antiwar sentiment of the last twenty years and that America has come around to the same feeling of urgency.

It may be argued that there is a more immediate and concrete reason to fight Germany or to try to ward off its assault, which is the instinct of self-preservation. Both England and America feel threatened in their national existence by the conquering ambition of Hitler and the Teutonic world. But the tendency is to create an identity

between the survival of England and America and the preservation of what we call civilization. In so far as the nations opposed to Germany have an idealistic reason to
fight this war, that reason lies in their belief that their
defeat would mean not only the domination of the world
by a single power, Germany, but the disappearance of
civilization itself.

Those who entertained another view, the isolationists
of the Wheeler type in America, for instance, or the
collaborationists in France, formed a minority. Even they
did not try to oppose openly the popular view that there
is a basic antagonism between Nazi Germany and civilization. They merely pretended that this civilization can be
saved in spite of a German victory, either by insulating
certain areas of the world against the Nazi influence (the
American isolationist thesis) or by collaborating with Germany in order to modify the spirit of the victor and
thereby prevent the total disruption of civilization (point
of view of many French partisans of collaboration).

These minority views, however, have not been strong
enough to influence very perceptibly the prevalent conviction that the resistance to Germany represents indeed
a fight for the defense of civilization.

This belief has grown steadily since the beginning of
the war until it has reached the point where it has finally
been possible for President Roosevelt to overcome the
inhibitions against everything connected with the First
World War and to establish a link between the war of
1914-1918 and the war of today.

Speaking on November 11, 1941, the twenty-third anni-
versary of the 1918 Armistice, President Roosevelt expressed himself as follows:

"A few years ago, even a few months, we questioned, some of us, the sacrifice they [the soldiers of

the last war] had made. . . . Today we know the answer, all of us. . . . We know that these men died to save their country from a terrible danger of that day. We know because we face that danger once again on this day. . . . 'What did it get you?' People who ask that question . . . forgot the one essential fact which every man who looks can see today. They forgot that the danger that threatened this country in 1917 was real, that the sacrifice of those who died averted that danger. Because the danger was overcome they were unable to remember that the danger had been present. Because our armies had been victorious, they demanded why our armies had fought. Because our freedom was secure, they took security of our freedom for granted and asked why those who died to save it had to die at all. . . . Whatever we knew or thought we knew a few years or months ago, we know now that the danger of brutality, the danger of tyranny and slavery to freedom-loving people can be real and terrible. . . . We know why these men fought to keep our freedom—and why the wars that save a people's liberties are wars worth fighting and worth winning—at all cost. . . . We know that it was in literal truth to make the world safe for democracy that we took up arms in 1917. It was in simple truth and in literal fact to make the world habitable for decent and self-respecting men and women that those whom we now remember gave their lives. *They died to prevent then the very thing that now, a quarter of a century later, has happened from one end of Europe to the other.*"

Thus after twenty-six months of war, President Roosevelt found it possible not only to rehabilitate the participation of America in World War I, and to present World War II as a renewal of an identical conflict, but also to reassert boldly the long-derided slogan of Wilson: "to make the world safe for democracy."

This speech is significant as a milestone in the evolution of American opinion which only a few months before, as the President said, could not have accepted the notion that twenty years of denial of the validity of the First World War could be reversed to the point where fighting a second time for the same objectives would appear commendable. But the most important aspect of this speech is that, by showing the continuity of the conflict, and the permanence of the issue (to save democracy actually means to save civilization), it reinforced the dominant idea that the opposition between the Western World and Germany is a constant, regardless of whether that country is ruled by Kaiser Wilhelm II or by Adolf Hitler.

By presenting the two world wars as two acts of the same drama, President Roosevelt repudiated the whole attitude of mind of the last twenty years and condemned as fundamentally erroneous all the theories which, by one method or another, have mistaken what was in reality a mere truce with the opening phase of an eternal era of peace.

By the same token, this speech formulated once more the priority over all others of the problem of Germany. It raised by implication a multitude of questions, none of which are particularly new, but all of which are made more acute by the Hitler phenomenon and by the extremity of the danger in which the opponents of Germany find themselves.

These questions can be summed up as follows:

1. Are the German people so essentially different from other people of the West that there will always be periodical conflicts between them?

2. Are the German people merely susceptible to being misled by dangerous leaders, and if so, is there a method by which they can be cured of this peculiar susceptibility

and made to conform to the universal trend of Western civilization?

3. Granting that the German people are moved, from time to time, by certain dynamic or demonic impulses which project them outside the boundaries of Western civilization, can a merger between this aspect of Germanism and the principles of civilization be conceived? If there are two Germanys, or if the Germans have "two souls" as they often say themselves, can a synthesis be found between the two which would ensure their permanent integration into the broad historical current of the West?

4. If not—if we must assume an irreducible conflict between Germanism and civilization—what prospect have we got to face in the future?

Before trying to answer these questions, it might be worth while to define what we mean when we speak of *our* civilization, or even of civilization as a general phenomenon. In other words, do certain current expressions such as "the future of civilization," "the defense of civilization," "the threat to civilization," and the like correspond to a set of definable concepts, or are they mere propaganda slogans which we use, especially in time of war, for the purpose of giving more prestige and more nobility to our prosaic struggle for survival?

1. Standards of civilization

It should be noted first of all that we use the word civilization in two different senses. When we speak of *a civilization,* like the Mycenaean, the Aztec, or the Chinese, we have in mind the characteristic development, over a definite period of time, of a certain people. We think of that development in terms of social customs, of industry, of art, of religion, and more generally under all the aspects

which are properly those of an organized human society.
We associate the history of a civilization with the behavior of a living organism. A civilization grows, flourishes,
falls into decadence, and dies. Some civilizations have
disappeared without leaving any trace. Others are known
only by very faint vestiges, such as the Etruscan, of which
practically nothing tangible has survived except a few
potteries and vague legends.

On the other hand, there are civilizations such as the
Phoenician, the Greek, or the Roman, the influence of
which has outlived the physical disappearance of the people whose name they bear.

The distinction between a civilization which has disappeared without leaving any influence and one which
has survived itself is obviously arbitrary. In most cases a
civilization which like the Greek is still a potent source of
inspiration for us today was itself the heir to many others
that preceded it. What we identify as a source of our
present civilization is seldom the original fountainhead.
But the important fact is that certain civilizations can be
recognized as having permanently contributed to the shaping of our concept of civilization, while others (like the
Aztec or the Sumerian) are either too episodic or too re-
mote in time to have any verifiable influence today.

This brings us to the second meaning of the word *civilization*.

Taken in its modern sense, civilization connotes a gradual process of improvement in the behavior, and perhaps
in the nature, of man. We oppose the civilized man to the
savage or the barbarian. Civilization is a movement away
from the most primitive toward the more complex forms
of society. It cannot be dissociated from the relatively
modern notion of progress. But as no movement or progress can be measured if there are no standards of meas-
urement, it follows that the very concept of civilization

implies the recognition of standards. It can even be said
that the ability to establish standards is the test of a civilized society.

The concept of civilization contains another notion,
which is that of continuity or tradition. Standards cannot
be considered as such if they are not supported by experience. They must have withstood the test of time, and even
if in the course of time they are modified, their validity
depends on their permanence. In so far as the Western
man is concerned, the value of this sense of continuity is
shown by his regard for history. Barbarians or savages
have no sense of history. Non-Western civilizations view
their own past as a kind of static background of fixed traditions or moral teachings. The Western man alone has
what might be called an anxiety about his own past, as if
he felt that not only his consciousness of the present but
his hopes for the future were conditioned by his knowledge and recognition of his own origins.

When, therefore, we speak of civilization we signify a
belief that we are the heirs to the sum total of all efforts
of the civilizations which have preceded us in so far as
they have established standards and values which have not
only stood the pragmatic test of time but which contain
elements of further progression by ourselves and future
generations.

Civilization, in other words, contains the dual concept
of preservation and further expansion of whatever has
been found valid and beneficial—or let us say good—and
the constant fight against the forces which tend to destroy
the principle of continuity inherent in human consciousness.

It follows that it is not possible for us to conceive of a
civilization measured by other standards than our own,
and any attempt to deny the validity of these standards or
to replace them by others is in fact equivalent to a rebel-

lion against civilization itself. The opposition between the civilized man and the barbarian is fundamental. Some people may believe that a periodical triumph of barbarism against civilization is healthy, but this is a romantic view. The fall of Rome has not prevented the process of civilization from being carried on by other people, and first of all by the descendants of the barbarians themselves, but that does not make the fall of Rome less of a disaster. To believe that anything that happened was good for no other reason than that it did happen, is to renounce all criticism and all judgment. The triumph of barbarism, even if it is temporary, can be looked upon with complacency only by those romantic minds who find some sort of enjoyment in the abdication of ordinary common sense.

2. *The highroad of civilization*

Even a superficial analysis of the standards or values which we recognize as basic to civilization would be beyond the scope of this book. Such fundamental concepts as justice, freedom, equality before God or before the law, charity or neighborly love, tolerance and the right of rational criticism, the notion of the individual, and of the rights of the citizen in an organized society have a very long history. The prophets of Israel, the Apostles of Christ, the Doctors of the Church, the philosophers of ancient Greece, the jurists and the political historians of Rome have all contributed to establishing the foundations of our present concepts of civilization.

Geographically speaking the cradle of civilization is the shores of the Mediterranean. For the sake of historical chronology we are in the habit of making a distinction between the Ancient world and our own. After the fall of Rome there was indeed a formidable gap of several centuries during which the essential principle of continuity was suspended. There was a relapse into barbarism. But there is no greater proof that civilization is based on immutable values than the fact that Christianity, as a unifying force, was the only vehicle through which the traditions of the Ancient world could be perpetuated and carried on into the Middle Ages. Through the universality of Christianity, the inheritance of the Ancient Mediterranean world was carried northward. The Renaissance was a movement which gave a kind of official recognition to this inheritance. Through it what we now call Western civilization established itself as a continuation of the Mediterranean civilization.

The survival or rediscovery of classical civilization affected the whole of Europe and no demonstration is needed to prove that the ideological history of the people who inhabit that continent is a prolongation of the classical ages. However diverse may have been the "national" histories of these people, they have one aim in common: the constant reassertion of the principles of Greece, Rome, and of Christianity, and the persistent effort to repudiate barbarism.

The movement of European civilization was not uniform. One people after another took the lead. After the miraculous blossoming of the Italian republics during the Renaissance, for instance, the role of torchbearer was taken up by France—for many centuries the most powerful as well as the most "civilized" nation in Europe. England somewhat later assumed an equally prominent part. Later on still America added her contribution by emphasizing the notions of progress, of material well-being through mass production, of democracy considered both as a political formula and as a spiritual force. What is called the American dream is a manifestation of Western thinking. It has its roots in Europe quite as much as in America and its reverberations in the outside world are as powerful as, for instance, the influence of rational thinking and the right of free criticism which originated in Greece over 2,500 years ago.

What we call our Western civilization is the total sum of a prodigious amount of research, discoveries, and positive gains made by the many generations which preceded us in as many fields as there are forms of human activities. But it is also the exercise of a choice. We could not call ourselves civilized if we accepted all our past, all our present, and, a fortiori, all our future. Fatalism is antithetic to the very spirit of Western civilization because it excludes criticism.

In spite of the various assaults launched against rational criticism in recent years, in spite of a romantic tendency to abdicate before the so-called irrational forces, it remains that it is quite impossible to conceive of any civilization, or for that matter of any human thought at all, if reason is given up as a criterion. The argument is often heard that we have reached a point where scientific methods and rational thinking have failed and that Western civilization is in a kind of impasse from which it cannot emerge except by the discovery of some new spiritual values, or of a new *mystic* springing from the depths of the irrational. The drab materialism of Karl Marx, the theatrical pessimism of Oswald Spengler, and the frantic divagations of Adolf Hitler are given as proofs that the highroad of civilization is now blocked and that nothing less than a total reform of the Western man can possibly offer a solution to the problems that besiege us.

Even some of the most stable and fervent partisans of tradition, like the bulk of the American educators, newspaper commentators, and other leaders of opinion, seem to accept implicitly or explicitly the premise that nothing short of a revolution of the human soul is now required. The magazines and the newspapers are full of appeals for a spiritual regeneration of the world, or of cries of despair because nothing of the sort seems to be in sight. There is a constant recurrence of the idea that the Communists, but more especially the Nazis, have *found something* and that we, the champions of civilization, have not. The whole doctrine of Hitler is wholeheartedly condemned, but at the same time many honest democrats and sincerely civilized men and women talk about Hitlerism with envy. The general idea is that however bad Hitler and his doctrine may be, the German people have nevertheless found in their leader and in his teachings a source of inspiration and a strength which we lack. If only we could invent something as powerful as Hitlerism, but which would be turned toward the good of mankind instead of toward its destruction . . . if only we could find a new source of inspiration, a new dynamism to match that of the Nazis. . . .

This kind of thinking runs as an undertone in the speeches, in the writings, and in the conversations of many people. In so far as it compels us to analyze the causes of our difficulties and to improve the structure of our own society, such criticism can do only good. Unfortunately there are many instances of this way of thinking which reveal no real solidity of purpose, no recognition of the true elements of the problem, but rather a queer masochistic tendency, a propensity to give up the normal and arduous process of critical reasoning and to abdicate before the easy prestige of the oldest sophistry of all barbarism, which is that what succeeds is right in itself—because it succeeds—and that the final criterion of all human endeavor is force.

The most interesting and extreme manifestation of this tendency is to be found in the philosophy of a man like Marshal Pétain since the armistice of June 1940. Leaving aside the political motives which may have inspired the head of the French state, the important fact, from the point of view of this discussion, is Pétain's interpretation of the defeat and the lesson which he has drawn out of it for the conduct of the French people. According to Pétain the defeat was not only a national disaster but it was well deserved. The defeat in his eyes was a punishment. The French having sinned for over one hundred and fifty years, it appeared just to the aged hero of Verdun that they should now suffer. There is no reason to believe that Pétain has any fondness for the Germans and for the Nazis. The most that can be said is that he has been taken in by the aspect of Nazi propaganda which presents Hitler as the champion of the world crusade against Bolshevism, and that he hopes to accomplish a counterrevolution in France under the protection of the German machine guns.

But even this presupposes that Pétain sees in Hitlerism an *alternative* to the kind of civilization which has made France what it is from the very beginning of its history. Whatever may be the opportunistic reasons of Pétain for choosing to collaborate with Hitler, the very fact that he can recommend such a course proves his total incomprehension of what is really at stake in the present struggle. To detach France from England and America and to join with the Reich is not a mere reversal of alliances. Should that detachment become permanent, it would mean that France would cease to belong to the group of people who have carried civilization forward up to now. It would mean that France would be engulfed in this latest rebellion of barbarism against classical civilization. It would mean in fact that France would cease to exist.

I do not know what place Marshal Pétain will occupy in history because all depends on how events turn out and therefore on who writes that history. But it can already be said that Pétain enjoys the singular distinction among all the rulers that France has known in her long history, of being the first one not to recognize a barbarian when he sees one and the first one to accept the idea that the victor must be right because he has conquered, and the vanquished wrong because he has suffered defeat.

Such blindness and such dereliction might indeed justify the old Germanic idea that civilization is synonymous with decadence and that the time has come once more for the healthy brutes to launch their final assault against the tottering fortresses of the West.

Granting that Marshal Pétain represents an extreme point of view which may be more the aftereffect of a catastrophic disaster than the result of considered thinking, his attitude raises the central problem of this war, of its objectives, and of the conditions of peace. It raises the question of whether the German people can eventually be integrated permanently in the system of Western civilization, whether Hitlerism is an abnormal and temporary phenomenon as dangerous to the spirit of true Germany as it is to the spirit of civilization, or whether Hitler and the National-Socialist doctrine represent something which is fundamentally German—the most recent and most violent expression of a conflict which not only antedates Versailles but has its roots in a permanent opposition between the German outlook, the German destiny, and the outlook and the destiny of the Western people.

3. The five German revolts

As I have noted before, many people, especially in America, have been taught that the problem of Germany in its relations with the rest of the world began at Versailles. Hitler himself has greatly contributed to the magnification of this period of history in which he himself has played a part. The denunciation of this treaty was the main platform of the program which brought him to power. It became an obsession with him. He made it an obsession for the Germans, and thanks to his fanatical persistency and to the passive complacency of an uncritical world, Versailles became an obsession for everybody else. But this distortion of perspective has had the effect not only of falsifying our judgment on contemporary events but of making us forget that the problem of Germany and Germanism has very deep roots, a long history, and that its present manifestation cannot be understood if one refuses to consider the real essence of that problem.

The opposition of Germany and the West is neither new nor artificial. This opposition has been recognized by most German thinkers as fundamental. In a sense, it is part of Germany's mission not only to create a counterpoise to Western influence but eventually to supersede it. The whole history of the German people is marked by a series of rebellions which have assumed different forms, but have one common aim: the disintegration or overthrow of the whole structure of Western civilization.

Peter Viereck in his book, *Metapolitics,* lists five such revolts in the last two thousand years. The first took place some 1,500 years ago when the "blond barbarians of the North" brought about the collapse of the Roman Empire. Hermann the Cheruscan (Arminius) defeated the Romans at the Battle of Teutoburg Forest (A.D. 9). "Hermann," writes Viereck, "symbolizes the first of the five great Germanic revolts against the West." [1]

The second revolt was carried on by the Saxons, fighting in the name of Wotan against Charlemagne, who had tried to unify Europe through Christianity. It may be said in passing that Charlemagne is hailed as a great hero by both the French and the Germans, and rightly so. His was the only successful attempt ever made to blend the Roman heritage and the Germanic into one European empire.

The third revolt took a very different form. Luther was

[1] *Metapolitics,* Knopf, 1941, p. 10 *et passim.*

its initiator and the Reformation its result. The outside
world has emphasized the religious aspect of this split in
the Christian world, but the rebellion against Rome was
also a rebellion against the Renaissance and therefore
against the classical heritage of the West.

Viereck writes:

"Germany's fourth major revolt against the West
began in the late eighteenth century with the anti-
rational literature of the pre-romantics known as
'Storm and Stress' (Sturm und Drang) and ran through
the great romantic school of 1800 and through the
neo-romantics (the decadents) of the 1890's. In politics the same great wave of this fourth revolt surged
through the War of Liberation and the Revolution of
1848." [1]

The fifth revolt is taking place now. It may be said that
it is not only the most violent, but also the most compre-
hensive in the sense that Hitler and the doctrine he
preaches constitute a kind of perfect synthesis of all the
earlier revolts. In the Nazi dogma we find reunited the
primitive warlike spirit of Arminius and his hordes; the
Wagnerian medievalism of the Saxons rebelling against
Charlemagne, the Christian emperor; the religious fanaticism of Luther's followers; the irrationalism of the German romantics of the last century; and finally the scientific
militarism inaugurated by Frederick the Great and perfected by the creators of the modern Reichswehr.

4. Germany on the sidelines of history

It is often claimed that the reason the German people
constitute such a problem in the modern world is because
they have arrived too late at a stage of political maturity.

[1] *Metapolitics,* p. 14.

Unlike the other European nations they have been deprived of certain normal opportunities, such as being able to take part in the great movements of world colonization that started in the fifteenth century. Moreover it is said they were not united as a nation, before Bismarck. In fact that unity has been realized only by Hitler.

The tendency of the Western nations is to judge the history of Germany by the same standards as their own. According to this view, the trouble with the Germans is that they have been deprived of the advantages for betterment which have been the natural share of other "civilized" people. They are like a child who has not been able to go to school and whose bad manners should therefore be excused.

Historically it is perfectly true that the Germans have not benefited directly by the main achievements of Western civilization. In particular they have had but a small share in the two greatest periods of European emancipation: the Renaissance and the eighteenth century. While the whole of Western Europe was awakening to the new magic of Italian art, poetry, science, and of a more subtle concept of life, Germany was absorbed by religious strife and well-nigh devastated by the Thirty Years' War. As for the influence of the eighteenth century as expressed by the English and French schools of philosophy, it was practically negligible in Germany because it was definitely foreign and reserved to an elite. The fact that Frederick the Great prided himself on being a friend and pupil of Voltaire created no link between French philosophical and prerevolutionary emancipation and the stagnation of the Germans taken as a whole. Frederick the Great despised what was properly German, including the language of his people, which he called "that coachman's language." And this snobbishness on the part of the King of Prussia and of German polite society in general was to help considerably the prophets of the romantic school, like Father Jahn,[1] in their efforts to "awaken" the soul of true German nationalism, and all those mystic apologists of Teutonic purity who for over one hundred and fifty years have preached the cult of primitiveness and denounced the civilization of the West as the sink of all iniquities and all corruption.

It is often said that the Germans taken collectively, and often individually, show all the signs of suffering from a national inferiority complex and that the explanation for this phenomenon is to be found in their history. The fact that they have been by-passed, so to speak, by the main currents of civilization of the last five or six hundred years, that they have been deprived of certain opportunities, that they have been retarded—through no fault of their own— in the normal development of a nation, all these factors account, it is said, for the explosive qualities of the German soul and for the brutal manifestations of it that we see once more threatening the safety of the whole world.

Germans themselves seldom like this psychoanalytical explanation of their own case. Although one of the key arguments of their defense is to pose as the eternal victims of an eternal and iniquitous conspiracy (and who better than Hitler has played up this theme of the German people persecuted by the whole world?) it is also a fundamental dogma of Germanism that civilization is a form of decadence, a perversion, and a kind of cancer of the human race which must be cured by the assertion and the eventual triumph of a people not bound nor corrupted by the restrictions and the niceties of civilized life.

It is strange that Jean Jacques Rousseau, who is the spiritual father of a certain form of romantic concept of democracy (man is born good, therefore the will of all is good), should have also inspired the German romantics who conceive the nation, or rather the Volk, as some sort

[1] See Peter Viereck, *Metapolitics*, Chap. IV.

of mystical power, half God, half monster, the most fantastic and irrational vagaries of which should be respected and obeyed because there is no other absolute. But the foolish proposition of Rousseau that man being born good, civilization is therefore a corrupting factor, is what seduced the German romantics. This part of Rousseau's doctrine was not taken up seriously by the Western World (except if one wishes to consider Marie Antoinette's experiments in the simple life of Trianon, and other movements toward a return to nature, including perhaps Thomas Jefferson's futile attempt to establish a rural democracy). But the German romantics and their disciples made this proposition of Rousseau the basis of the doctrine that it is the mission of the master race to sweep away the dusty ruins of the Christian-Greek-Roman-French-English-American way of life and all it stands for.

If this is the effect of a nation suffering from an inferiority complex, the case is a very advanced one and it would appear that it is becoming increasingly difficult to cure, for the simple reason that the patient—that is, the German people—far from believing that he is ill, has been told by a whole series of leaders (of which Hitler is only the latest) that there never was anything wrong in Germany except when that country succumbed to the fatal lures of reason, to international law, and other *antinatural* concepts.

5. *Romanticism as a national policy*

The Germans are the only people who pretend to be incomprehensible to anyone not born a German. Sometimes this assertion is made boastfully, sometimes with regret. One must accept the premise that it is sincere, and not merely an easy way of evading many of the troublesome questions which are constantly asked about the Germans, and addressed to the Germans by other people.

To cloak oneself with mystery, to say that one is different and one's soul so exceptional that none can understand
one, is of course one of the familiar affectations of the
romantic. For nearly one hundred years, during the whole
of the nineteenth century, Europe's heartstrings were torn
by the laments of the poets and forlorn souls suffering
from what the French called *le mal du siècle*, a disease
which has produced a considerable amount of literature—
some of it very good. The exploitation of the misunder-
stood soul has been thorough and is today practically
exhausted. Dr. Freud having contributed greatly to the
transformation of our vocabulary and therefore of our
thoughts, we do not speak of *mal du siècle* any more, nor
even of *ennui,* but of maladjustment, which is less con-
ducive to Byronic exaltations.

The romantic of the nineteenth century found great
pleasure in his own complaint. The fact that he was tor-
mented by the uncontrollable and mysterious yearnings
of his own unexplainable soul allowed him considerable
leeway in his relations with society. The Bohemian artist
is the banal incarnation of an attitude toward life founded
on the belief that the full expression of the human spirit
is normally accompanied by a good deal of intemperance
and irregularities of various kinds.

It goes without saying that the romantics caused very
little harm to society and that their contribution to the
"decline of the West" is definitely negligible. To break
feminine hearts, to get very drunk or even to indulge in
opium, hashish, and cocaine may not be commendable
from the point of view of bourgeois morality and social
hygiene, but the fact that the romantics have usually been
strictly interested in themselves and very little in what
was going on around them has made them relatively innocuous.

But when we speak of the romantics of England, France,

America, and other Western countries, we should not forget that across the Rhine, romanticism took a very different form. Under its Germanic aspect this explosion of
sentimental emotionalism, of inflated egotism, and poetic
license translated itself into something forceful, aggressive,
bloody, racial, and barbaric. Viereck quotes Gustav Pauli
as follows:

"Romanticism is Germanic and reached its purest
expression in those territories which are freest from
Roman colonization. Everything that is regarded as
an essential aspect of the romantic spirit, irrationalism, the mystic welding together of subject and object,
the tendency to intermingle the arts, the longing for
the far-away and the strange, the feeling for the infinite and the continuity of historic development—all
these are characteristic of German romanticism and
so much so that their union remains unintelligible
to the Latins. What is known as romanticism in
France has only its name in common with German
romanticism." [1]

The most important difference between the romanticism of the Western countries and German romanticism
is to be found in the fact that whereas on one side of the
Rhine romanticism remained within the frame of laws
and restrictions generally accepted by the Western people,
this same movement in Germany became a philosophy
of life, affecting politics as well as art, science as well as
economics. Western romanticism had a great effect on the
shaping of the individual, at least for a while. It had little
effect on the political history of the countries concerned.
In Germany, on the contrary, romanticism became all-
embracing and served to explain or justify some of the

[1] *Metapolitics*, p. 19.

most extreme and dangerous contradictions of modern Germany.

For example, it is not to be doubted that Walter Scott had a profound influence on millions of his contemporaries. So did Byron and Shelley, and in France such writers as Chateaubriand, George Sand, and Victor Hugo. But neither in England nor in France can one find the equivalent of a Richard Wagner or even of a Goethe, that is, of artists serving at once to create and as a part of what the Germans call *Weltanschauung*.

The specific meaning of the word *Weltanschauung*—in itself a sort of Teutonic metaphysical battle cry—has been described many times. I merely wish to point out that the whole trend of German poetry, philosophy, and scientific thinking of the last one hundred and fifty years or so seems to have been toward establishing further impassable barriers between things essentially German and things not German. In other words, the great romantic discovery that man is ever lonely, ever incomprehensible, ever victimized by the rigors of a disciplined society, that true expression of the divine ego can be found only through breaking all codes of morality and all laws—all this rebellion of the individual against his surroundings which was characteristic of the two or three generations preceding ours, has been transmuted by the Germans into a national theme. The whole German people now visualize themselves as the incarnation of all the symbols of the great romantic age. They are at once the chosen people, the master race, and the victim race (compare this with the attitude of mind of the Montparnasse or Greenwich Village artist). They are a force of nature and also the superachievement of man-the-hero. They are wild and fearless, ruthless and cruel. But they are also the tenderest people on earth, the most loving of children and helpless animals. They cultivate and admire with equal fervor sentimentality and boorishness, individual acts of kindness and organized cruelty.[1]

All these contradictions which the Germans would not condone in another people, they justify for themselves because it is the fundamental theme of romanticism that the ego is the supreme law unto itself, it being understood that other egos can under no circumstances be considered as having equivalent rights nor even equivalent value. Such an admission would imply necessarily the existence of such things as justice, morality, law, and other anti-romantic notions.

[1] Although Thomas Mann is an ardent anti-Nazi and profoundly imbued with the democratic spirit of the Western World, there was a period of his life, during the First World War, when he expressed himself like most German intellectuals of that period, that is, like an exponent of anti-Western romanticism. In view of what Thomas Mann now stands for, the following quotation is all the more indicative of the power of this philosophy in Germany.

"That conquering warring principle of today—organization—is the first principle, the very essence of art. . . . The Germans have never been as enamored of the word civilization as their western neighbors. . . . Germans have always preferred *Kultur* . . . because the word has a human content, whereas in the other we sense a political implication that fails to impress us. . . . This is because the Germans, this most inwardly directed of all peoples, this people of metaphysics, pedagogy, and music, is not politically but morally inclined. In Germany's political progress, it has shown itself more hesitant and uninterested in democracy than the other countries. . . . As if Luther and Kant did not more than compensate for the French Revolution! As if the emancipation of the individual before God and as if 'The Critique of Pure Reason' were not a far more radical revolution than the proclamation of the rights of man! . . . Our soldiering spirit is related to our morality. Whereas other cultures, even in their art, incline toward a civilian pattern of ethics [*Gesittung*], German militarism remains a matter of German morals. The German soul is too deep to find in civilization its highest conception. . . . And with the same instinctive aversion it approaches the pacifist ideals of civilization, for is not peace the element of civil corruption which the German soul despises? . . . Germany's full virtue and beauty unfold only in wartime. . . . The political form of our civil freedom . . . can only be completed . . . now after certain victory, a victory in tune with the forces of history, and in the German sense, not in the Gallic, revolutionary sense. A defeated Germany would mean demoralization, ours and Europe's. After such a defeat, Europe would never be safe from Germany's militarism; Germany's victory, on the contrary, would assure Europe's peace. . . . It is not easy to be a German, not as comfortable as being an Englishman or as being a

6. Hitler, an old-fashioned romantic

It is interesting to note that Adolf Hitler is the perfect example of the romantic hero made accessible to the greatest possible number. He is curiously unmodern. *Mein Kampf* is not a book of the future, nor even of the present. It belongs definitely to the latter half of the last century—to that rather indecent school of writing which began with the *Confessions* of Rousseau and produced the greatest quantity of unregulated intellectual exhibitionism that the world has known in the same amount of time. The very title of the book is revealing—*My* Struggle. It is a subjective outburst in which the author is totally unable to dissociate his own story and his own self from the events around him. Hitler is constantly sorry for himself, and finds an obvious enjoyment in describing his difficult youth, how he was made to suffer because no one recognized his genius as a painter, how hard and unjust the world is to the poor and unknown, and at the same time how marvelous it is to have been poor and unknown and to be now on the way to ruling the world.

Many pages of *Mein Kampf* are, in their very banality, models of this kind of self-centered and maudlin literature

Frenchman and living with brilliance and gaiety. Our race has great trouble with itself . . . it is nauseated by itself. However, those who suffer the most are worth the most. . . . There is something deep and irrational in the German soul which presents it to more superficial people as disturbing, savage, and repulsive. This something is Germany's militarism, its moral conservatism, and soldierly morality, which refuses to acknowledge as the highest human goal the civilian spirit. . . . The Germans are great in the realm of civilian morality but do not want to be submerged by it. . . . Germany is the least known of all European peoples. . . . But it must be recognized. Life and history insist upon it, and the Germans will prove how unfeasible it is to deny, from sheer ignorance, the calling and character of this nation. You expect to isolate, encircle, and exterminate us, but Germany will defend its most hated and innermost 'I' like a lion and the result of your attack will be that much to your amazement you will one day be forced to study us." (Thomas Mann, "Thoughts in War," Sept. 1914, quoted by Janet Flanner, in *The New Yorker*, Dec. 20, 1941.)

which was so much in fashion in the last century and which still survives in the outpourings now usually confined to personal diaries.

Hitler, describing his troubles with his father in his early youth, writes:

> "I did not want to become an official. Neither persuasion nor 'sincere' arguments were able to break down this resistance. I did not want to become an official, no, and again no! . . . The thought of being a slave in an office made me ill; not to be master of my own time, but to force an entire life-time into the filling-in of forms." [1]

I wonder how many times the reader has come across precisely this kind of stuff, or how many readers perhaps have themselves been tempted to write in this vein about their own childhood.

Hitler, like all romantics, is inordinately proud of his own childish conflicts and does not shy at telling us what a bad little boy he was.

He goes on:

> "What ideas this must have awakened in a boy who was anything but 'good' in the ordinary sense of the word! The ridiculous easy learning at school left me so much spare time that the sun saw more of me than the four walls of my room. When today my political opponents examine my life down to the time of my childhood with loving care so that at last they can point with relief to the intolerable pranks this 'Hitler' carried out even in his youth, I thank heaven for now giving me a share of the memories of those happy days. Woods and meadows were the battlefield where the ever-present 'conflicts' were fought out." [2]

[1] *Mein Kampf*, p. 12.
[2] *Ibid.*, pp. 12-13.

Thus the great romantic—left over from another age—depicts himself with a time-tested mixture of naïveté, complacency, and smugness. Nothing is left out: the conflict between young Adolf, the budding genius, and his unimaginative father; the old cliché of comparing the office clerk to a slave; the implication that the author's intelligence is way above the average, so that "learning is ridiculously easy"; the quaint admission (future historians please note) that young Adolf was already not exactly a "good boy" and that anybody who cares can see in his early "pranks" a premonition of what the future Führer of all Germans would do when he reached manhood. And there is, of course, the unavoidable touch about the woods and the meadows where the eleven-year-old Adolf repaired with his "conflicts."

But there are other passages in *Mein Kampf,* as well as in Hitler's speeches, where the frustrated artist expresses aspects of romanticism which are considerably less innocuous and not in conformity with the outworn and mild father-and-son motif. Those are the passages where Hitler preaches the great rebellion against law, against reason, against independent criticism, against charity and tolerance. Those are the passages where Hitler gives a new meaning to the word liberation. "For liberation something more is necessary than an economic policy, something more than industry: if a people is to become free, it needs pride, and will power, defiance, hate, hate, and once again hate." [1]

The son of the Austrian official who rowed with his father because he would not let him paint has now merged his own individualistic romanticism with the romanticism of the German Volk.

[1] Speech of April 1933, *My New Order,* p. 49.

7. *Hitler, loud-speaker of the German soul*

This merger is so complete that it has baffled most of the foreign statesmen who have come into contact with Hitler. For the Western mind it is difficult to conceive that an individual, the leader of eighty million men, should in fact be so totally an incarnation of something as organic and undefinable as the German Volk that he ceases to be recognizable as a personality.

In another chapter I have referred to Hitler's mediocrity both in his appearance and in his thoughts and writings. I have mentioned the paradox that the man who now threatens to dominate the whole world is a kind of transfiguration of the "mass man," of the most commonplace type without any of the characteristics which we are accustomed to look for among the men who influence the course of history.

But this very shadowiness of Hitler's figure, his lack of style, of measure, his inability to limit himself, either in his speeches or in his conquests, the vagueness of his purpose (because after all it is Hitler's opponents who have decided that his plan is something as definite as world domination)—the whole impression of something blurred, uncontrolled, and totally reckless which the name of Adolf Hitler brings to the consciousness of the foreigner, all this is what makes Hitler so indissolubly united with an aspect of the German temperament that tends to overshadow all others.

H. R. Knickerbocker quotes an interview he had with Dr. Jung in October 1938, which I believe quite illuminating on the problem of the relation of Hitler to Germany.

"I asked [Dr. Jung]: 'Why is it that Hitler, who makes nearly every German fall down and worship him, produces next to no impression on any foreigner?'

" 'Exactly,' Dr. Jung assented. 'Few foreigners respond at all, yet apparently every German in Germany does. It is because Hitler is the mirror of every German's unconscious, but of course he mirrors nothing from a non-German.' " [1]

An illustration of this was given by no less an authority than Dr. Hermann Rauschning in an interview given to the *New York Times* on November 9, 1941.

"One strength of Hitler," said Dr. Rauschning, "is that in Hitler's presence a man feels the complications being cut out of his mind, and we are such a complicated people, there is relief in that." [2] He described an occasion when he had gone into Hitler's office at the same time as Baron von Neurath, the Foreign Minister.

"The Foreign Minister was like a schoolboy who has been sent for by his chief master he knows not why. *To be small, to be obedient, to merit no punishment, was his aim. Why? I cannot tell you,* yet I know how he felt. I was myself like a schoolboy in Hitler's presence. In Danzig I opposed him and what he stood for. *In his presence I never opposed him. I think I might have found it impossible.* He causes fear. *I do not know why.* And I have heard Herr Dr. Schacht, the Finance Minister, say that when he left Hitler it was with a feeling that he *was bigger, braver than he had been before.* He said that for some time after returning to his office, he felt braver, bigger, as though he could accomplish the impossible."

[1] *Is Tomorrow Hitler's?* H. R. Knickerbocker, Reynal and Hitchcock, 1941, p. 46.

[2] Note that Dr. Rauschning is, like all Germans, a believer in the romantic concept of the Germans being complicated and somewhat unexplainable to anyone, including himself.

Now Dr. Rauschning is definitely not a follower of Hitler today and he has shown that he was aware of some of the implications of the Nazi revolution. But Dr. Rauschning is a German, and from that point of view, his testimonial regarding the effect produced by Hitler on men not known to be particularly emotional, such as von Neurath and Dr. Schacht, not to speak of Dr. Rauschning himself, is illuminating. No wonder that Dr. Jung in his interview with Knickerbocker could compare Hitler to a seer, to a tribal witch doctor, to a new Mohammed, and call him the Messiah of the German people.

> "He [Hitler] is the loud-speaker which magnifies the inaudible whispers of the German soul until they can be heard by the German's conscious ear. He is the first man to tell every German what he has been thinking and feeling all along in his unconscious about German fate, especially since the defeat in the World War, and the one characteristic which colors every German soul is the typically German inferiority complex. . . . Hitler's power is not political; it is *magic*." [1]

Hitler himself has expressed many times the idea that there existed between himself and the German people a mystical tie, that he was not only their spokesman and ruler but their living incarnation. Hitler believes he is in fact the German people, the visible and acting representation of the Volk, this "collective organic mystical entity which is greater than the sum of its individuals." [2]

To the Western mind used to words like *people* or *nation,* it is almost impossible to understand what a word like *Volk* means to the Germans. It does not merely signify the total sum of the individuals of German birth, nor does

---

[1] *Is Tomorrow Hitler's?* p. 46.
[2] Viereck, *Metapolitics*, p. 196.

it imply what might be called a political sublimation of the notion of a definite collectivity of men. The *Volk* is an all-embracing word, the connotations of which are at once organic, lyrical, and metaphysical. The Volk is not comparable to anything else. There are not several Volks. The French, the English, the Americans are not Volks. Only the Germans form a Volk—*the* Volk.

The Volk is bound by no law, except that of nature, but nature in turn finds its most perfect expression through the manifestations of the Volk. The Volk is superior to everything conceivable and particularly to all other human groups. The Volk's mission is to impose its metaphysical domination over the world because it is better qualified (by its own standards, which are the only ones recognized) to do so.

8. The mass man scorns the mass

Anyone who has the unrewarded courage to read Fichte or Hegel must be struck by the painstaking effort of these two prophets of modern Germanism to rationalize the irrational and to try to explain in plausible language certain impulses which if they were described in unphilosophical terms would hardly retain the attention of anyone. Fichte and Hegel are true romantics, and German romantics at that, which means that they have the ability to the highest degree to confuse obscurity and depth, complication and insight, and especially what they feel as Germans with what they think is just and right for the whole of mankind. Their contribution to the formation of the concept of Volk as a metaphysical reality should not be minimized. They have by the same token greatly enlarged the field of what Rebecca West calls "Teutonic confusion."

Hitler has brought down to a popular level the teaching of these prophets of modern Germanism which had already been made more accessible by Gobineau, Houston Chamberlain, and especially Richard Wagner. But in bringing such ideas to the masses, one should not think that Hitler has made them either clearer or sounder. Quite the opposite. If Hitler has a claim to a real talent, it is his understanding of the art of debasing the intelligence of the masses. In order to assure the triumph of the Volk-idea both in Germany and in the world, Hitler has no hesitation at all in recommending that the Volk should be lied to, deceived, and fooled by its leader, that is, by the incarnation of the Volk itself.

Hitler writes in *Mein Kampf:*

"But if nations fight for their existence on this planet, that means if they are approached by the fateful question of 'to be or not to be'—all reflections concerning humanity or aesthetics resolve themselves to nothing and are excluded; because all these ideas are not floating about in the world ether, but come from the imagination of man and are connected with him. His departure from this world also dissolves these ideas into insubstantial non-existence; *for Nature does not know them.* But in mankind too, they are characteristics of only a few people or rather races according to the measure in which they originate from their feelings. Humanity and aesthetics would even disappear from a world inhabited by men as soon as it lost the races which are the creators and bearers of these ideas." [1]

In other words, the Germans alone are able to determine what is "humane and aesthetic." Were they to disappear, mankind would apparently be totally unable to conceive such ideas. It follows that a race endowed with such nat-

[1] *Mein Kampf,* p. 229.

ural gifts cannot be submitted to any international rule of morality.

This is the level to which the ideas of Fichte concerning the sacred amorality of the state and the turgid romanticism of Richard Wagner are brought down through the practical mind of Adolf Hitler. All the highfalutin metaphysics and apocalyptic poetry so dear to the Germans and their admirers finally end up in Hitler's recipes on the art of propaganda, in which he makes the interesting discovery that this great Volk may be divine but is certainly deprived of intelligence. "The great masses' receptive ability is only very limited, their understanding is small, but their forgetfulness is great," [1] writes Hitler. And again: "The people, in an overwhelming majority, are so feminine in their nature and attitude that their activities and thoughts are not motivated less by sober consideration than by feeling and sentiment." [2]

The foreigner may sometimes wonder how Hitler can possibly reconcile this obviously sincere scorn for the intelligence of the people—an attitude of mind which makes him appear as one of the greatest cynics of all times—and his fanatical glorification of these same people and of himself as their living incarnation. Hitler offers the strange spectacle of a Messiah despising the Chosen People which he leads because the inner logic (if such a word can be used here) of the whole German conception of ruthless amorality makes it necessary that the Chosen People themselves should be treated like beasts. Thus the theory of racial superiority, of the divine right of the German Volk to rule all other people, and similar ideas nurtured by a long line of pre-Nazi prophets, when finally expressed by Hitler and his friends end up in a series of contradictions:

Hitler is a witch doctor, a seer, and a new Mahomet.

[1] *Ibid.*, p. 234.
[2] *Ibid.*, p. 237.

He is the reincarnation of Barbarossa and Siegfried. He is the heir of Charlemagne, Frederick the Great, and Bismarck. He is the nearest thing to a god that such a large number of supposedly rational human beings have wanted to recognize in many centuries. But his mind is that of a very cheap type of underdog, such as this civilization of ours can too often produce, and which creates gangsters or, at best, second-rate cynics.

9. Hitlerism, a German synthesis

Hitlerism has brought about the perfect synthesis between apparently irreconcilable concepts: the romanticism of the last century and the machine efficiency of the present day. One has been made to serve the other. The "blue flower" has turned into a Stuka propeller. Goebbels, Rosenberg, and other Nazi doctrinaires have created what they call "steel romanticism." Heroism, death, sacrifice, purification by the sword and by blood, the final rest in Valhalla, all these Wagnerian themes so vague but so poignant for the Germans have been turned magically into some sort of spiritual fuel for the panzer divisions and the bomber planes.

Other contradictions have been solved, or rather made to act as forces directed toward the same aim. The Germans have now succeeded in combining a condition of chronic hysteria with perfect efficiency. Whoever has listened to the crowds greeting a speech by Hitler knows what I am talking about. It is frenzy, but it is organized frenzy. The delirium has been regulated like everything else. Heroism on the battlefield seems, by many accounts, to be of the same order. German heroism is never gratuitous. The German hero seems to remain thoroughly conscious of being part of something organic, larger than himself, larger than his regiment, larger than the German

Army or perhaps even than the sum total of all the Germans dead and alive. The German hero does not seem to find in death that final loneliness so characteristic of the Western attitude toward death. Through death he reintegrates himself even more completely into the metaphysical All called the Volk.

Through Hitler, the Germanic tendency to identify brutality with strength, cruelty with manliness, hardness with determination, has been brought to perfection. William L. Shirer in his *Berlin Diary* shows his astonishment at the capacity of the Germans for being at once so kind and so brutal. He writes:

> "The German has two characters [always the two-souls theme]. As an individual he will give his rationed bread to feed squirrels in the Tiergarten on a Sunday morning. He can be a kind and a considerate person. But as a unit in the Germanic mass he can persecute Jews, torture and murder his fellow men in a concentration camp, massacre women and children by bombardment, overrun without the slightest justification the lands of other peoples, cut them down if they protest and enslave them." [1]

The remark of Shirer concerning the difference in behavior between the German acting as an individual and the German acting as a unit in a mass brings up a point which is of general importance.

All men, to whatever nation they belong, tend to act differently as persons and as members of that nation. The greatness or validity of a nation as a civilizing factor can be measured by the degree to which it approximates the recognized standards of usual morality which are applied to individuals.

[1] *Berlin Diary*, William L. Shirer, Knopf, 1941, p. 585.

It must be admitted that all nations, including those that most ardently profess their attachment to a code of morality, have a tendency to behave much more like organized gangs of brigands than like communities of civilized men. Formulas of exception, such as "sacred egotism," "my country right or wrong," "the undisputed primacy of patriotism," are called for to justify actions by the state which have no excuse whatsoever according to ordinary ethics. The nation or the state is admittedly somewhat beyond good and evil, and dealings between states or nations are conducted according to rules that would lead the ordinary citizen to jail if he applied them in his personal dealings with other citizens.

But this being admitted, there are nevertheless very important differences among the various nations in the manner they practice or tolerate international immorality. It also makes a great difference whether the individual citizen belongs to a nation which condemns international gangsterism (though it may resort to it at times) or to one which glorifies it and considers it as the fundamental law of nature and the national guiding principle.

There is no reason to suppose that the individual German as a human being is essentially different from the individual Frenchman, Englishman, or American. The capacity for cruelty, kindness, brutality, or pity is probably fairly evenly divided among men who on the whole belong to the same biological stock and have been submitted to the same broad influences. This is why people are right, at least in theory, who say that it is at once unreasonable and dangerous to treat the Germans as if they belonged to a different species from the rest of the white race. Germans who have emigrated to America have given ample proof of their adaptability to a society which condemns practically everything now associated with the name of Germany.

This is why, also, these same people are right—always in theory—in assuming that the way to solve the German problem is to separate the German people who are individually identical to all other men, from those who lead them astray and pervert their morals. The First World War was fought on the assumption that once the Kaiser and the military clique of Germany were removed, the German people would automatically renounce war and the practice of force. Today Hitler has been substituted for Kaiser Wilhelm and the same idea prevails: once Hitler and the Nazis are out, the rest of the world will have no difficulty in dealing with the German people on a basis of mutual understanding and in a spirit of human brotherhood. The prevalent idea, especially in America, is that the only reason why the good German, that is, the one who feeds squirrels in the Tiergarten and would adopt democracy, cannot exorcise the bad German who shoots hostages and puts Jews in concentration camps, is Adolf Hitler and his friends.

Even President Roosevelt and Winston Churchill, who both must have some understanding of the fundamental problem of Germanism, like to spread the notion that the real reason this world of ours is threatened with destruction is because some eighty million innocent Germans have fallen prey to a bunch of unscrupulous gangsters.

If only the problem of Germanism were as simple as that!

But I think that the time has come to take a more realistic view of the situation which confronts us.

10. The German problem

The truth is that whereas the individual Britisher or American—whether he is a decent citizen or not—belongs to an order of society which openly and constantly recommends law, moral discipline, tolerance, order, and other *civilized* virtues, the German unfortunately has been submitted for centuries to a series of influences which have taught him that the great mission of the Teutonic people is to overthrow the Western World, to rid themselves of its moral discipline, of its rationalism, and of its concept that there is a law above men.

This has been going on, under one form or another, since the Romans had to erect Maginot Lines against the hordes of the East. And unfortunately, the modern German is far from being on the mend as compared with his ancestor of the time of Arminius. Quite the contrary. Back of him there is now over one hundred years of romantic and militaristic education; one hundred years of pan-Germanic propaganda and barbaric exaltation. The modern German is farther away from the trend of Western civilization than was even the German who fought the war of 1914-1918. He is farther away because Hitler and National Socialism are not an accidental outbreak, the temporary and feverish expression of a sentiment of revolt of an oppressed people: Hitler and National Socialism are the final blossoming of a very long evolution, the most perfect synthesis of the aspect of Germanism which finds satisfaction in the irrational romanticism of Richard Wagner, in the heretic racial scientific divagations of Houston Chamberlain, Gobineau, and Rosenberg and in the militaristic ruthlessness of Clausewitz, Treitschke, Ludendorff, Banse, and Haushofer.

We should stop and think. What would be the effect on the morality of the average American citizen if high officers of the United States Army wrote the kind of books which form the bulk of German military literature? In these books, war is presented as the supreme aim of the nation. These are not mere technical books, such as those published by army officers the world over. As is usual with everything German, they overlap into other fields. They deal—and have always dealt—with what we now call "total war," that is, a form of warfare which engulfs the whole of the nation and the whole of man. These books teach that war must be not only ruthless, but cruel if necessary. They advocate the suspension of all laws of humanity under the pretense that the worse a war is, the sooner it will come to an end—the sooner the enemy is exterminated, the sooner the peace will reign. Treachery, deceit, absolute ruthlessness are preached; ordinary laws of humanity and decency are scorned.

People for whom it has become a parlor game to quote passages out of *Mein Kampf* to show the immorality of Hitlerian Germany overlook the fact that Hitler is comparatively mild compared with a good many German military writers whose works form part of the popular education. These military writers are more sinister than the romantic Nazis of the Hitler or Rosenberg type, because they assume an air of scientific authority to demonstrate the necessity of concentrating the whole effort of the nation toward war, and a type of war which knows no law, and no restriction whatsoever.

The combination of German military dogmatism and the fanatical exaltation of the Nazi whirling dervishes is the overwhelming force which dominates the German soul of today. The outside world must realize that, under such a regime, it matters little whether Fritz or Hans is kind, humane, appreciative of the higher values of life, and in general civilized. All these tendencies are combated by the surroundings in which the Germans live. The highest entity in which they are asked to believe and to which they belong, the German Volk, is presented to them as a negation of these values, as the great force which will destroy them.

Human nature being what it is, a mixture of good and

bad, this appalling thing called Germanism is certainly not sufficient to destroy in every German all the good that is in him as in any other man. But to expect anything but brutality, stupidity, and barbarism from this same German when acting as a unit in the mass is expecting too much. Germanism, in its most positive manifestations, is one of the most dangerous forms of human destructiveness that history has known. The trouble with it is that the sinister aspects of Germanism, far from being on the wane, are obviously in the ascendant. Hitler is the last phase of an evolution toward total evil which has been pursued under the various incarnations of the primitive Teutonic tribe, the German concept of state, Prussian militarism, and the notion of Volk for several centuries.

11. The "two souls of Germany"

I am well aware of the theory of the "two souls" of Germany as expressed in the often-quoted passage of Goethe: "Two souls, alas, dwell in my breast together; the one wants separation from the other." The whole personality of Goethe is cited as typical of this ability or desire of the German mind to split, and there is the great Faustian theme in which the symbol of the German psyche can be recognized.

There is the fact that Germany has produced philosophers and artists, as well as eminent individuals in all walks of life, who have expressed an aspect of Germany radically antithetic to the one described in the preceding pages. Germany is not wholly anti-Western. Germany, like a giant pendulum, oscillates between attraction to the West and repulsion from it. Germany's friends as well as many Germans believe in fact that the whole problem of Germany is how to stabilize this perennial swing be-

tween German rebellion against the West and cooperation with the West.

No one denies that that pendulum movement exists,
nor can anyone be blind to the fact that we are witnessing
one of its sharpest and most dangerous swings. In fact this
time the whole Western World is definitely threatened
by it. Adolf Hitler is mincing no words about it. His purpose is the destruction of the Western World and what it
stands for and there is no reason to suppose that he will
not carry out his plan if he can.

This being so, the question is whether this excess will
be followed by a swing in the other direction. If Nazi Germany is defeated in this war, can we expect a period during which the other soul of Germany will again manifest
itself?

This is obviously the hope of most liberals in the Anglo-
Saxon countries. It is also the hope, quite naturally, of all
the Germans who are out of Germany, fighting Nazism,
but who want their country to be saved eventually. This
is a natural hope because it is reasonable to expect that
after a movement as extreme as National Socialism has
spent itself or been destroyed, a period of moderation will
follow.

This may well happen, but looking back on German
history one is not reassured. If one admits the theory of
the two Germanys, and of a kind of oscillation between
the good and the bad, the constructive and the destructive
(from the Western point of view), one cannot escape the
conclusion that the bad overweighs the good to such an
extent that it is difficult to adopt a purely statistical attitude toward such a problem.

It is not easy to weigh with the same scales a quartet of
Beethoven and a panzer division, a page of Goethe and
the practices of the concentration camps. But for that very
reason there is a fallacy in the reasoning of those who pre-

tend that Bach, Beethoven, Schiller, and Goethe atone, in a certain way, for the brutality and ruthlessness of Germany in the realm of politics and war.

The root of the problem is not the outcome of the struggle between the two "souls" of Germany. The root of the problem is the fact that such dualism exists at all and that on it hinges the fate of the whole civilized world.

No other nation has thought of basing its policy and its world outlook on a case of schizophrenia. No other nation has tried to justify its quasi pathological manifestations of brutality, lawlessness, and ferocity on the presumption that the whole world was leagued against it in some sort of fabulous plot. No other nation has complained so much of being treated unjustly not only by fate but by every other single nation, whether powerful or weak. No other nation has practiced with such consummate skill and persistence the double blackmail of trying to inspire pity as a victim and terror as a bully.

Again I wish to state that I do not believe that this kind of diseased fermentation in which the Germans are maintained by their cultural leaders makes the individual German necessarily different from other people. But unfortunately it is not with individual Germans that the world has to deal but with this solid, organic, barely human thing called the German Volk. And the chances are that it is with this German Volk that the rest of the world will have to deal not only during the war but after.

This brings us back to the questions raised at the beginning of this chapter. If answers can be given to them at all, it would appear that these answers are not very comforting.

The German people, acting as a people, are giving no sign that they wish to find some sort of synthesis between themselves and the civilization of the West. The reason for this is that such a synthesis is inconceivable. German-ism is out to eliminate Western civilization and to sup-plant it with something totally hostile to it. Germanism cannot be blended with Western civilization.

Hitler is not merely an accident in the evolution of Germany. He is not a gangster nor even a "usurper," as Napoleon was called by his enemies. No one denies that Hitler is a legitimate German phenomenon, the final product of a very long Teutonic will to rebel against the rule of the West.

The removal of Hitler might plunge Germany into a condition of chaos. It might end the war. It would not solve the German problem, because the roots of Hitlerism go far deeper than the immediate events which seem to have given birth to it.

The solution of the German problem is not visible to-day because there is no indication whatsoever that the German people are ready to repudiate the dual heritage of romanticism and militarism of which the Nazis are the perfect synthesis.

Moreover, even if one should imagine that after the present rebellion (presupposing, of course, it is checked) Germany should swing back to a phase of collaboration with the West, this would not be reassuring in the long run. What is wrong with Germany, what makes the prob-lem of Germanism so much more disturbing and danger-ous than any other we have to face, is precisely this faculty of the German soul to move in and out of the orbit of civilization. As long as the Germans (and this applies to some of the best of them) stick to the romantic idea of their dualism, the chances for a durable solution of the German problem will be small indeed.

The world is one and no progress is conceivable if all nations do not accept and understand the fundamental fact of the unity and universality of civilization.

National idiosyncrasies and diversity are not only tolerable, they are necessary to civilization itself. What is not tolerable is the existence of a chronic rebel in our midst.

The purpose of this war is to quell a Germanic revolt against two thousand years of civilization. It is not the first one. Our position has obvious analogies with that of the Roman Empire when it was attacked by the ancestors of the present Germans. Our chances of resisting successfully the onslaught seem, however, to be considerably better than those of the Romans. In spite of many obvious deficiences—which are political, spiritual, as well as material—the countries of the Western World and those siding with them have a resiliency and resources which the Roman emperors of the decadence lacked completely.

But even if we obtain total victory over Germany, it will not necessarily mean that a solution of the problem of Germany against the world will be at hand.

That solution implies the fundamental transformation of the German outlook on all the essential questions which for so many centuries have faced humanity.

The Germans, as they are, have given no proof of being able to shake off the deadly burden of what they believe is their national destiny: the periodic rejuvenation of mankind through barbarism.

Part VI

AMERICA AND THE WORLD

CHAPTER I

America and the "Grand Proportions of History"

THE Western World and all that it stands for cannot be saved from a Germanic rebellion without the help of America. This has been true since the Battle of the Marne in 1914. But this truth has become apparent to America itself only in 1941.

The danger of course has become infinitely greater and more urgent through the astounding successes of Germany's partner in Asia, Japan.

These successes are so considerable and the disasters suffered by the United Nations in the Pacific are so pressing that many people are inclined to believe that the real peril to America is not Germany but Japan.

But the truth is, of course, that Japan could never have expanded so rapidly and so dangerously if the United States and England had not been obliged to maintain a very large part of their forces in the West in order to contain Germany. If Japan has been able to defeat the combined forces of the United Nations with relative ease up to now, it seems to be due much more to the weakness of these forces on the spot than to the power of the Japanese military machine. Hirohito's fortunes are intimately tied to those of Hitler.

It remains however that the disasters suffered by the

United Nations in the Pacific have created a situation the ultimate consequences of which defy the imagination. In less than three months Manila, Hongkong, Singapore, Batavia and Rangoon have fallen. By the time this book is published Australia may well be invaded and India attacked. In one hundred days the Japanese have broken down the strategic barrier which separated the Pacific from the Indian Ocean. This means—at least in theory—that there is nothing to stop the advance of the Japanese until they reach Suez. There are no fortifications, no important naval force, no substantial army to oppose them if they wish to pursue their conquest westward. This means that it may take only a few months perhaps for the Japanese to become the masters of a section of the earth which it has taken centuries for Western man to explore and colonize.

Without going into a discussion of the merits or the faults of Western Imperialism, one can recognize, however, that ever since Marco Polo's travels, the Western man's accomplishments between the Red Sea and the China Sea represent a rather remarkable success both materially and culturally. The record is certainly not all white: far from it, but I believe that it is fair to say that on the whole, humanity in general has profited from the efforts of the West to develop the richness of the East, and to establish a link between the civilizations of the Orient and our own.

But all this today is suddenly threatened by a new conqueror. Japan as a world power is less than ninety years old. It has very little experience in ruling other people and has shown mostly up to now its military ability. Japan has often been compared to Prussia and there is nothing to prove that Japan believes in anything else but conquest by the sword. How the Japanese will behave when they have to deal with the complex problems of ruling other people is therefore hard to predict.

What will happen if and when Japan attempts the conquest of India, for instance? Will this produce a national reaction such as took place in China? Or will it cause civil and religious wars among the people of India?

What will happen if the two Axis partners, Germany and Japan, join hands somewhere in the Near or in the Middle East? Will it mean the dawn of a new world era dominated by two great military States? Or the beginning of a new conflict between these two States for the exclusive domination of the planet?

One can speculate indefinitely on the possibilities opened in this direction. For the present however one can limit oneself to the following conclusions: 1. The Japanese victories could not possibly have happened without Germany's successes in Europe and the subsequent threat to America. 2. Materially and morally the blow inflicted by Japan on the Western nations is the greatest that they have suffered collectively through the whole history of the Occident. 3. Hitler is openly out to destroy the kind of civilization upheld by the Anglo-Saxon countries, but the chances of his succeeding have been tremendously increased by the Japanese contribution, not only from the purely military point of view, but because a Japanese conquest of the East would have racial and political repercussions which can hardly be imagined at the moment. 4. America finds herself encircled, and threatened with isolation from her allies. The width of the oceans, considered as a protection up to now, turns out to be a real peril; because if it is true—as generally admitted now—that the only way to reverse the tide of adversity is by taking the offensive, the distances which separate America from the main battlefields constitute a serious handicap. America would be in a better position to win this war were the Atlantic no larger than the Channel and the Pacific no broader than the Mediterranean. 5. In spite of Japan's fantastic successes, they probably cannot be consolidated except through a German victory over England and America. Germany, therefore, remains the heart of the coalition and the most powerful as well as the most dangerous of the Axis partners.

From the American point of view the pattern of the First World War was deceptive. It started definitely as a European conflict. During the first years the American people were quite sure that it was their duty to remain neutral. Their sympathies were divided to a much greater extent than they were to be twenty years later. The Germany of the Kaiser had violated treaties and behaved pretty badly in the conquered territories. Even if one discounts the exaggerations of Allied propaganda, this remains substantially true. But on the whole the American people looked upon the war in Europe with little sense of danger to themselves and certainly with no feeling of responsibility. By no stretch of the imagination could America be connected with the complex diplomatic crisis which brought about that war. If a feeling of partisanship developed in the hearts of large sections of American public opinion, it was for two main reasons: first, because sentimentally many Americans were definitely on the side of the Allies, and second, because the Germans were foolish enough to accumulate such a fantastic series of errors and outrages against American citizens and against American rights that it became practically impossible for President Wilson not to declare war on Germany.

Many people saw that a Germany victory would constitute a threat to the security of the United States but public opinion by and large was not aware of the seriousness of the danger, and the Administration carefully avoided emphasizing this angle of the situation. So much so that when

Woodrow Wilson finally called upon Congress to declare war upon Imperial Germany the main reason given was that through submarine warfare, Germany had violated international law.

Wilson in his war message to Congress of April 2, 1917, declared:

"International law had its origin in the attempt to set up some law which would be respected and observed upon the seas, where no nation had right of dominion and where lay the free highways of the world. By painful stage after stage has that law been built up, with meager enough results . . . but always with a clear view, at least, of what the heart and conscience of mankind demanded. This minimum of right the German Government has swept aside under the plea of retaliation and necessity and because it had no weapons which it could use at sea except these which it is impossible to employ as it is employing them without throwing to the winds all scruples of humanity or of respect for the understandings that were supposed to underlie the intercourse of the world." [1]

And further on in the same message, Woodrow Wilson spoke as follows:

"There are, it may be, many months of fiery trial and sacrifice ahead of us. It is a fearful thing to lead this great peaceful people into war, into the most terrible and disastrous of all wars, *civilization itself seeming to be in the balance.*" [2]

[1] *Woodrow Wilson, Life and Letters,* Ray Stannard Baker, 8 vols., Doubleday, Doran, 1927-39, Vol. VI, p. 510.
[2] *Ibid.,* p. 513.

Except for this tentative admission that civilization might be threatened by the ruthlessness and lawlessness of the German Imperial Government, there is no trace in Wilson's message that the war constituted a real menace for America. Wilson wished to give the impression that he resorted to war for moral or legalistic reasons, because the neutral rights of the United States, as he understood them, were being violated. This was his main preoccupation all along. This is so true that during a certain period before the entry of the United States into the war, the bitterest conflict developed not with Germany but with England. It may now be argued that this conflict could never have led to war, even if it had become much more acute, but judging by the record, there is no doubt that Wilson's indignation against England's methods was as sincere and as intense as his indignation against Germany.

We know today that the safeguard of the freedom of the seas does not involve merely, as Wilson contended, a moral and juridical problem. As far as America is concerned, freedom of the seas means something much more vital than that. America in fact cannot hope to remain independent and secure if the seas should be controlled by a power or a group of powers hostile to the United States.

But a truth which has now become obvious was not at all clear in 1917, and although Woodrow Wilson actually went to war to preserve the principle of the freedom of the seas, there is reason to doubt that he saw clearly the practical implications of that principle. The greatness of Wilson was his capacity to interpret the world he lived in in terms of moral values, and to enable the common man to put some idealism into the drabness of a war that was becoming less and less inspiring as the years went by. But Wilson's limitations were equally remarkable. These limitations have been diversely qualified, but I think they can be summed up by saying that he lacked the historical sense which would have enabled him to grasp the full implications of the conflict in which the United States and the rest of the world were then involved.

Happily, however, and as if some unconscious knowledge was inspiring them, the American people did act in 1917 precisely as they should have acted had they had as clear a vision of what they were doing as they have today. It matters little now what were the motives for which the United States went to war in 1917, whether (1) to defend international law and the freedom of the seas; (2) to liberate the world from autocratic regimes such as the German Imperial Government and establish democracy everywhere; (3) to save the war investments of several American banking firms; (4) to pull England's chestnuts out of the fire; or (5) to establish eternal peace on earth. The important fact is that America did go to war against Germany in 1917 and thus established itself for the first time in history as a vital factor in the balance of world power.

I know well that the expression "world power" is very distasteful to American ears because it connotes greed, imperialism, and conquest. But to shirk the responsibility of power because some of the exercises of power can be objectionable from a moral point of view is another way of abusing the gift of power—by the sin of omission.

At any rate, whatever the Americans may have thought about it or desired, there is no doubt whatever that from 1917 onward, the whole balance of power in the world has been changed by America.

I would like to add that this change is not only material. It is not merely American economic and financial resources, nor American man power, that have altered the old equilibrium. As important as all these changes is the

one brought about by the political, moral, and philosophical intrusion of America into the world.

1. The spread of Americanism

It has become a habit, especially in America, to denounce the influence of foreign *isms*. Communism, Fascism, Socialism, and the like are recognized as world-wide
ideas, the spread of which produces world-wide problems.
But there is a tendency to minimize or overlook another
ism which in many ways has been more successful and
more revolutionary than all others: Americanism.

The spread of Americanism, over the world did not
begin with the First World War. The prestige of certain
aspects of American life and of certain American achievements, some good and some bad, goes much farther back
into the nineteenth century. But if the outside world, and
particularly Europe, have long been curious about America, this curiosity was hardly more than vicarious. As a
dominating influence on the destinies of the whole Western World, America really began to make its influence
felt with the First World War. From the day that the German armies were "miraculously" stopped on the Marne in
September 1914, the process of America's involvement in
the affairs of Europe began and never stopped in spite of
all efforts on the part of the Americans themselves to
revert to their isolationism after the First World War was
over. But even if isolationism had been more successful,
even if the twenty years of aloofness that extend roughly
between 1921 and 1941 could have been prolonged, the
expansion of Americanism would not have been less. The
truth is that the dynamic quality of Americanism as a world
force is as much a cause of the failure of isolationism as
the outside threat of Germany and Japan. A nation that

radiates as much influence and in such different ways as America cannot isolate itself, even in the absence of an enemy. Nations are like people: only the weak and the invalids can live like recluses. Those who are normally strong, or very powerful, cannot help but entangle themselves with the lives of other people in direct proportion to their power and vitality.

The influence of Americanism throughout the world is difficult to define because Americanism itself is difficult to define. It is not a political doctrine like Fascism nor a *Weltanschauung* like Germanism. It does not propose itself as a solution to other people's troubles, although many Americans of the type of Woodrow Wilson or Cordell Hull feel deeply that the world would profit if it followed the example of America. They are not actively messianic, but they are grieved and somewhat surprised that other nations are not reasonable enough to let themselves be persuaded by the American example.

Americanism is a way of life. But there is a constant misunderstanding between the Americans and other peoples as to what is meant by the American way of life.

Americans are rather apt to forget that the adoption by other people of American methods and tastes does not mean the adoption of American thoughts and ideals. It is easier to export Hollywood films and Coca-Cola than the spirit of the Bill of Rights or the political philosophy of Jefferson and Lincoln. The pre-eminence given by Americans for so many years to the businessman and to the businessman's point of view has been greatly instrumental in distorting the true meaning of Americanism as a powerful element in the building up of Western civilization under its modern form. Because Americans have themselves put forward their own businessmen as the supreme expression of Americanism—because even today, the same aura of respect and awe surrounds what is called a big executive as is the case in Germany for a general—it is extremely difficult for the outside world to have a clear perception of what the contribution of America to the general trend of civilization has been in the past and what it can be tomorrow. That America has something more important to offer the world than the philosophy of success has not always been easy to grasp.

The outside world, and more particularly Europe, thinks of America and Americanism very much in the terms of material achievement and very little in any other way. This of course is natural, because it would be foolish to deny that America's most obvious achievements have been in this direction. During the last fifty years, but much more markedly since World War I, the whole world has undergone a process of "Americanization," the extent of which is hard to realize because it is so diversified and, in a sense, so obvious.

In certain fields, such as industrial mass production, American methods have asserted themselves in such a manner that other countries have had but one of two choices: either buy American products or copy them. Certain islands of resistance, such as the automobile industry in France before the war, only showed the futility of the struggle.

But Americanization of other countries showed itself in more striking ways when it came to putting to use purely American methods. Some Americans admire the efficiency of the Germans. Others, even more naïvely, are left breathless by the achievements of Soviet Russia. But leaving aside the political differences which separate these countries, the truth is that neither Germany nor Russia could have got where it is today if it had not conscientiously set itself to imitate American methods of organization and production.

The case of Russia is particularly striking. Anyone who

is somewhat familiar with what has actually happened in the U.S.S.R. since Lenin decided to industrialize that vast country by force can detect the influence from America. It manifests itself in such ways as the pride in the factories, the electric power works, and the dams, all reminiscent of what used to be American boastfulness as a national trait. The only country in the world where one could conceive of the publication of a magazine like *Fortune,* outside the United States, is Soviet Russia.

Or to put it another way: if one can imagine America going on pretty much unaffected even if Communism disappeared from the world, it is much more difficult to envisage what would happen to Soviet Russia deprived of America as a model.

But in other countries besides Russia, such as England, France, Italy, and even Spain, the process of Americanization has been constantly on the increase ever since 1919. Had there been no Hitler and no Second World War, the chances are that the tendency toward an even greater Americanization of Europe would have continued if only because over a third of the business transactions of the world was carried on by America.

It is important to repeat, however, that this process of Americanization was very fragmentary. What the Americans have a tendency to take for granted, such as the improvement of the mechanical commodities of life, was precisely that which surprised the Europeans the most. By exporting such things as motor cars, refrigerators, radios, and other good gadgetry, America falsified, quite unintentionally, the real and important meaning of its contribution to this civilization of ours.

No one who has a refrigerator, a radio, and a car is in a position to say that these things are immaterial in comparison with the higher things of life. There is something profoundly irritating in a new school of thought, particularly virulent since America went to war, which preaches that the trouble with the American people is that they have spent the last twenty years in willful blindness, crass materialism, or selfish hedonism, thus neglecting the true values of life which are the constant fight for freedom, sacrifice, heroism, and so on.

Henry R. Luce wrote in *Life* magazine on December 22, 1941:

"This is the day of wrath. The disaster which befell America on December 7th, 1941, was an episode. But it was also a sign. It was a sign of all the weakness and wrongness of American life in recent years. The thousand-odd dead at Pearl Harbor that first day were not merely the victims of Japanese treachery. They were the victims also of a weak and faltering America that had lost its way and failed the world in leadership." [1]

To condemn the America of the last twenty years is just as futile and unfair as to condemn France for the same period. That both the Americans and the French, along with most other people, were slow to grasp the danger that confronted them is not to be disputed. But it is not *they* that sinned. Their trouble—our trouble—is that we have tried to live along like civilized human beings in spite of the fact that in our midst there was a people, the Germans, intent on bringing us all down to their level of barbarism. It may have been foolish. It certainly was improvident and dangerous. It was not wicked nor sinful. In any event the choice has never been and should not be, I hope, between freedom and a refrigerator, brotherly love and good food, tolerance and air conditioning.

Nevertheless it so happens that America's success in producing contraptions which have improved the material

[1] *Life*, Vol. II, No. 25.

comfort of a large number of people coincided with the withdrawal of its influence in other fields (political isolationism). As a result there has been an increase in the world-wide modern tendency to oppose the wickedness of materialism to the hypothetical holiness of some kind of sacrificial heroism now required from humanity to save itself.

To sum up: whereas the American way of life as seen by most foreigners expresses itself in terms of more bathtubs, more commercialization of everything (including religion and sex appeal), more money and more success measured by money, the American way of life perceived by the Americans themselves has another meaning. This meaning is considerably more valuable for the good of our Western World at this moment than is usually realized.

Of course Americans are not interested merely in the higher aspects of Americanism. In fact they themselves have considerable difficulty when they try to express what this thing is which they possess and think worth while and could share with other people. But I believe that only Americans—and perhaps not a majority of them—are beginning now to have a dim perception of the kind of spiritual and intellectual support they can give, and must give, to the structure of Western civilization if it is to overcome the present Germanic revolt and carry on into the future.

2. *Americanism versus Germanism*

The opposition between Germanism and Americanism is more fundamental and irreconcilable than that between Germanism and any other national outlook, and this in spite of the fact that the Americans have a tendency to prefer the Germans to other Europeans.

This may seem a paradox. I have already noted that one of the basic traits of Americanism is opposition to Europe en bloc, and that to be American is, to a certain extent, to be anti-European. Nevertheless the American temperament shows different reactions toward the various peoples of Europe. There has been on the whole more admiration and sympathy toward the German people than toward any other because the kind of Germany that the Americans usually knew was indeed more hospitable, cleaner, and more efficient than, for instance, England or France. Moreover the Germans had pushed the process of superficial Americanization farther than any other European people. This quite naturally incited the American to believe in the progressiveness of Germany. Finally German science and German methodology have had a profound influence on the American system of education.

I should mention also the natural sympathy of the Americans for the underdog. The Germans have played up that theme for twenty years. Hitler's theory that Germany has been forced to take justice into her own hands against a wicked world may be somewhat threadbare by now, but one cannot forget the response that such a theory found in America up to a very recent past. American generosity accepted the picture of a victimized Germany and admired all the more the courage and patience of the hard-working, efficient German people.[1]

But in spite of all the superficial favors that have been lavished on Germany by a certain form of American sentimentality, it remains that it is impossible to conceive of two outlooks more radically different in all essential respects than the German and the American.

Even the French, notwithstanding their position as

---

[1] If it is a characteristic of the Germans always to be sorry for themselves, it is an American one to be sorry for someone else. A long list could be drawn of the people who have stirred the compassion of America, such as the Armenians, the Belgians, the Hindus, the Jews, and the Germans themselves. If this is an American "weakness," it is certainly less distasteful than the German self-pity.

hereditary enemies of the Germans, could stand a certain amount of Teutonic influence without necessarily losing their identity as Frenchmen, and provided also that this influence was not the kind that exerts itself through organized looting, military oppression, and the shooting of hostages. As for the English, experience has shown that they are extraordinarily apt at compromising even with the devil without suffering very much by it themselves, thanks to their unique faculty of believing that things will come out all right for them in the end, somehow or other. If at times they can be compared to the ostrich, it is not so much for their ability to bury their heads in the sand in order not to see the danger as for the elasticity of their stomach which enables them to tolerate the coexistence of any ideas and any systems without indigestion.

But the Americans, by the very nature of their make-up as a nation, cannot show such tolerance toward the set of doctrines which form the basis of present-day Germany. The doctrine of racialism, for instance, which constitutes the cornerstone of Nazi philosophy, is obviously incompatible with the American concept of the nation based on the equality of races. Nothing is further from Hitler's ethnological ideas than the process of the "melting pot."

The same applies to America's conception of Christianity as opposed to the tendency of the Germans to institute a kind of state religion founded on the mysticism of blood and soil, the sword, racial purity, and other non-Christian concepts.

America's attitude toward the problems of religion is unique in the sense that although the Americans as a whole cannot be considered as particularly devout nor even very much interested in religious problems, they nevertheless consider themselves as a thoroughly religious people and more specifically a Christian one. The word *Christian*, in America, has been extended in its meaning. It is connected with the notion of democracy (as the Americans understand it), of humanitarianism, with a general outlook on life which includes being a good citizen, a good family man. It embraces the American concept of progress (in both the moral and material sense). American Christianity seldom concerns itself with mysticism or with higher problems of dogma. The average American, so curious and questioning in all other fields of thought, is strangely passive in matters connected with religion. The Christian point of view, in the peculiarly broad and undefinable sense that is given to it in America, is accepted without discussion as the only one valid nationally. The church, or rather the churches, have retained their place institutionally, in spite of the fact that they have lost ground constantly as a means of binding the individuals together socially. There is no state religion in America, but there is a kind of diluted and polymorphous national religious point of view which is called Christian, and which is all the stronger because it is so thoroughly adogmatic, diffuse, and indistinguishable from Americanism itself.

It should be remembered too that America, contrary to all European nations, has not known the classical conflicts between church and state. For this reason it is all the more difficult for the Americans to understand and accept such conflicts, especially when they assume the virulent form that opposes the Nazi dogma of the supremacy of the state and of the race to the Christian concepts. Perhaps more than any other Western people the Americans will generally tend to blame the state rather than the church when there is a clash between them.

In the case of Nazi Germany, the persecution of the churches has certainly aroused more indignation in America than in any country in Europe. One might even say that these persecutions have shocked the ordinary American more than they seem to have shocked the churches themselves. At any rate, this is certainly true as far as the Catholic Church is concerned, whose attitude in the present world conflict has not given the impression that it was blinded by a sense of righteous indignation.

The opposition between America's political outlook and that of the Germans is even more profound. Indeed it would be impossible to conceive of two points of view more radically and totally incompatible than that of the Americans and the Germans.

It would be tedious to review in detail the points of antagonism between the two systems, but certain broad differences may be recalled.

One of the most striking characteristics of the American system of government and of the political philosophy that supports it is the fact that they were established by men who had the opportunity and the ability to think of what they were doing not only in terms of the present, but with an eye on the future and a competent knowledge of the past. More than any other document of its kind, the Constitution is the product of intelligence. It was worked on by men who were not subject to the pressure of public passion and who, consciously and conscientiously, set out to study the lessons of history in order to build a system that would eliminate some of the most glaring defects of government, as shown by past experience, and that would endure.

Such an undertaking could have been attempted only in America at that time, that is, in a new country where a new nation was being born. The authors of the American Constitution were inspired by precedents, but these precedents were taken outside of the American experience and therefore chosen objectively. England, France, Rome, and Greece furnished ideas to the authors of the Constitution, but what made their work so profoundly original was pre-

cisely the unique opportunity given to them to prefabri-
cate, so to speak, a new system of government for a new
nation.

The Bill of Rights, as well as most of the documents
which have served to build up the political philosophy of
the American people, proceeds from the same principles.
Taken altogether, the Constitution gives the impression
of a construction based on as much reasonableness as it is
possible for human beings to apply to such an effort under
the most favorable circumstances.

For instance, two of the cardinal principles of the American system—the notion of "government by law and not
by men," and the general concept of check and balances
—are typical of a high form of rationalism as well as of
plain human understanding. The ideas may not be original and indeed they have been the subject of debate from
Aristotle to Montesquieu, but the important fact is that
the authors of the American Constitution were able to put
to a practical test abstract political thoughts.

Contemporary Americans have a tendency to attribute
to the Fathers of the Constitution some kind of superhuman powers. They are collectively endowed with an
insight into the future which has given to their work the
magic of divinely inspired documents. The prevalent idea
is that the American system, as it has been handed down
from the past, is so good that it can hardly be improved
and that it will very likely endure forever.

This patriotic mysticism probably cannot be helped, but
it has the inconvenience of befogging, and in a way dwarf-
ing, the work accomplished by the creators of the American system. These men were not superhuman. They were
merely, in general, intelligent and very well-informed.
They received no divine inspiration, but they had the rare
opportunity of being able to exert their intelligence with-

out too much interference from the mob and with the minimum of pressure from prejudices.

The result is certainly not perfect and there is no telling how long it can endure, but it is so much better than any similar construction that the Americans can certainly be excused for thinking that it took a special intervention of Providence to give them a system of government not completely unreasonable.

That fact alone—that the Constitution is the product of rational thinking by reasonable men—opposes the American system to the German on all scores.

The guiding principle of the American system is the recognition that men are rational beings and that there is no way to accomplish any good except through the process of reason. The guiding principle of Germanism, as it has developed for over one hundred years and has found its perfect expression in Hitlerism, is irrationalism.

It may be argued that there are many aspects of Americanism which are irrational too. The set of beliefs, for instance, which support the faith in democracy are, like all beliefs, difficult to rationalize completely. There will always be people who will argue that there is no way of proving that freedom is better than slavery, order under the law preferably to tyranny by force, tolerance more commendable than organized repression. It is true that democracy and everything it stands for appear preferable only when one loses them. But if it is often difficult to prove by the logic of words why one thing is better than another, the fact remains that certain things are better than certain other things. The kind of modern sophistry which has tried to undermine democracy under the pretense that there was no standard by which one could prove why freedom was better than tyranny, nor why Hitler was less democratically representative of the German people than is Roosevelt of the American, nor why the German doctrine of might makes right was not just as sound as the notion of abstract justice—this type of sophistry has not changed the reality in which we find ourselves. It has only wasted an incalculable amount of time for those who have taken an interest in it, that is, a very large part of the educated public in Europe and an even larger one in America, for over twenty years.

The important thing to keep in mind is that the American people, however irrational they may appear in some respects, remain purposefully dedicated to the fundamental principles which inspired the founders of their nation one hundred and fifty years ago. And first among these principles is the conviction that human beings have no better guide than reason, with all the rigors that the exercise of reason implies.

Speaking to the German soldiers on December 21, 1941, Adolf Hitler said: "After fifteen years of work I have achieved as a common German soldier and *merely with my fanatical will power* the unity of the German nation and have freed it from the death sentence of Versailles."

This language is very far from that of the *Federalist*.

3. The growth of America as a world power

When one considers the problems of America in its relation to the outside world from the classical point of view of power, the fact that the United States is now at war with Germany and its Axis partners appears as the unavoidable and perfectly logical development of this century.

The war of 1914-1918 exhausted all the Allies as much as it exhausted Germany. But the policy of pacifism and compromise which was followed by England and France during the years that preceded the Second World War— while the Germany of Hitler was feverishly arming—had as a result that the strength of Germany was relatively much greater in 1939 than it was in 1914. This strength should not be measured in armaments alone—although the superiority in this field was tremendous. One must take into account also the psychological and moral factors.

When Germany went to war in 1914, it had but one ally: the Austro-Hungarian Empire, which was more of a liability than an asset. In a short while the most powerful nations of the world, France, England, Russia, Italy, Japan, were aligned against it. As the war progressed, Germany gained no important ally, except Turkey, while the Allied camp finally comprised nearly all the nations of the world, including the United States.

But when Hitler went to war in 1939, only two major powers were opposed to him: England and France. Italy was in his camp. Russia was more than neutralized. In less than a year, practically the whole of continental Europe was under German domination. The French Army, the most dangerous threat from the German point of view, was destroyed. England for several months literally stood alone facing Germany.

At the end of June 1940, there was no reason to believe that Hitler had not won the war. All the mistakes of 1914 had been avoided. There had been no "miracle" of the Somme, nor of the Marne, nor of the Seine. Hitler had entered Paris. There was no more French Army.

Moreover there was no British Army either. A few hundred thousand men had escaped from Dunkirk, leaving behind all their equipment. The situation which had been the dream of all German strategists for so many years had come true. Germany had defeated all the armies opposed to it. It had no enemy to fight. As Hitler said at the time: "I see no reason why the war should go on."

If one accepts the thesis of the periodicity of Germanic rebellion against the Occident as one of the dominating themes of history, it can be said that in the summer of 1940, the German revolt initiated in 1914 had finally succeeded. Hitler was right, from his point of view, to consider the struggle over. In the minds of most Germans, including Hitler, domination of the land meant domination of the earth. The old theory of Admiral Mahan had been superseded by the *geopolitics* of Professor Haushofer, who had showed that once Germany ruled continental Europe, the powers that controlled the sea, and particularly England, would finally have to surrender. The weapons of modern warfare, and particularly the airplane, coupled with the formidable possibilities of production of a continent like Europe working as a unit under one master race, would give the victorious Germans such superiority that no sea power could match it.

At the time of writing, no definite answer can be given to the question of whether a power that possesses superiority of land armaments can finally defeat the powers that control the seas. The quarrel between Mahan and Haushofer is not settled. It probably will not be settled conclusively in this war, first of all because military theories (like all theories) are finally wrecked by human experience, and second, because as this war develops, it tends to become amphibious on both sides. The Germans may not be considered a sea power, but their submarines and their planes compensate their lack of surface craft. Besides, the Japanese are their allies. They have a powerful navy. On the other hand, the Allied powers are fighting on land as actively as on the sea and the chances are that as the war progresses it will become more and more difficult to determine the respective superiority of each side in any particular domain. They tend toward an equilibrium now.

But if this is so today, it does not make it less remarkable that in the summer of 1940, after the defeat of France, Hitler was not able to complete successfully the last and most successful of all Teutonic rebellions against the West.

The immediate reasons for this are not all apparent as yet. Strategic and psychological mistakes were obviously made by the German command. According to the logic of a people conditioned by the conceptions of land warfare, there was no reason—in fact no excuse—for England, deprived of the French Army and without any army of her own to speak of, to carry on the fight. England should have conceded defeat when France did. The German High Command and most experts in other countries certainly thought that there was no other choice. For England to prolong resistance appeared futile and—to some—nearly criminal.

England, however, decided not to give in, and the story of what happened need not be repeated here. After fighting alone against apparently hopeless odds, England began to organize its defenses, to make an army, to produce armaments. It began also to receive help from America in a way that made its position every day less precarious. In the spring of 1941, Hitler added Russia to the list of England's Allies. In December 1941, America was finally plunged into war by the Japanese aggression on Pearl Harbor and the war declaration of Germany and Italy. By the end of 1941, less than two and a half years after the Second World War began, a year and a half after the defeat of France, the appalling handicap under which the Western coalition had started was practically wiped out. Germany had a strong ally, Japan, and a weak one, Italy. Arraigned against it there was once more a strong bloc of nations whose resources in man power and raw materials were potentially greater than its own. The Allies were still due, according to logical calculations, to suffer many more reverses and many setbacks, but by the beginning of 1942 an objective appraisal of the situation taken as a whole showed that the chances of success of the great German revolt of the twentieth century were much less good than in the summer of 1940.

How this came to pass, how it happened that once more Germany actually failed to obtain victory as it had failed in 1914, is written in the events which took place after June 1940.

It is currently said that the magnificent and unexpected awakening of the British people achieved this. And this is true. But back of this new "miracle" there is a logic. The reason why the British, under the inspiration of Winston Churchill, resolved to sacrifice all they had rather than surrender may appear as one of those extraordinary acts of blind heroism which, once in a thousand times, are repaid. But if it was indeed heroism, and of the purest kind, it was not blind nor even reckless. The men who led England at the time may or may not have been clearly conscious of the fundamental factors which influenced their decision. But had they been, they would not have acted otherwise.

It is not detracting from the heroism of the British leaders to say that they could not have decided to fight on after the fall of France had they not been sure that sooner or later America would have to stand by them.

There is nothing selfish in such calculations. In fact such thoughts or intuitions can come only to men of Winston Churchill's or Franklin Roosevelt's type, who, however different they may be in many respects, are endowed with the rare gift of being able to visualize the events and their development from the point of view of what Churchill himself calls "the grand proportions of history."

I have not the pretention to know whether Roosevelt's and Churchill's conceptions of history coincide. The chances are that on many points they do not. But it is obvious to anyone who has read their speeches and their books that they view the broader aspects of the present conflict very much in the same manner. Both men are not only sincere but practically immutable in their conviction that this war cannot be understood as a mere episode of our times; that the only way to judge it and cope with it is to situate it in the perspective of centuries; that therefore, in spite of its apparent complications, it can be reduced to fairly simple terms. It is the fight between two conceptions of life that cannot possibly be reconciled. Such a fight has occurred before. The fact that it is recurring today in such a cataclysmic form shows the power and permanence of the forces at work.

4. No choice for America

There is no hindsight in saying today that America's participation in this war was certain enough, from the very day it began to enable the British to base their course of action on that eventuality. This was predetermined as far back as 1917 when it was shown, more or less clearly, that even then the nations of the West might not have been able to resist this first act of the twentieth century German revolt without the help of America.

From then on there was no question of America's being able to remain neutral in case of another war provided there was a danger that Germany might win. Events which seem to prove the contrary should not deceive us. The only reason why the Senate of the United States could repudiate the Covenant of the League of Nations and Versailles in 1920 was because there was no danger in sight. The reason that, for the next twenty years, America could practice isolationism, and wrap itself up in neutrality acts and other forms of restriction, was because democracies are ultrasensitive to immediate currents of opinion and incredibly inert when it comes to long-range views. A speech of yesterday or a news item in today's newspapers will be enough to swing a parliamentary majority which will remain totally unmoved by an appeal based on more vital but less immediate contingencies.

But ever since Hitler came to power, it can be said that American opinion has been kept on the alert in such a way that it has never been allowed to go to sleep for one day.

This was done first of all by the American press. No other country has had a corps of foreign correspondents comparable to that of the United States during the last ten years or so. Not only were these men and women competent technically and highly conscientious, but it so happened that, with a handful of negligible exceptions, they were unanimous in their diagnosis of the situation in Europe. They started ringing the alarm as soon as they looked at Hitler and the Nazis and they have never stopped since. What that diagnosis was is written in their cables and in their books. By and large, allowing for individual variations, it coincides with the thesis of this book: that Hitlerian Germany is out to overthrow what we call civilization and cannot be stopped except by force.

These ideas have become so banal by now that one feels a scruple in wasting paper to write them on. But one should not forget that those who made them understandable and popular—the American correspondents abroad—started in an atmosphere of disbelief and suspicion. It took courage to describe what Nazism was about, seven years ago. The proof of it is that in the meanwhile the European press, whether British or French, was carrying on its soporific messages to the public with the result that the French, for instance, in spite of being nearer to the enemy than anyone, never grasped the real nature of the peril that threatened them—not even after they were actually at war with Germany, not even after the defeat, as far as their leaders were concerned.

But the American correspondents alone could not have accomplished the job of forcing American opinion to look at the facts. The greatest credit must go to President Roosevelt, who started a one-man relentless campaign of popular education regardless of the opposition and even the hatred it created. Those who remember the reaction that followed the famous speech of October 5, 1937, in which the President suggested that aggressor nations should be put "in quarantine," can measure the magnitude of the task accomplished. History may find that the part played by Franklin Roosevelt in awakening the American people was as great as that played by Winston Churchill in England. Moreover it required the coincidence that two such men should be at the helm of their respective nations to enable the Western World to resist the Hitlerian onslaught against it.

It is not within the scope of this book to review the evolution of American opinion from the time it voted the first Neutrality Act in 1935 to December 1941 when Congress declared war unanimously on the Axis powers. In preceding chapters I have tried to describe the underlying opposition to war that permeated all the people engaged in this war, under one form or another. The history of the evolution of American opinion from a position of rigorous aloofness to all-out war can be written in terms of this antiwar sentiment. The story would be one of a long, step-by-step resistance against the complete involvement in war, finally made impossible by the aggression of the Japanese at Pearl Harbor.

But a broader view of the situation would show that America's reluctance to go to war and all the efforts made to avoid this outcome were as useless from the very start

as were the efforts of all other countries in the path of the
German rebellion.

America had been aligned against Germany in 1917 and
served to defeat it then; there was no doubt that it would
be aligned against Germany again in this second attempt.
The growth of American power during these twenty years
of truce and the relative weakening of European members
of the Western coalition against a new German attack
forced America into the position of becoming the most
important factor in this second coalition.

From the day that war started in September 1939, it
became obvious that America's material support was indispensable to compensate the Allies' inferiority in this
respect. By the time France fell in June 1940, the chances
that Germany could be prevented from winning the war
without America's full participation were practically nil.
Such expressions as "all-out aid to Britain," "methods
short of war," "America, arsenal of democracy," and the
distinction made between a "shooting war" and other
kinds of war, mark the steps by which public opinion came
around to accept what it had known to be unavoidable
all along. The choice for America never was between making war on the side of England or keeping out of war.
The choice was between the quasi certainty of a German
victory if America stayed out and a good chance of preserving the continuity of this civilization if America threw
in its lot against Germany.

CHAPTER II

The Road before Us

THE philosophically minded may find consolation in
the thought that the complex and all-embracing crisis which it is the destiny of this generation to live
through is not the first one that humanity has known.
Several times before, as history records, there have been
upheavals as profound as this one, wars and revolutions
which in the eyes of their contemporaries marked the end
of an era, and perhaps the end of the world. Our ancestors
had even more reasons than we to be scared and disarmed
by such convulsions. Their limited knowledge of history
led them to exaggerate the magnitude of the disasters
which afflicted them. They lacked points of comparison.
But more especially they lacked the remarkable optimism
which is characteristic of the modern man. Being more
aware than we are of the wickedness of mankind and more
inclined to believe in the visible manifestation of Divine
Justice, they could never be sure that a great crisis was not
a punishment from God. Neither could they be certain
that the wrath of the Almighty would always be tempered
at the last minute by His compassion for the frailty of
man and that He would give man another reprieve.

Up to only a few hundred years ago our forefathers
were anything but bullish on the prospects of humanity.
All through the Middle Ages the end of the world had

been prophesied many times and although it had not come, few were those who would have dared to bet heavy odds against an abrupt, final, and not too distant intervention of the Creator which would bring to an end the story of Adam on this earth.

Today, for a variety of reasons, we do not believe that the end of the world is at hand. We do not even think that humanity, or even a considerable portion of it, can be wiped off this earth, although the now-combined forces of war, starvation, and disease can be focused on certain sections of the map at the will of a conqueror and with devastating results. Before this war is over, we may see whole nations exterminated. We may see others so crippled in their moral and physical health that it may take several generations for them to recover. We already see that what was considered a normal standard of nutrition, heat, light, clothing, and general comfort for a man of the twentieth century can be lowered to the level of chronic suffering. We know that hunger, maltreatment, mental and physical torture can become the normal condition under which millions of men, women, and children live, and that it is the plan of their masters that they should go on living in this manner. We know that slavery can be reinstituted—and that it is reinstituted now over large sections of Europe. We see that centuries of arduous progress in the direction of more humanity and more intelligence can be wiped out in a few years, that entire peoples can be made to act against their better self and think against their own reason. The youth of Germany, for instance, can be taught to follow blindly on the path of death and destruction the call of a fool, whose abysmal mediocrity is mistaken for genius because it is seen through the fantastic deformations of a neurosis attuned to that of a whole nation. We know that in our midst some have become vulnerable to poisons to which, up to recently, there was reason to believe that intelligent men had been made immune. Serious books and articles are written about the "Jewish problem" as if the very fact that such stuff is printed and read were not already a proof of the progress of the perversion that these writings pretend to eradicate.

War is a great stultifier, and for America as for any other country at war, it will be hard to avoid the dishonesty, the prejudices, the lies, and the blind passions that breed so naturally under the cloak of patriotism. If the war is long, it will be harder for the Americans to maintain their standard of thinking than their standard of living. As with all other people engulfed in this war before them, the tendency will be toward a lowering of the moral and intellectual level, all the more difficult to resist, or even detect, in that the movement downward will be unanimous, a byproduct of national unity.

But in spite of this, the chances are that the hardships of America will be less, in the process of winning this war, than those suffered by its Allies. Even when America devotes 50 per cent of its productive capacity to the war, the way Germany has been doing for six or seven years and England for a shorter space of time, the consequences for the individual American citizen will not be so severe by a wide margin. Restrictions are already in force and many more will follow. The ordinary citizen will have to give up many things which, although not essential, have become symbolical of America's better way of life. Motor cars, radios, refrigerators, mechanical appliances of all kinds, and in general all such objects which the average American has considered more or less indispensable will be unobtainable. But this will not cause real suffering. As far as one can predict there will be enough food, enough heat, enough light, and enough clothes. America, in other words, will remain considerably better off than its partners in this war, and be relatively unexhausted at the end of it.

These predictions are naturally based on the assumption that the war will be won by the Allies. Should there be another outcome, it goes without saying that the relative advantages which America is expected to maintain throughout the coming years would be wiped out. One can confidently expect that the Axis powers, if they are victorious, will plunder America with the same thoroughness with which they have plundered Europe.

1. It is hard to wake up

But as things stand at the moment this book is written, the reasonable prospects are that Germany's latest rebellion against the West can be defeated as well as Japan's provided the full moral and physical force of America is thrown in. No piecemeal effort can ensure that result and it would now be futile to rely on other nations to do the actual fighting. America may have to take the major brunt of the war before it is won.

There is no doubt that the American people as a whole are not eager to assume the responsibility which is now thrust upon them. The attack on Pearl Harbor and the reverses in the Far East certainly dispelled many illusions and tore some of the fabric of wishful thinking. But in spite of this, there is no certainty that the mass of the people are quite aware as yet of the vital character of the conflict. I have already noted how Pearl Harbor, although analogous to Dunkirk, has not had such a deep and lasting effect on the American mind. The leaders of opinion, and first of all the President, are no doubt aware that when they say that the very existence of America is now at stake and with it the whole future of Western civilization, they are not using a figure of speech. They know that the peril is real, that in all their history the American people have never had to face anything comparable to it, that it is really the first time that this nation is indeed threatened by forces that intend to destroy it, and that *can* destroy it.

But this realistic view, if it exists in the leaders' minds, is naturally slow to penetrate the consciousness of the people. For them, in spite of Pearl Harbor, the loss of Singapore and of the Dutch East Indies, the issue of the war is not in doubt. They believe that the war will certainly be won for the sufficient reason that America has now got into it. They believe that it was unfortunate that the Japanese and the Germans should have forced the United States into war and thus deprived them of the advantage of choosing for themselves the moment of going to war. They have thus lost the initiative. This awful Damocles sword, the entrance of the United States into the war, which the Americans thought they held firmly in their hands, and which was, in a sense, the strongest weapon that America possessed before December 7, 1941, has been wrested from them and made harmless by the treachery of the Japanese attack. But in spite of this reversal, the bad effects of which are as great from the psychological as from the military point of view, the mass of the American people still think that the loss of initiative is only temporary, and that automatically it will come back to them, not so much through an enormous material and moral effort on their part as by the natural effect of some sort of immanent justice which makes it impossible for the American people not to be stronger than any other people on earth and therefore in the predestined position of always being victorious in the end.

Hanson W. Baldwin, military critic of the *New York Times,* wrote as follows, the day after Manila fell to the Japanese:

"We are still complacent. We still display what Homer Lea described in a book of the same name as 'the valor of ignorance'; we are still 'slothful with fat pride.' Far too few of us understand that this war upon which we are joined is a war to the death, a war for life itself, a war the outcome of which is by no means certain. . . . But above all they [the recent defeats] should awaken the American people to the fact —which to too many of them seems fantasy—that we *can* lose the war, that nothing is foregone except struggle. We *can* lose the war; but we won't—if the nation works and sweats and bleeds for victory."

The day before this article was published, on January 2, 1942, the *New York Times* presented a series of eight photographs of men and women interviewed in Times Square on New Year's Eve, under the caption, "Wishes for the coming year."

Here are the wishes of these eight citizens:

A young woman: "I wish that the war will be over soon, with the United States the victor."

A middle-aged man: "I wish good luck for everybody and a short war with a United States victory."

A middle-aged woman: "I wish that the war will be over quickly so that our boys will not have to fight."

A young man: "I wish the war would end quickly and of course victoriously for us."

A young woman: "I wish for a solid month's vacation starting right now."

A soldier: "I wish for a speedy victory."

A young man: "I wish that there will be no difficulty in my entering college."

Another young man: "I wish that I had all the money in the world so that I could buy the things I want for myself and my friends."

It would be unfair to attach too much importance to these eight answers. They do not have the scientific pretensions of a Gallup poll. The only curious fact is that America's most authoritative newspaper should choose to publish these particular samples of *voces populi* at such a moment.

In the same paper, Hanson Baldwin wrote:

"And the elements making for a survival in a predatory world are a concentrated singlemindedness upon one aim—victory—a complete national willingness to subordinate all else to this end, and a vigor and energy of purpose that no pain or toil or trouble, no reverse or defeat can dampen."

In France during the period called the "phony war" people were encouraged to be not only confident but optimistic. They believed in an ultimate victory arrived at by the magic and automatic interplay of predestination. Those who had a pessimistic view of the situation were denounced as defeatists and as working for the enemy. Unfortunately these accusations were most of the time well founded, because the great majority of the French "realists" had no solution to recommend except some sort of compromise with the enemy or capitulation. A handful of them, without despairing of success, thought that this success could be achieved only by a radical transformation of the conditions of living and especially by a fundamental change in the attitude of mind of the people. This could not be done. The French, within a space of a few days, saw the whole fabric of their peaceful life torn to shreds. With practically no warning, war and destruction were upon them. Within a few hours, people who had been enjoying the miraculous monotony of an easy life in a great city like Paris were fleeing on the roads, suffering from hunger, thirst, fatigue, and terror. Those who had been "slothful with fat pride" were now running for their lives in an atmosphere of panic and shame.

This was the end of the "phony war" in France as well as the end of war itself.

It would be foolish to liken the situation in America today to that of France then. Roosevelt is not Daladier. American public opinion has a few bad leaders, but it has many good ones who are wide-awake. The standard of the American newspapers has undoubtedly suffered by the process of stultification which accompanies unfailingly the state of war, but compared with the French press during the beginning of the war, it might be said that American journalism is making a sincere effort to resist the frightful temptation to deceive a public, which still finds it very hard to believe that there is actual danger.

Nevertheless one has to recognize that America must, like every other nation before it, go through the queer evolution which was called the "phony war" in France. It is a phase of adaptation to war rendered all the more difficult and painful because this world—as I have tried to show in previous chapters—had sincerely renounced war. The Americans, in this respect, were like the French. Most of them knew in their bones that they could not escape war. But up to the very day that the Japanese attacked Hawaii, they actually did not believe that it could happen. There were too many reasons, all apparently very valid, why the Japanese and the Germans should not provoke America—as there were too many reasons back in 1939 why the Germans should not force England and France to go to war against them. But these reasons, however plausible, were superficial and even irrelevant. It may be that, in the long run, the Japanese will not be able to sustain their war effort for the same reasons that the Germans will not be able to sustain theirs. But it is now clear that the Japanese gamble is not crazier than the German. It is not crazier than the whole attempt on the part of the German world to overthrow reason,

Christianity, and everything for which classical civilization stands. The Japanese have other motives than those
of the Germans, but their aim is identical. Given the
premise that the deep significance of this war is an assault
on the Occident, there is nothing absurd, nor perhaps
even foolhardy, in the Japanese decision to strike at America and the British Empire now.

2. *Toward a new world outlook*

The Japanese break-through in the Southern Pacific was
analogous to the German break-through at Sedan. The
United Nations command was as unprepared for this move
and as stunned by it as was the French command when the
panzer divisions crossed the reputedly impassable River
Meuse. The only difference, luckily for America, is that
Malaya is considerably farther from any American vital
center than are the Ardennes from Paris.

In spite of these obvious geographical advantages in
favor of America, in spite also of the immensely superior
resources of the country, one cannot help but feel that tremendous changes must still take place in the public mind
before the urgency of the peril is fully realized and before
the corresponding efforts necessary to meet it are made.

Some of these changes concern the acceptance of restrictions, as well as a training of public morale in order that
the reaction to the good and bad news of the war will become more rational. The French never had time to learn
the difficult art of resisting the impulse to be either over-
optimistic or desperate in the presence of the kind of war
news that was dished out to them by a hopelessly incom-
petent information ministry. As for the British, it has
taken them many months to reach the levelheadedness
and equanimity which is one of their strongest weapons
now. There is no reason to believe that, allowing for

differences of temperament, the Americans will not attune themselves to this new and distorting vision of reality which comes through the fact that a nation goes to war.

But there are other changes more difficult and more profound which may have to be accepted by American opinion if this war is not to end in some sort of unpredictable chaos.

These changes affect certain fundamental problems of America as a nation and its relation to the rest of the world. They involve a whole series of instinctive reactions and possibly a reappraisal of the whole destiny of America as one commonly views it through the orthodox teachings of history and popular prejudices.

For instance, the American people will have to answer the following questions:

Should America renounce forever the policy of isolation? If this is answered in the affirmative, should America accept boldly the responsibility of asserting its leadership in the reconstruction of the world which will follow this war if it is not won by Germany and its allies?

History shows that America has always been torn by two conflicting tendencies in its dealings with the outside world. The first one is called isolationism.

Isolationism is an expression of what has been called the American dream. In other words it is a conception of American destiny according to which the most sacred national duty is to preserve this nation from outside interference in order to create on this continent a better world. According to this theory, the rest of the world, and more particularly Europe, can only breed revolutions, wars, and misery. America is the predestined land on which a new and regenerated humanity can hope to purify itself from the dangerous tyrannies and corruptions of the Old World. America, therefore, must be insulated as much as possible.

Consider these words by Herbert Hoover spoken on September 16, 1941:

"To most Americans, Europe consists of magnificent cities, cathedrals, cafés, art, music, literature, great universities and monuments to heroism and human progress. Men among them have fought and died for liberty to lift the dignity of man. From them all we have received magnificent heritage of human thought.

"But other forces make the fates of these people. Here are 400,000,000 people on the Continent divided into twenty-six races. They are crowded cheek by jowl in an area less than two thirds of the United States. Suppose each of twenty-six of our states had its own language, its own racial inheritance, its own economic and political problem.[1]

"And suppose through all these races for centuries have surged the forces of nationalism, of imperialism, of religious conflict, memories of deep wrongs, of age-old hates, and bitter fears. . . .

"In contrast here in America during these 400 years since our beginnings *we have grown steadily apart from the ideas of Europe. Every one of our ancestors came here to get away from this dread turmoil.* Ours has been a continent of magnificent resources. . . ."

Herbert Hoover is not exactly an original thinker. That is why it is interesting to find in his words such a pure expression of America's persistent dream to constitute a

[1] This kind of fallacious comparison between Europe and America can produce only incomprehension. It is as vital for Europe to preserve the principle of its national and cultural diversity under some form or another as it is important for the forty-eight states of the Union to be united. To apply the American regime to Europe would be as fatal to Europe as the separation of the forty-eight states of the Union would be fatal to America.

kind of refuge for the downtrodden and an escape for the just.

The isolationist Utopia has broken down time and time again. America has taken part in all the major wars since the end of the eighteenth century. But after each such excursion there has been a return to the dream of aloofness and escapism.

It might be said in passing that the wish to be left alone by other nations is not exclusively American. Most of the twenty-six European nations of which Hoover talks, with the exception of predatory Germany, would have liked nothing better than to remain isolated from every other nation. For instance, I know no people, including the Americans, in which the isolationist spirit was more obvious and more passionately expressed than in the French.

What is peculiar to America is that it should have been possible to transform a perfectly normal though unrealizable dream into a national policy. The reason why this has been possible is both geographic and historical. For the longest part of its history, America was at once too far away and too weak to clash with the big powers of the world. Moreover Europe during the whole of the nineteenth century, that is, during the major part of America's development, was engaged in industrial and usually peaceful developments. America was one of the beneficiaries of this development, not a rival. Later on, after the First World War, America found itself suddenly in a position of such strength and wealth in relation to the other large nations that it could actually impose its aloofness as a national policy. Thus the continuity of the isolationist policy was made possible (1) because America was weak for the early part of its history, and (2) because it became so powerful after the war of 1914-1918 that there was no challenger to this power before the advent of the present Axis coalition.

In contrast with this isolationist current, there has always existed in America a spirit of reform which has sometimes taken the more intensive form of the crusade. This tendency springs from the same deep sources according to which America is a favored land in which a chosen people are destined to create a better life. While the isolationists conclude from this premise that it is America's duty to insulate itself, the reformers feel that it is America's mission to set an example for the whole world and have the whole world benefit by it.

There are as many shades of the missionary conception of America as there are of isolationism. Some believe that America's intervention in the affairs of the outside world should limit itself to philanthropic works. Others think that America should lead what might be called a normal international life and subscribe to the same kind of obligations as other nations. There are those too who go further, and think it is America's destiny to impose its ideas and its methods on other people, by persuasion or, if need be, by force. This sentiment does not emanate from any conscious imperialism, but on the contrary from the conviction that *Pax Americana* is the best way to give security and prosperity to the planet.

The two contradictory currents of isolationism and reform have had, up to now, one trait in common: They took too little account of the reality of the world as it is. The fundamental reason for this, as I have said before, is that America has been up to now in the privileged, or unfortunate, position of being able to ignore most of that reality. The chief reason that the partisans of the League of Nations failed in 1919 to swing American public opinion to their side is the same reason that the isolationists who dominated the policies of the United States for the next twenty years also failed to avoid war. Wilson had promised the American people that the Versailles Treaty and the Covenant of the League of Nations would show that Europe, at last, was repentant of its past errors and that the people of the Old World were now ready to mend their ways. The Versailles Treaty and the Covenant fell short of these promises and the American people rejected them. Similarly the isolationist theory was founded on the improbable premise that it was enough not to want certain things, such as war, for them not to happen.

3. Roosevelt leads the way

But today of course all this irrealism has been swept away, temporarily at least, under the impact of the war.

No doubt the two contradictory tendencies of isolationism and universal reform are still alive. The American people have not quite made up their mind as yet to accept unreservedly the new destiny that is thrust upon them.

It is true that President Roosevelt has done it for them. In his message to Congress of January 6, 1942, the following passages stand out:

"I know that I speak for the American people—and I have good reason to believe I speak also for all the other peoples who fight with us—when I say that this time we are determined not only to win the war but also to maintain the security of the peace which will follow. . . . We are fighting today for security, for progress and for peace, not only for ourselves but for all men, not only for one generation, but for all generations. We are fighting to cleanse the world of ancient evils, ancient ills."

Clearly President Roosevelt has made his choice. Isolationism, as far as he is concerned, is dead and condemned, and it is obviously his purpose to persuade the American people that there is no turning back. It is his conviction that winning this war would be hardly worth while if, after it is won, America withdrew from the peace, as it did in 1919. President Roosevelt, and with him an increasing number of his compatriots, are becoming thoroughly awake to the realities that confront them.

It may not matter much for the moment whether they interpret these realities in the same manner as I have done in this book. Most spokesmen on the side of the United Nations are loath to admit that the German people are really united behind Hitler and that National Socialism expresses something profoundly satisfactory to the German soul. They prefer to keep up the fiction that the Germans and the Japanese are the victims of militarism and that everything will go smoothly the day the Germans are liberated from the oppression of their present masters.

This kind of talk may still be necessary to placate democratic sensitiveness and the spirit of tolerance and human brotherhood in the name of which this war is waged. But there are signs that the democratic leaders are much more aware than the leaders of the last war of the implications of the present conflict. There is no question this time of a peace without victory. Moreover, there is a realization that the "ancient evils" and the "ancient ills" of the world, whatever may be their complexity and ramifications, have a way of becoming explosive and dangerous through the German problem. That problem is a fact. It will probably be easier to seek for its solution when Hitler is removed. But the mere removal of Hitler will not solve it. Whether one likes to recognize it or not, the United Nations are fighting Germany as well as Japan, and the defeat of Germany and Japan must be achieved before any sense of security can be restored to this world.

4. *Without America the West cannot be saved*

What that solution will be, as well as the solution of the other questions raised in this book, is not discernible now. The fact that there is such wide interest, particularly in America, in the future peace and in the world of tomorrow springs from a variety of motives: the first one is the real and deep abhorrence for war which exists in this democracy. The thought of peace is an incentive to carry on the war. The second is the indestructible American faith in human progress, according to which it is impossible to accept a war—even if it is one in which one's very existence is at stake—without the ulterior intention of making war serve to create a better world.

"We of the United Nations," said President Roosevelt in the message already quoted, "are not making all this sacrifice of human effort and human lives to return to the kind of world we had after the last World War."

This American desire to utilize this war as a means of transforming the world into something better is one of the main reasons why the entrance of the United States into the war has had such far-reaching psychological consequences. The outside world has for a long time been considerably more conscious than the Americans themselves that there is literally no salvation for Western civilization without positive leadership and inspiration from America. The time has now come for the Americans to understand and accept this truth.

The German conquest has dislocated the continent of Europe morally, politically, and economically to such a degree that there seems to be no other desire left among the conquered people than to get rid of the Germans, and in the meanwhile keep alive somehow or other. Beyond these aims, which are already difficult enough to achieve, there is no room for constructive speculation concerning the future. Europe today is in no condition to think of the Europe of tomorrow. To all intents and purposes, the Germans have indeed succeeded in wiping out civilization from continental Europe, at least temporarily.

England it is true is unconquered. But England has been too harassed and in a sense too abandoned for many months to be able to do anything more than recreate its own soul. And that indeed was enough.

This does not mean that Western civilization is forever doomed in Europe. In fact it is not possible to conceive of what we have called civilization without Europe. But the rehabilitation of Europe can hardly be achieved without the help of America.

This help can manifest itself in two essential ways: as an inspiration and as a moderating factor.

That America can act as an inspiration needs no demonstration. That it can also serve as a moderating factor in the reconstruction of the world of tomorrow is less obvious.

The very fact that America has come into the war so late has compensating advantages. It is physically intact at a moment when the other belligerents, friends and foes alike, are either thoroughly exhausted or feeling the strain of their effort. But more important still, America has moral reserves which have hardly been tried as yet. It is true that the cobwebs of twenty years of complacency and irrealism have not all been swept away. There is still a tendency to be very much alarmed for a very short time when some bad news breaks and to go back to sleep as soon as possible. President Roosevelt has not succeeded, at the time of writing, in communicating to all the necessary feeling of permanent urgency and relentless effort. But the chances are that the Germans and their allies will take care of that.

In any event it is not unreasonable to expect that America will see the war through by a process of internal adaptation which will not involve a radical break with the past. This adaptation to war will have drastic results and each citizen will feel it, but there are no signs as yet that this will mean structural changes in the political system or a different orientation of the American point of view on fundamental principles. For this reason, America will serve as a sort of bridge between the past and the future which is now in the making. It will assure the continuity of civilization, a role which no other nation is in a position to play now.

5. "On the side of life"

I have raised several questions in this book concerning the major trends which are discernible in these times of war and revolution. My purpose has not been to answer these questions, for the simple reason that I do not believe that anyone today can make a synthesis of the contradictions which they imply.

For instance, one of the worst evils of these times is nationalism. To say that nationalism is dangerous only when it becomes aggressive and excessive like the German brand of it does not answer the problem. Even if we suppose the elimination of German nationalism we shall still be faced with the problems emanating from the practice of unlimited national sovereignty and with the passion aroused in the heart of each human being whenever that ultrasensitive spot—patriotism—is touched.

It is perfectly obvious that, in time of war at least, patriotism is the supreme virtue. It is not obvious that we can rid ourselves of wars as long as no formula is found to prevent patriotism from degenerating into the kind of extreme nationalism which is today the greatest single force capable of moving men.

I have raised other questions concerning the position of

capitalism and socialism in relation to the evolution of democracy. It seems to me that what I have called the collectivist trend is an imperative which operates regardless of the political and philosophical systems. There is no reason to believe that the modern man can reverse the trend toward greater integration of the individual into an organized society. This is made necessary by the development of our industrial achievements and the interdependence among all men. But the practical consequence of this evolution appears to point toward certain curtailment of individual initiative and freedom which affects the capitalist as well as the worker, the farmer, and the clerk.

We are faced therefore with an apparently insoluble dilemma: either we have to set as our aim an increased production, a better distribution of goods, a better and more secure life for all, but at the cost of restricted freedom and possibly of a general lowering of the spirit of enterprise; or else we will sacrifice efficiency and the benefit of organized society for the sake of preserving individual freedom, which, as we know, is the condition of all human progress.

I say that this dilemma is *apparently* insoluble because it may resolve itself, so to speak, in the mere realities of the world of tomorrow. Contradictions exist as long as no synthesis has emerged out of life itself, and it is not necessary to be able to think of a solution for that solution to exist.

On the other hand, the dilemma of freedom versus efficiency, as well as the other conflicts mentioned in this book, may have no solution. This brings up a remark of general application concerning a peculiarity of human nature: It is indeed strange that whereas each of us accepts the existence of insoluble personal problems, we can hardly bear to think that there may be no ideal solution for the problems of humanity as a whole. Individuals go on living with equanimity, resignation, and often cheerfulness in spite of chronic bad health, money difficulties, inextricable family troubles or mental sufferings of one kind or another. Yet each of these individuals who so bravely bears his own personal problems without being able to solve them cannot suffer the idea that there may be no way of curing the ills of the world. If we can accept the thought that perfect happiness for the individual is not accessible on this earth (and who but a fool can think otherwise), we must believe nevertheless in the reality of the millennium.

It would be a great waste of time to argue whether this belief makes sense or not. But the fact that it exists and that, in modern times, it has constantly gained strength is a mystery which reaches to the very roots of the genius of man. It is a mystery, but also a tremendous force which explains why men, in spite of their individual cares and sufferings, are nevertheless able to rise above them at certain times, for the sake of greater things than themselves. It explains why men will fight and die against desperate odds and thus preserve the grandeur and dignity of voluntary sacrifices.

Everything we have been made to believe in is threatened. Each man's security and his very life are threatened. We cannot think of our children without a sense of anxiety. We do not know what the future has in store for us and much less for them. We are not quite sure of what to do except fight our enemies until we obtain victory. But when our enemies are crushed, we know that it will mean only the beginning of a new gigantic task. This world of ours has to be rebuilt. It may be that we should bless Hitler and the German revolt against us for having forced us to see that this world must be remade.

As yet, we have no clear idea of how that should be

done. But if we have no blueprint—or perhaps too many of them—it cannot be said that we do not know what we want. Before the United States went to war, one of the favorite criticisms against the British was that they had no war aims and that they could not describe the future peace. Now that the Americans are taking their share of the struggle, I believe that many things which seemed obscure or irritating to them as onlookers are now very much clearer. If all the questions raised by this conflict cannot be answered, nor the future prefigured, the fact remains that there is no doubt about the general orientation of this war. Democracy now does not seem quite so futile or so lifeless as one thought before one had to fight for it. That it is not good enough as it is, is recognized. The purpose of this war, however, cannot be anything else but to make democracy work, for the simple reason that in the word *democracy* is contained the best of two thousand years of human effort toward a better world. The very fact that we do not pretend to have a ready-made solution to all the problems that confront us today and to those that we shall have to face tomorrow is proof of the vitality of the democratic process. The ambition of democracy is constant improvement; it does not hold the promise of some fabulous millennium either next year, or the year after. Herein lies its strength.

If we win this war, there will be a tremendous reaction in the world against what is not democracy. Failing victory, there can be no other outcome to this struggle except chaos and death.

If these things be true, it follows that this war is not fought on either side to preserve what has already ceased to be. The real difference between us and the Nazi-controlled coalition is this: whereas they wish to eliminate us and with us more than two thousand years of painful effort toward something constantly better than ourselves, and to substitute for it the crude and foolish rule of naked force, we on the other hand are willing to go on criticizing our-selves and mending our ways the best we know how.

As Rebecca West writes in her recent book, *Black Lamb and Grey Falcon:*

"My civilization must not die. It need not die. My national faith is valid. . . . I know that the English are as unhealthy as lepers compared with perfect health. They do not give themselves up to feeling or to work as they should, they lack readiness to sacri-fice their individual rights for the sake of the corpo-rate good, they do not bid the right welcome to the other man's soul. But they are on the side of life, they love justice, they hate violence, and they respect the truth. It is not always so when they deal with India or Burma; but that is not their fault, it is the fault of Empire, which makes a man own things outside his power to control. But among themselves, in dealing with things within their reach, they have learned some part of the Christian lesson that it is our dis-position to crucify what is good, and that we must therefore circumvent our barbarity. This measure of wisdom makes it right that my civilization should not perish."

The road we must follow is not new. It is the road of reason. Those who feel that they cannot live without the intoxication of something irrational and romantic like a fundamental regeneration of mankind or a new spiritual revelation, will be disappointed. This civilization of ours, the one which Rebecca West says must not die, is infinitely rich and generous. It contains all the inspiration we need for a thousand years to come.

We believe that a world is in the making before our eyes. The aims for which we toil seem very distant and sometimes dim, but we know that there is no hope of reaching them except through victory.

Index

S